IMAGES
of America

INDIANA'S HISTORIC NATIONAL ROAD

THE WEST SIDE, INDIANAPOLIS TO TERRE HAUTE

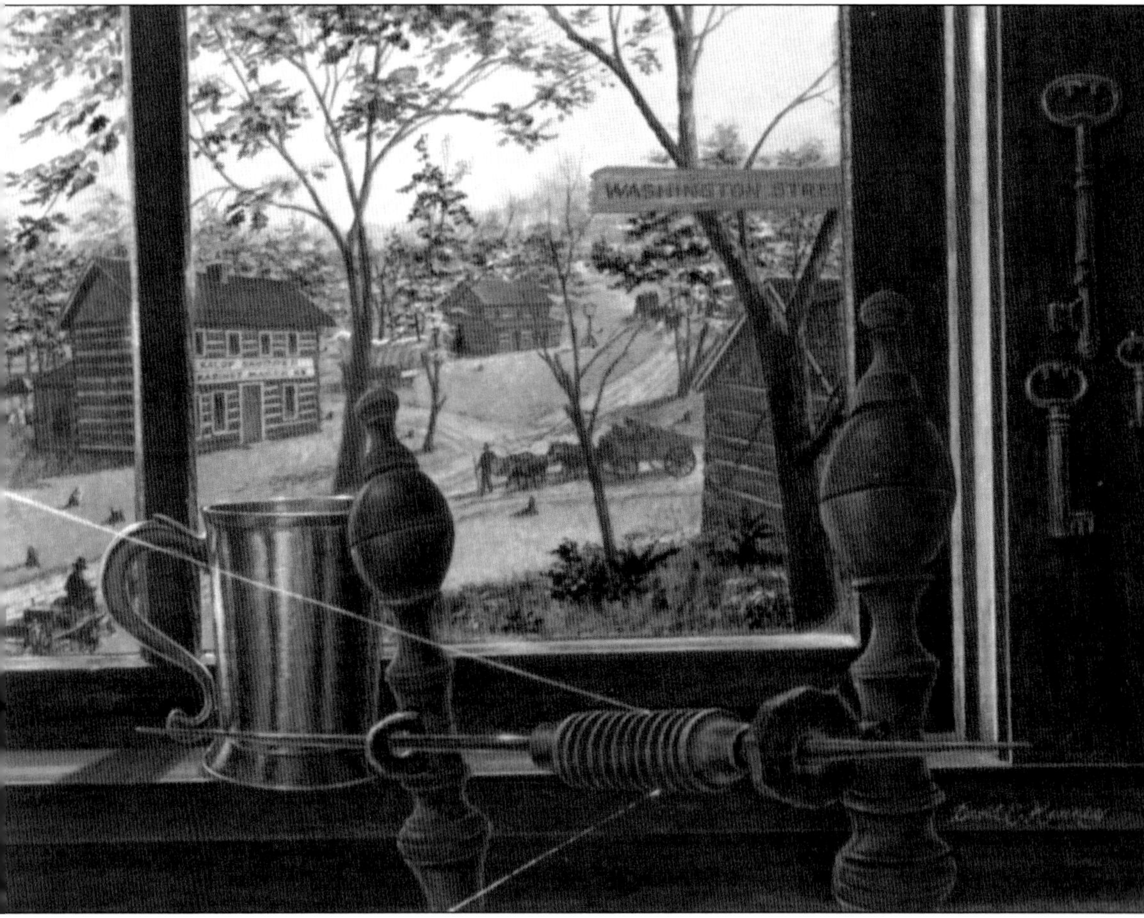

Artist David E. Kinney created the painting titled *Window on Washington Street, 1825*, depicting the National Road as it appeared in 1825, for the Indianapolis sesquicentennial celebration in 1971. The sign on the log cabin reads, "Kalop Scudder Kabinet Maker." Caleb Scudder was the first mayor of Indianapolis (1851–1854) and one of the city's first settlers, arriving in 1821. He established a home and cabinet shop on West Washington Street, where the first church, Sunday school, and fire department were headquartered. Stories of the rough-hewn road abound from this era and continued for the next 50 years. A letter dated April 8, 1876, and from Indianapolis Singer Sewing Machine traveling salesman W.D. McLain reads, "To say the roads are bad all over the territory does not half express the facts, it is simply impossible to travel by wagon. The mud is what 'Whoosiers' call 'belly deep' all over the state and the bottom is about to fall out." The Singer factory was located at 72 and 74 West Washington Street in the city. (Alan E. Hunter.)

ON THE COVER: In this Terre Haute view facing west from Eighth Street and Wabash Avenue, the wet streets are decorated for Elks Week 1936. On the back, this image is captioned, "All Duded Up for Elks Week." (Vigo County Historical Society.)

IMAGES
of America

INDIANA'S HISTORIC NATIONAL ROAD

THE WEST SIDE, INDIANAPOLIS TO TERRE HAUTE

Alan E. Hunter and Joseph M. Jarzen
for the Indiana National Road Association

ARCADIA
PUBLISHING

ISBN 978-0-7385-8862-9

Published by Arcadia Publishing
Charleston, South Carolina

Printed in the United States of America

Library of Congress Control Number: 2011939984

For all general information, please contact Arcadia Publishing:
Telephone 843-853-2070
Fax 843-853-0044
E-mail sales@arcadiapublishing.com
For customer service and orders:
Toll-Free 1-888-313-2665

Visit us on the Internet at www.arcadiapublishing.com

This book is dedicated to the members of the Indiana National Road Association (INRA), past and present, for keeping the spirit of the road alive. The mission of the Indiana National Road Association is working to preserve, protect, and promote the Historic National Road across the Hoosier state to save our history, interpret our heritage, develop tourism, and boost economic development. With an eye on its future and a firm grip on its historic past, INRA strives to preserve, protect, and promote the Historic National Road.

(Image courtesy of Alan E. Hunter.)

CONTENTS

ACKNOWLEDGMENTS

The idea for a roadway linking Eastern manufacturers with Western markets is as old as the country itself and was first broached by George Washington as early as 1755. It took until 1802, however, for the idea to take shape. Congress, in the act creating Indiana, required that five percent of funds received from public land sales in the Hoosier state be used to build public roads connecting the Atlantic Ocean to Indiana. In 1803, Congress made the first appropriation for a highway across the Allegheny Mountains to Ohio—the National Road. Beginning in Cumberland, Maryland, and running through six states, the road cost approximately $7 million and is known by many names: National Road, National Pike, Old Pike, Cumberland Road, Cumberland Pike, Highway 40, and Washington Street.

By the time the road reached Indiana, its national significance was well documented and many of the state's future leaders and budding politicians realized that it would be in their best interest to help build this thoroughfare. It is not uncommon for researchers to find the work crews littered with the names of Hoosier antebellum leaders. Just as we can never properly thank every one of those bygone pioneers for their contributions to the National Road, we can never properly thank all of the researchers, historians, documentarians, and collectors who have furnished material, past and present, for this volume. The best that we can do is try to acknowledge a few of them here.

The authors would like to thank many people who contributed images for this book. Individuals or organizations that deserve recognition are Sue King, Historic Knightstown, Cambridge City History Room, Rick Newton, April and Mark Riggle, Norma and Jim Bertsch, Jim Orr, Rhonda Hunter, Ron Sanders, Steve Barnett, Bill Raney, Mick Kissick, Tom Saunders, Kathy Miller, Western Wayne Heritage, Irvington Historical Society, Vigo County Historical Society, and Indiana Landmarks.

INTRODUCTION

If the east side of Indiana's Historic National Road can be best described as the pioneer experience, then what might best describe the west side must surely be 20th-century transportation. For the purposes of this book, the western region of the Historic National Road through Indiana is defined by that section located west of Meridian Street in downtown Indianapolis, through Terre Haute to the border with Illinois. The west side of Indiana's Historic National Road is home to the nation's first Union Station for railroads, the city's first (and current) airport, most of the automobile makers (who, for a time, rivaled Detroit in innovation and creation of motorcars), and, of course, the Indianapolis Motor Speedway, home of the Indy 500.

Beyond Indianapolis, travelers will find a much different experience than what they come across in the eastern region of the road. Natural landscapes are more prevalent, and smaller communities take the place of the pike towns in the east. Architecture from the 20th century—such as the Plainfield Diner, interurban station, and Works Progress Administration (WPA) post offices—are the landmarks seen along the road. Commerce is defined by companies that found their roots and became household standards, particularly in the 1900s, such as the Clabber Girl Flour Company in Terre Haute. Although Terre Haute and Brazil were some of the earliest communities in Indiana and along the Historic National Road, no longer is the experience of driving the western section defined as much by the rural-to-urban transitions that you find in the eastern section. This drive is noted more for its original road sections, where travelers will drive directly on the original concrete alignments of the road and pass over original concrete arch bridges built in the 1920s. They will pass through rural and forested environments where they will truly have the experience of what it was like to travel the road in a 1930 DeSoto.

Yet even through this difference in the experience, the early pioneer heritage can be witnessed, particularly when one travels past Rising Hall Estate on the Hendricks and Putnam County line, one of the Historic National Road's most impressive residences. It is this unique heritage and story of 200 years that make the Historic National Road significant and worthy of its All-American Road status through the National Scenic Byways Program.

The National Road is the nation's first federally funded interstate highway; it was commissioned by Pres. Thomas Jefferson in 1806. Today, the Historic National Road from Baltimore to East St. Louis is among only a select number of designated All-American Roads within the National Scenic Byways Program. These roads are considered the most distinguished of all nationally designated byways. However, the story of the road is about the people who traveled it, settled along it, and lived along it over the past 200 years.

Although natural beauty is an important quality, this scenic byway is not defined by it. Recreationally, there are many opportunities to explore the road and its resources. However, this road is defined by the man-made environment and footprints of millions of Americans whose lives have been impacted by their interaction with the road.

A traveler along Indiana's Historic National Road, which follows US Route 40 closely between Richmond, Indianapolis, and Terre Haute, today will find a landscape little changed since the heyday of the route in the 1940s. Historic towns with traditional Main Streets and tree-lined residential districts still give way to the productive fields and tranquil pastures that brought Indiana prosperity. From the Federal-style architecture of the 1840 Huddleston Farmhouse in the eastern region of the road to the 1940s Plainfield Diner, one can literally track the westward migration of the state and nation in the buildings and landscapes previous generations left in testimony to their hard work and creative spirit.

Sharing these stories alongside historical photographs provides a unique opportunity to tell the history of the road and hopefully encourage appreciation and energy to preserve the buildings that laid the background for the stories. May this book help orient you to the heritage of Indiana's Historic National Road through historical photographs of buildings that were constructed along it throughout its 200-year history. It will showcase the common people whose ancestors were the early pioneers who settled the towns and farmed the fields and were then captured on film living their daily lives—doing what we still do today—building a better future for themselves and their children.

Yet, the book will also attempt to open a window of understanding to look at these structures, not just as old buildings but also as artifacts of the past, of which we are only borrowers. The landscapes that separate these towns are not necessarily fields for future expansion of houses and big-box development, but they are part of local heritage steeped in farming and early settlement. We are responsible for ensuring the continued existence of these resources for people in the future to learn from and use.

The role of the Historic National Road as a nationally designated scenic byway is an important tool for the preservation and promotion efforts along the corridor in Indiana. By driving the Historic National Road, one may still experience firsthand a bit of the history that began when the United States was still only 30 years old. This book will help bring this history to you through the following pages that document the past 100 years through film and photographs. By reading these pages and viewing the photographs, may these hidden and unknown stories reveal themselves and allow the history of the National Road and the United States to start to come together.

One

Beginnings
Abraham Lincoln and the National Road

Abraham Lincoln spent his formative years from 1816 to 1830 in southern Indiana's Spencer County before leaving for Illinois. However, the future president returned to the state. As a circuit lawyer in Illinois, Lincoln occasionally appeared in Indiana on behalf of clients in legal matters. In 1844, in one of his first journeys back, he made speeches on behalf of Henry Clay as the Whig candidate for president. In 1847, Lincoln stopped in Indianapolis on his way to take his seat as a Whig member of Congress. Lincoln stayed at the Browning House, a prominent hotel on the National Road, where he was greeted by lawyers and politicians.

In the fall of 1859, after Lincoln rose to national prominence while campaigning and famously debating Stephen A. Douglas for the US Senate in Illinois, he spoke to a large crowd in Indianapolis at the Masonic Hall located on the National Road. His most celebrated visit to Indianapolis came in early 1861, on his way to assume the presidency on the eve of his birthday, February 11. Lincoln was met in Indianapolis by a large crowd, where he gave a brief speech, concluding, "Not with presidents, not with office-seekers, but with you, is the question, 'Shall the Union and shall the liberties of this country be preserved to the latest generation?' "

Standing in a carriage acknowledging his well-wishers, Lincoln made his way along Washington Street toward the Bates House, the most prestigious hotel of the day. From a balcony, he greeted a crowd of 20,000 people and made a speech that questioned the right of the Southern states to secede from the Union without the concurrence of the rest of the nation. The next morning, Lincoln and his son Robert were given a large breakfast by Gov. Oliver P. Morton and his family at the governor's mansion.

Just four years later, after his assassination in 1865, a funeral train paralleling the National Road bore Lincoln's body through the eastern half of the state. In Indianapolis, a mournful procession conducted the casket to the old statehouse on Washington Street in a pouring rain. Lincoln's body lay in repose atop a funeral bier in the rotunda, and an estimated 100,000 people paid their respects. To this day, Hoosiers feel a deep connection to the martyred president and cherish the brief time he spent in the capital city.

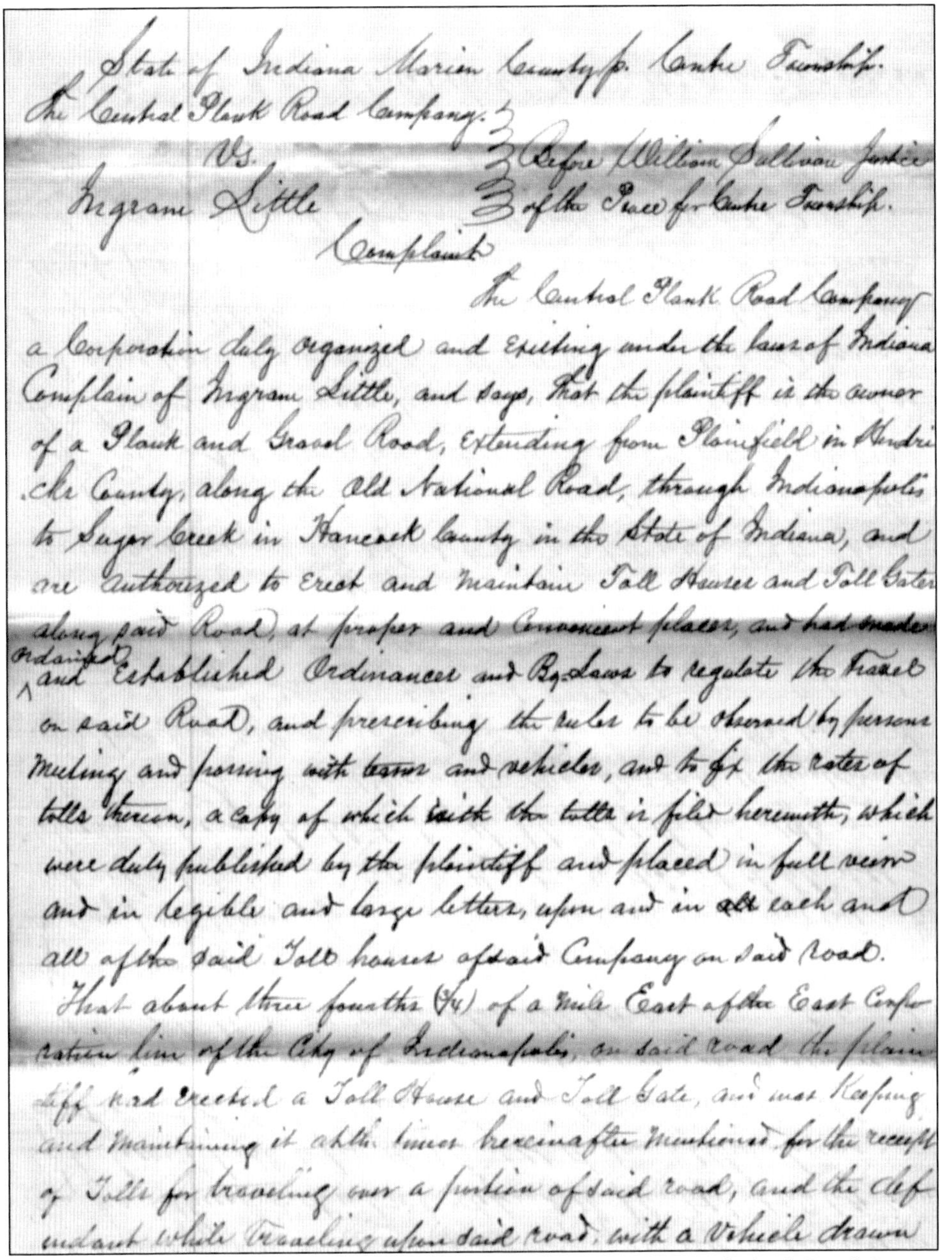
State of Indiana Marion County ss. Centre Township.
The Central Plank Road Company } Before William Sullivan Justice
Vs. } of the Peace for Centre Township.
Ingram Little }
Complaint
The Central Plank Road Company a Corporation duly organized and Existing under the laws of Indiana Complain of Ingram Little, and says, that the plaintiff is the owner of a Plank and Gravel Road, extending from Plainfield in Hendricks County, along the Old National Road, through Indianapolis to Sugar Creek in Hancock County in the State of Indiana, and are authorized to Erect and maintain Toll Houses and Toll Gates along said Road, at proper and Convenient places, and had made ordained and Established Ordinances and By-Laws to regulate the travel on said Road, and prescribing the rules to be observed by persons meeting and passing with teams and vehicles, and to fix the rates of tolls thereon, a copy of which with the tolls is filed herewith, which were duly published by the plaintiff and placed in full view and in legible and large letters, upon and in each and all of the said Toll houses of said Company on said road.
That about three fourths (3/4) of a mile East of the East Corporation line of the City of Indianapolis, on said road the plaintiff had erected a Toll House and Toll Gate, and was keeping and maintaining it at the times hereinafter mentioned, for the receipt of Tolls for traveling over a portion of said road, and the defendant while traveling upon said road, with a vehicle drawn

The cover of a 10-page, April 1864 Marion County court case, "Central Plank Road Company vs. Ingram Little," reads, "The Central Plank Road Company . . . extending from Plainfield in Hendricks County along the Old National Road through Indianapolis to Sugar Creek in Hancock County in the state of Indiana and are authorized to erect and maintain Toll Houses and Toll Gates along said road at proper and convenient places . . . and fix the rates of toll therein." The court case charges that Ingram Little "refused to pay the toll" on several occasions. The court case would set the toll rates and rules, thus, regulating the road from that point on. "No person shall either ride or drive over any bridge faster than a walk . . . No person shall horse race on said road, nor shoot craps on or along said road, or any bridge thereof." Ingram Little was found guilty and fined $24.65. (Alan E. Hunter.)

Abraham Lincoln defined the Civil War–era National Road in Indiana. He visited Indianapolis by rail on his way to assume the presidency on his first stop after leaving Springfield, Illinois, for the last time on February 11, 1861. His body retraced the route in reverse after his assassination on April 30, 1865. This photograph of Abraham Lincoln was taken by Alexander Gardner on November 8, 1863, just 15 days before he delivered the Gettysburg Address. (Alan E. Hunter.)

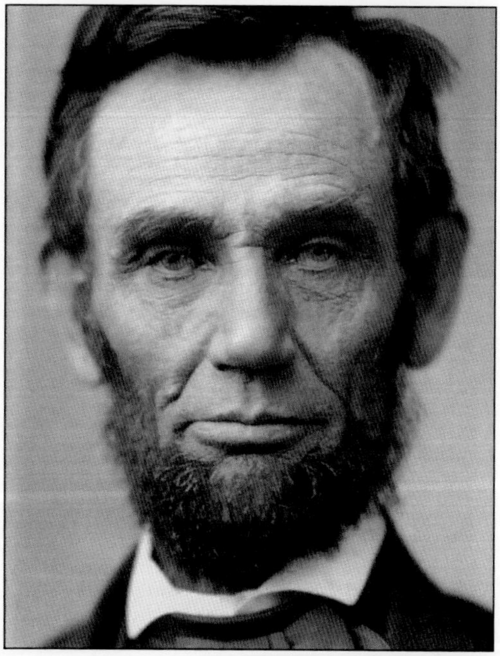

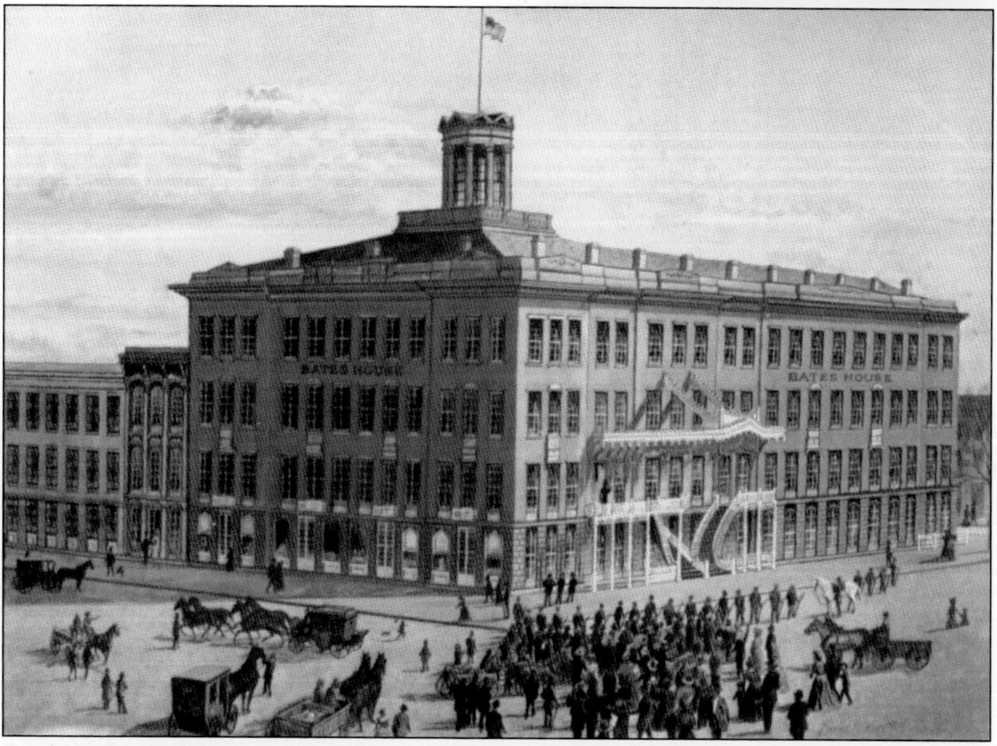

For the Indianapolis sesquicentennial celebration in 1971, David E. Kinney painted *The Day Lincoln Came*, depicting the Bates House hotel as it appeared the day Lincoln arrived in the Hoosier capital city. When the four-story Bates House opened in 1853, it was a favorite stop for travelers, politicians, and visiting celebrities. Notable guests included Mark Twain, Andrew Johnson, and Ulysses S. Grant. The Bates House hotel was razed in 1901. (Alan E. Hunter.)

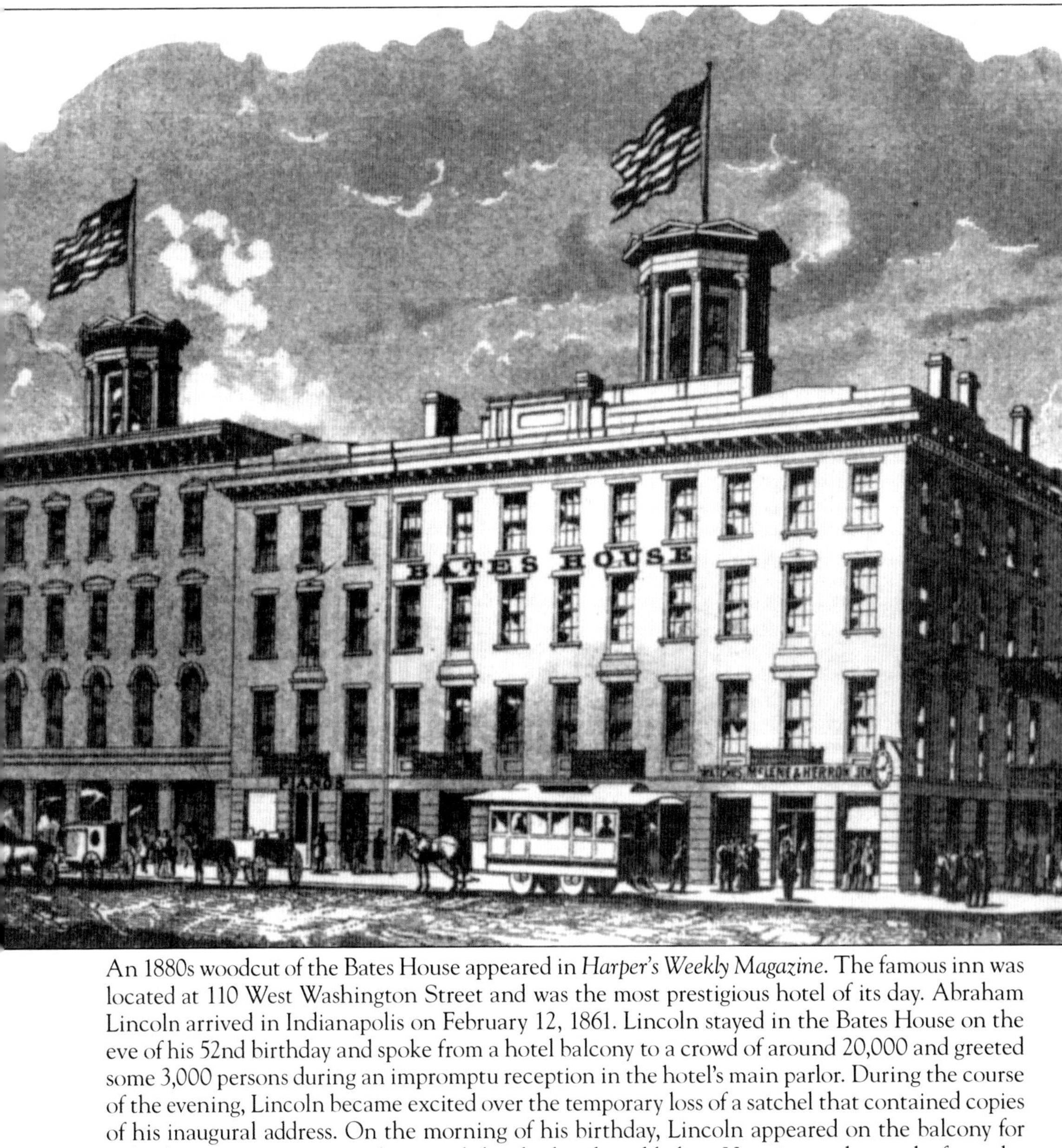

An 1880s woodcut of the Bates House appeared in *Harper's Weekly Magazine*. The famous inn was located at 110 West Washington Street and was the most prestigious hotel of its day. Abraham Lincoln arrived in Indianapolis on February 12, 1861. Lincoln stayed in the Bates House on the eve of his 52nd birthday and spoke from a hotel balcony to a crowd of around 20,000 and greeted some 3,000 persons during an impromptu reception in the hotel's main parlor. During the course of the evening, Lincoln became excited over the temporary loss of a satchel that contained copies of his inaugural address. On the morning of his birthday, Lincoln appeared on the balcony for a third time in response to the crowd that had gathered below. He reiterated remarks from the previous evening's address. (Alan E. Hunter.)

An 1860 campaign ribbon, like those that would have been worn by supporters in Indianapolis in 1861, shows a beardless Abraham Lincoln. Shortly before he arrived, Lincoln received a letter from 11-year-old Grace Bedell of Westfield, New Jersey, suggesting, "If you let your whiskers grow . . . you would look a great deal better, for your face is so thin." Over the next four years, Lincoln's whiskers did grow, resulting in the image so familiar today. (Alan E. Hunter.)

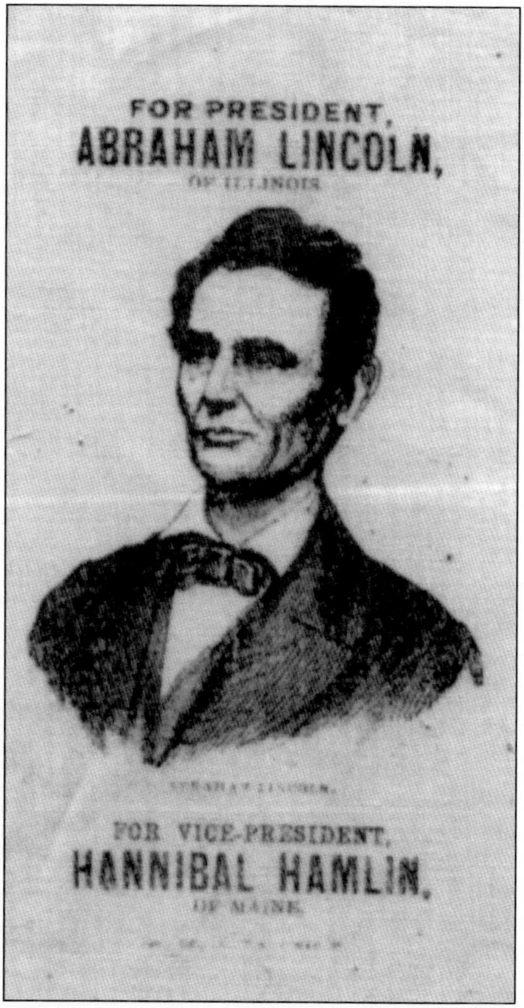

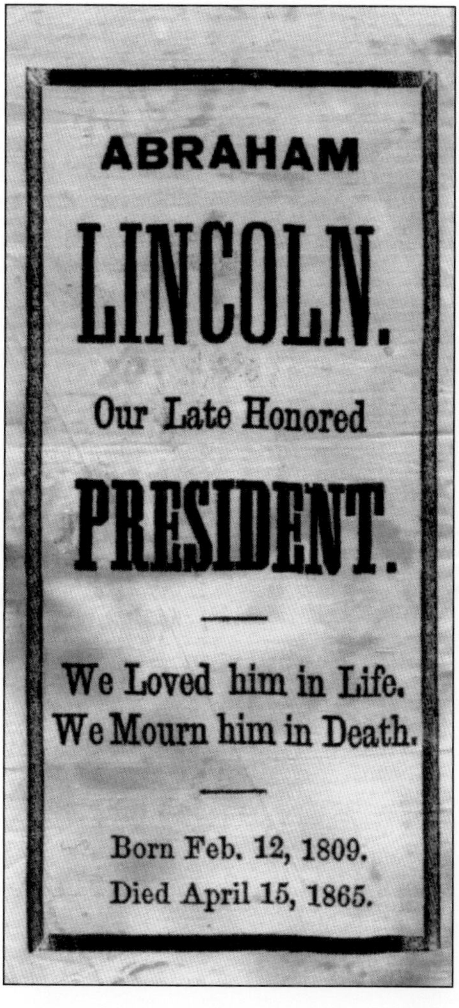

This ribbon was worn by bereaved mourners along the National Road as they watched the Lincoln funeral train roll slowly past in 1865. Around seven million people observed the funeral train. In Richmond, Indiana, officials estimated that 15,000 mourners turned out to see the train pass (a number greater than the city's population)—at 3:15 in the morning. This event changed the national landscape, shaped the American psyche, and elevated the Hoosier rail-splitter to secular sainthood. (Alan E. Hunter.)

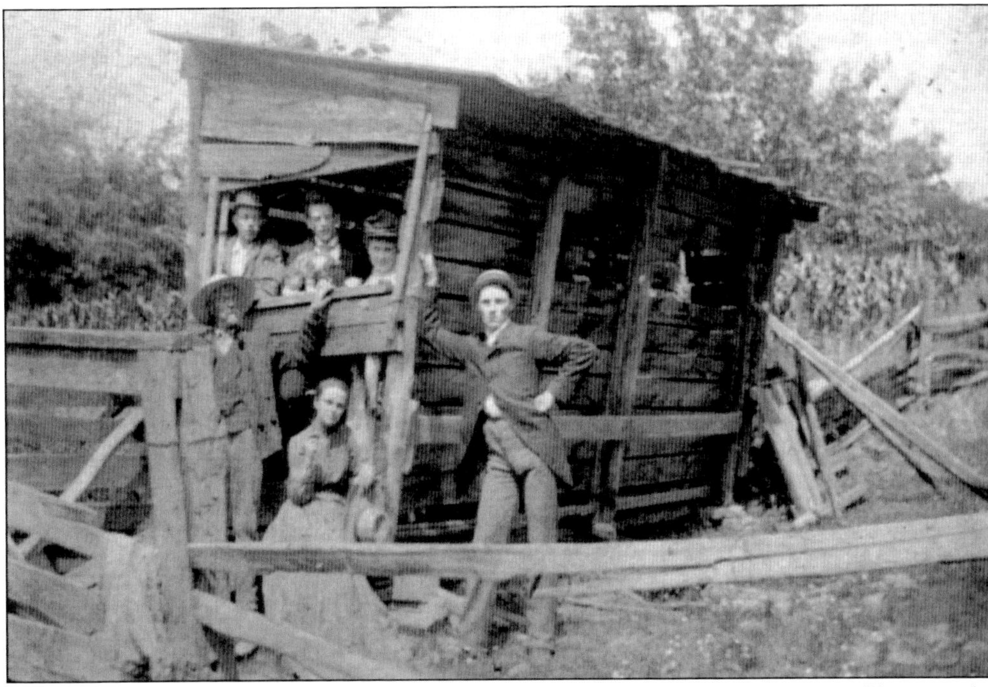

A July 1896 cabinet photograph shows the old Central Plank Road Company tollhouse. The building is falling apart, but four men and two women pose proudly. The photograph was taken the day the building was razed to make way for the widening of the road near Plainfield. The photograph was found with the court case papers for "Central Plank Road Company vs. Ingram Little." (Alan E. Hunter.)

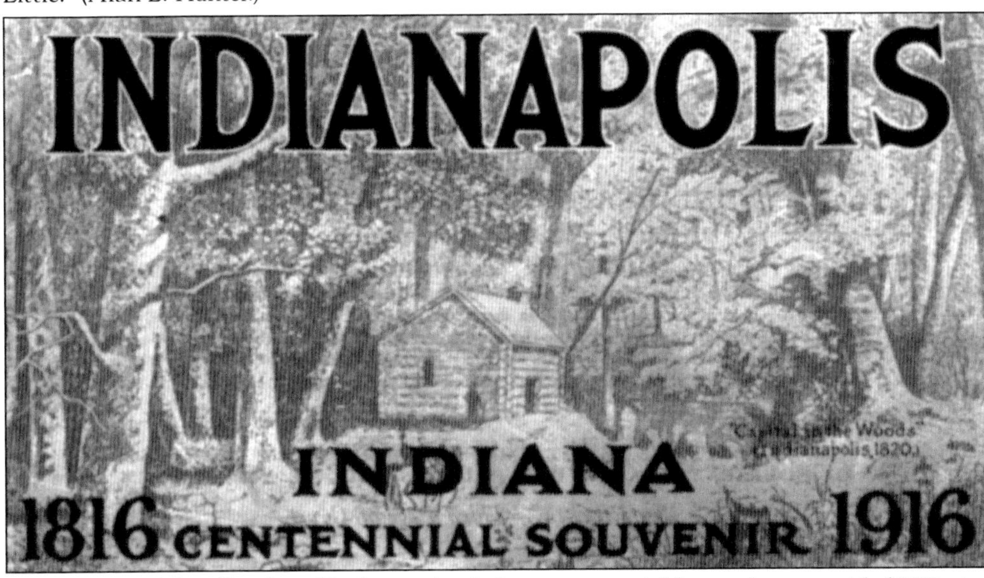

The program of the official 1916 Indianapolis, Indiana, centennial featured a scene titled " 'Capitol in the Woods' Indianapolis, 1820." The celebration was attended by Pres. Woodrow Wilson and his vice president, former Indiana governor Thomas R. Marshall. Poet James Whitcomb Riley, though in failing health, was the titular guest of honor at the mid-June event. Within six weeks of the official ceremonies, Riley was dead. (Alan E. Hunter.)

The official 1971 Indianapolis sesquicentennial program features the Indiana Soldiers and Sailors Monument as its centerpiece. The 150th birthday celebration was chaired by Mayor Richard G. Lugar, with the highlight being a visit by Pres. Richard M. Nixon, who called Lugar his "favorite mayor." (Alan E. Hunter.)

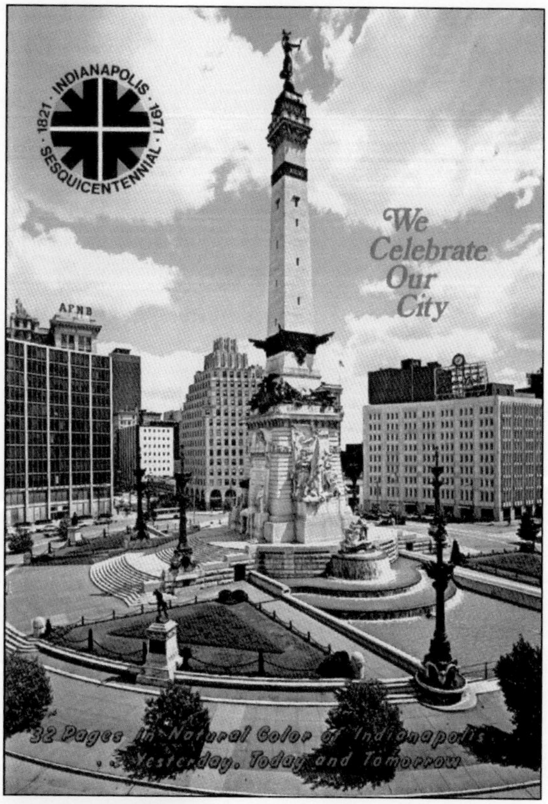

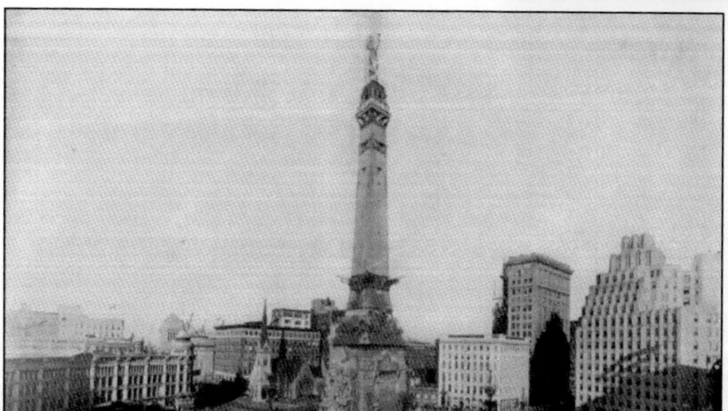

A 1940s-era Indianapolis visitor's brochure is titled *Places and Things You'll Enjoy in Indianapolis* and features an image of the Indiana Soldiers and Sailors Monument, the city centerpiece. Distributed by the Indianapolis Chamber of Commerce, the promotional copy boasts, "Here is a city of homes and churches, parks and boulevards, stores and factories, famous memorials, cultural and educational institutions, and theaters. A wealth of interesting and pleasant experiences await you here." (Alan E. Hunter.)

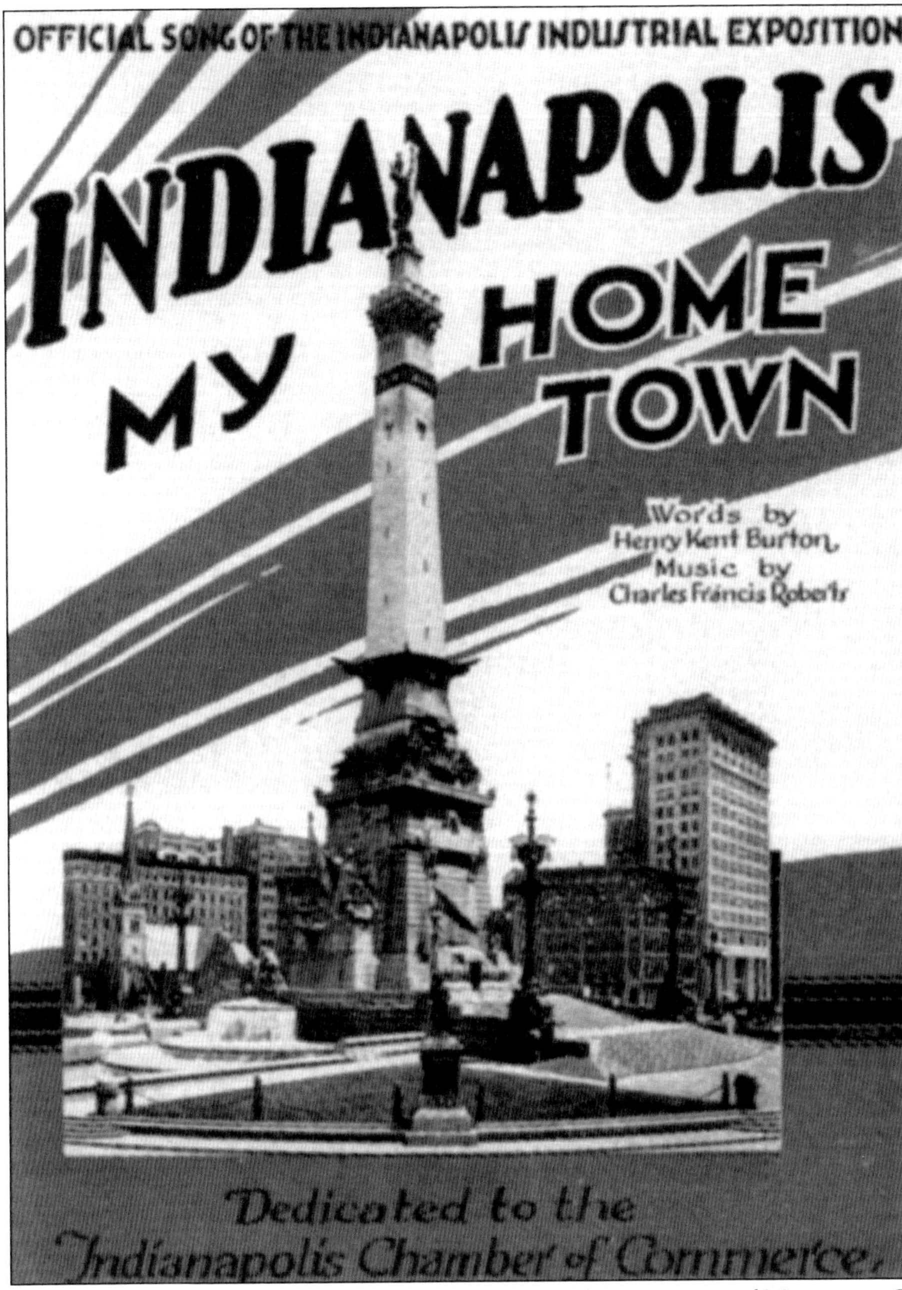

The 1921 sheet music for "Indianapolis My Home Town" has an image of Monument Circle for the cover. Written by Charles Frances Roberts and Henry Kent Burton for the Indianapolis Chamber of Commerce, it was the official song of the Indianapolis Industrial Exposition. The official slogan for the event was "A week for exploiting the industrial bigness of Indianapolis." During the exposition, 400 displays showcased 780 articles manufactured in Indianapolis. Samples were given away, and many items were manufactured on-site. Also on display were a gold-plated miniature printing press and the Duisenberg automobile in which Tommy Milton traveled the fastest mile ever by a human—135 miles per hour on Daytona Beach in Florida—at that time in 1920. (Alan E. Hunter.)

Two

INDIANAPOLIS
MONUMENT CIRCLE CORRIDOR

Indianapolis was selected as the site of the new state capital in 1820, and the city's layout was platted by Alexander Ralston, whose design included a three-acre circle, at the geographic center of the city, surrounded by an 80-foot street on which the Governor's Mansion was built in 1827. As Indianapolis grew, the area became a popular meeting place and was designated Circle Park. The four blocks surrounding the center were called the Governor's Circle.

Indiana was the first state, in what was then considered the American Northwest, to mobilize for the Civil War. President Lincoln initially requested that Indiana send 7,500 men to join the Union army. Before the war ended, Indiana contributed more than 200,000 men, 15 percent of the state's total population; 24,416 Hoosiers lost their lives, and more than 50,000 were wounded.

In 1887, the general assembly formed a monument commission to plan a marker to honor Indiana's veterans. Commissioners unanimously chose a design by Prussian architect Bruno Schmitz. Named supervising architect, Bruno earned a pay of five percent of the monument's total cost.

The cornerstone was laid on August 22, 1889, holding a copper box containing a list of all Indiana soldiers, newspapers, the Constitution of Indiana, a national flag, and other paraphernalia. Ceremonies included a speech by Pres. Benjamin Harrison, firing of artillery, and a parade. It was the first monument dedicated to the common soldier. The structure took 12 years to complete. The Indiana Soldiers and Sailors Monument was formally dedicated on May 15, 1902. Gen. Lew Wallace presided as master of ceremonies. There were speeches and parades. James Whitcomb Riley read his poem "The Soldier," and John Philip Sousa composed "The Messiah of the Nations" march for the occasion. The Christ Church choir performed "My Country, 'Tis of Thee."

In 1918, a museum opened in the basement of the monument, featuring artifacts and one of the finest collections of Civil War battle flags in the country. Monument Circle is guarded by bronze statues of four wartime leaders: George Rogers Clark, William Henry Harrison, James Whitcomb, and Oliver Morton.

The circle became a thriving business district, offering hotels, theaters, and shops. Today, the circle is also home to studios for local radio stations, financial institutions, the Columbia Club (one of the oldest social clubs of Indianapolis), and Indianapolis Power & Light Co. (IPL) corporate headquarters. The circle is the symbol of the city known as the "Circle City," and the city flag features a representation of Monument Circle.

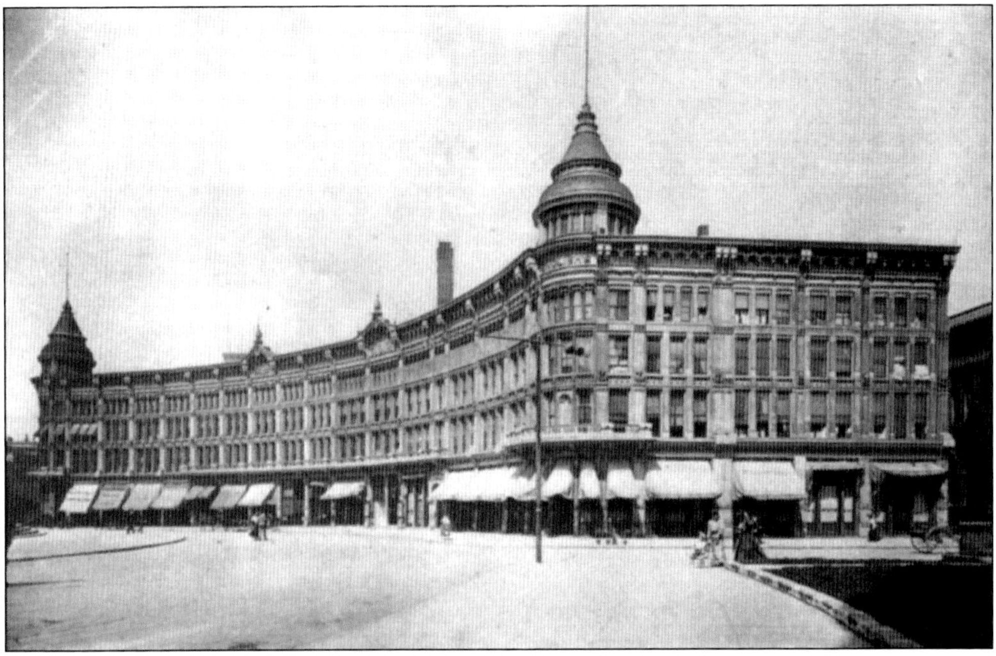

A 1925 view shows the English Hotel and Opera House on the northwest quadrant of Monument Circle. Opened in 1880 and built by namesake William H. English, the curved building stood four stories high and featured marble pillars and staircase and massive balconies, making it the ideal place for visiting politicians to speak to the crowds that naturally gathered below. The building was demolished in 1948 to make way for the J.C. Penney building. (Alan E. Hunter.)

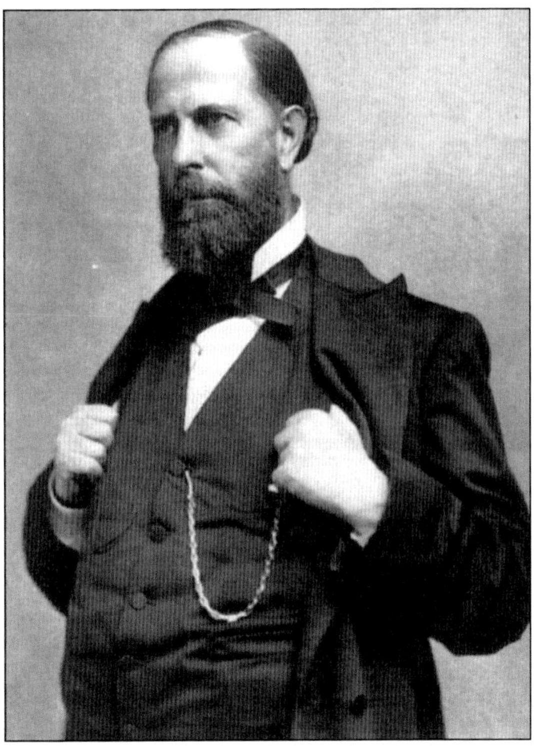

William Hayden English was an Indianapolis businessman, congressman, and 1880 Democratic vice presidential candidate credited with transforming Monument Circle from a place of residence to a place of business. By the time the English Hotel and Opera House opened in 1880, only two houses remained on the circle. English's development efforts caused remaining lots to be purchased quickly in the 1880s. (Indianapolis Public Library, Central Branch.)

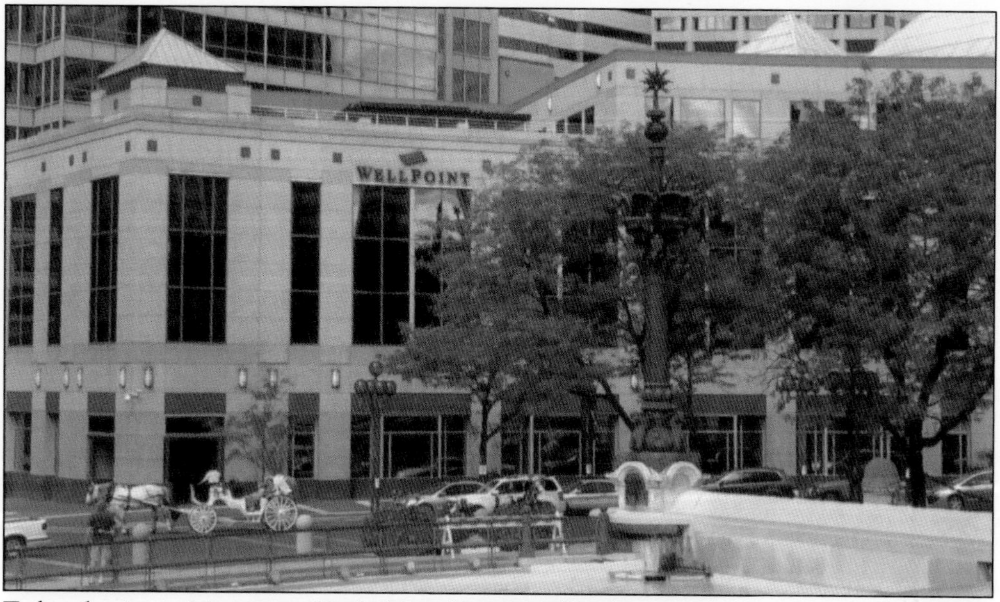

Today, the site on Monument Circle formerly occupied by the English Hotel and Opera House is home to insurance titan Wellpoint. Located a short walk from the Indiana Statehouse, Lucas Oil Stadium, Conseco Fieldhouse, Victory Field, and dozens of nightclubs, theaters, and restaurants, the circle remains the focal point of Indianapolis activity. A horse-drawn carriage passes in front of a couple having their picture taken at the famous landmark. (Tim Poynter-Spirit Photography.)

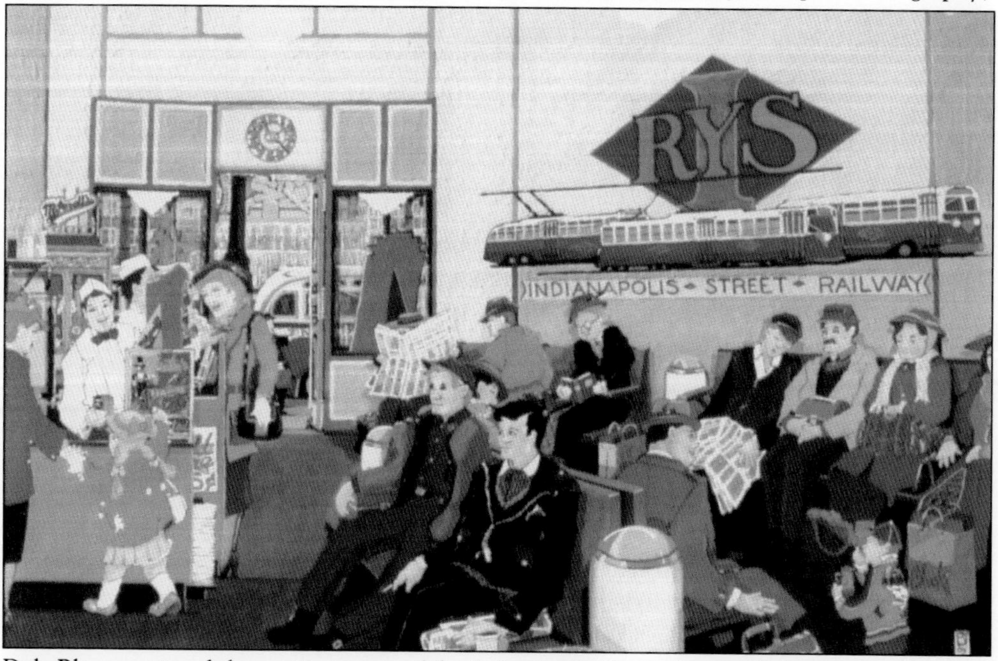

Dale Blaney painted the waiting room of the Indianapolis Street Railway's downtown departure hub. *Monument Circle Bus Station c. 1946* shows the crowded waiting room as it would have appeared just after the close of World War II. Men read their newspapers, as women tend the children. The shimmering waterfall of the Monument Circle fountain can be seen outside the glass entry doors. (Alan E. Hunter.)

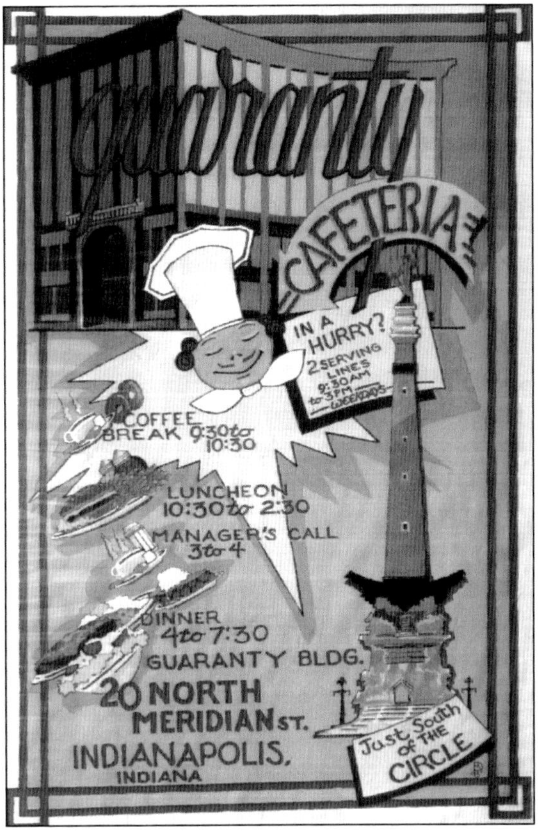

Dale Blaney's painting of the Guaranty Cafeteria is located in the Guaranty building on the circle at 20 North Meridian Street in downtown Indianapolis. The cafeteria's chef mascot is inset, and the text reads, "Guaranty Cafeteria In a Hurry?—2 Serving Lines 9:30 AM to 3 PM Weekdays—Coffee Break 9:30 to 10:30—Luncheon 10:30 to 2:30—Manager's Call 3 to 4—Dinner 4 to 7:30—Guaranty Bldg. 20 North Meridian St. Indianapolis, Indiana—Just South of the Circle." (Alan E. Hunter.)

A photograph from around 1900 shows the Indiana Statehouse located at 200 West Washington Street. The capitol building is home to the general assembly, the office of the governor, and the state supreme court. Erected in 1888, it is the fifth building to house the state government. In the left foreground, the 1890 statue of former vice president and Indiana governor Thomas A. Hendricks can be seen. The offices of the Rock Island Plow Company are in the background at left. (Alan E. Hunter.)

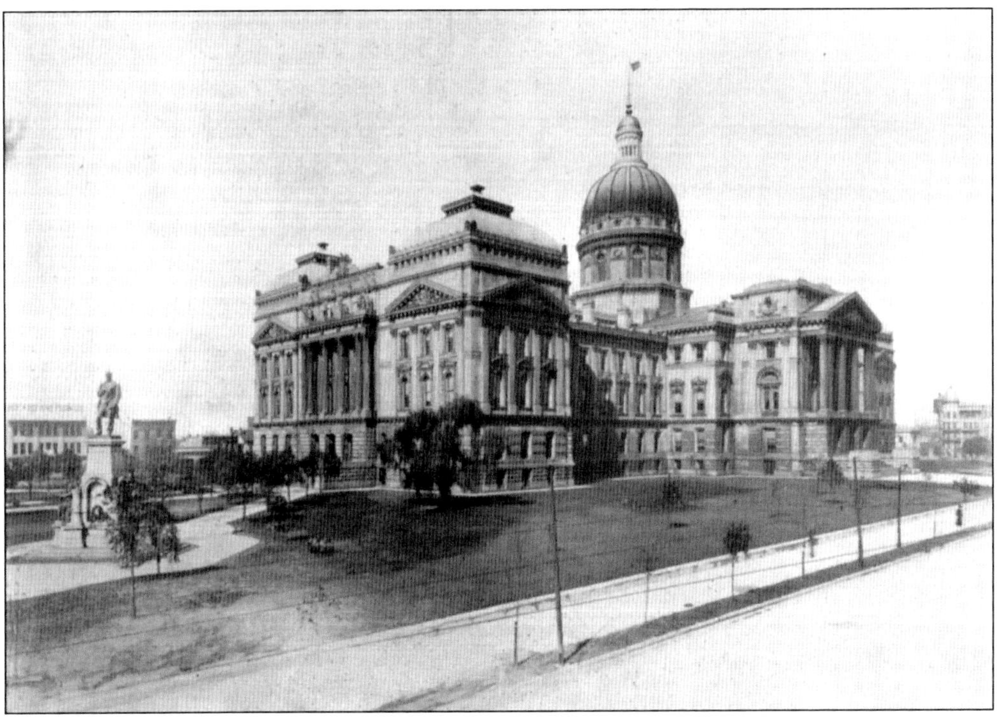

The Masonic Temple, shown around 1910, is located at the intersection of Washington Street and Capitol Avenue, just south of the Indiana Statehouse. A street vendor leans against a mailbox in front of the building as a uniformed policeman looks on. Next door is the Chas. Willig housewares store and Harmon & Hall hardware store. (Indianapolis Public Library, Warren Branch.)

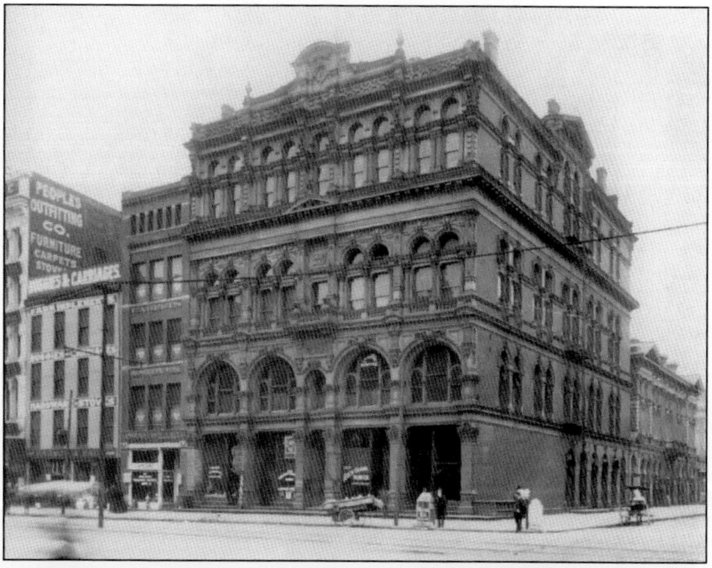

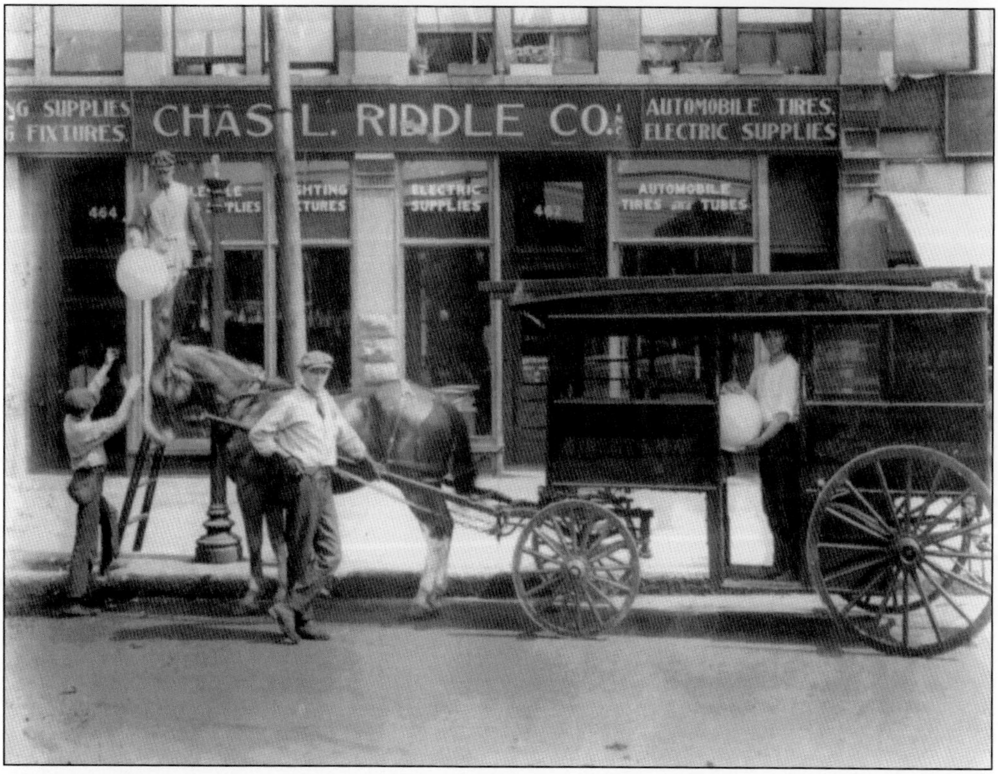

Cleaners in horse-drawn wagon No. 25 from the Merchants Heat & Light Co. are pictured washing streetlight globes in front of the Charles L. Riddle Co. at 462 West Washington Street in 1919. The Charles Riddle store sold automobile tires, tubes, and electrical supplies. Obviously posing for the camera, one man tends the horses while another man atop a ladder hands down the large milk-glass lamp globe to a coworker on the ground, and the last man waits with a clean globe inside the wagon. The photograph's original handwritten caption reads, "This simple job needed three men, a boy, a horse, and a wagon." (Indianapolis Public Library, Warren Branch.)

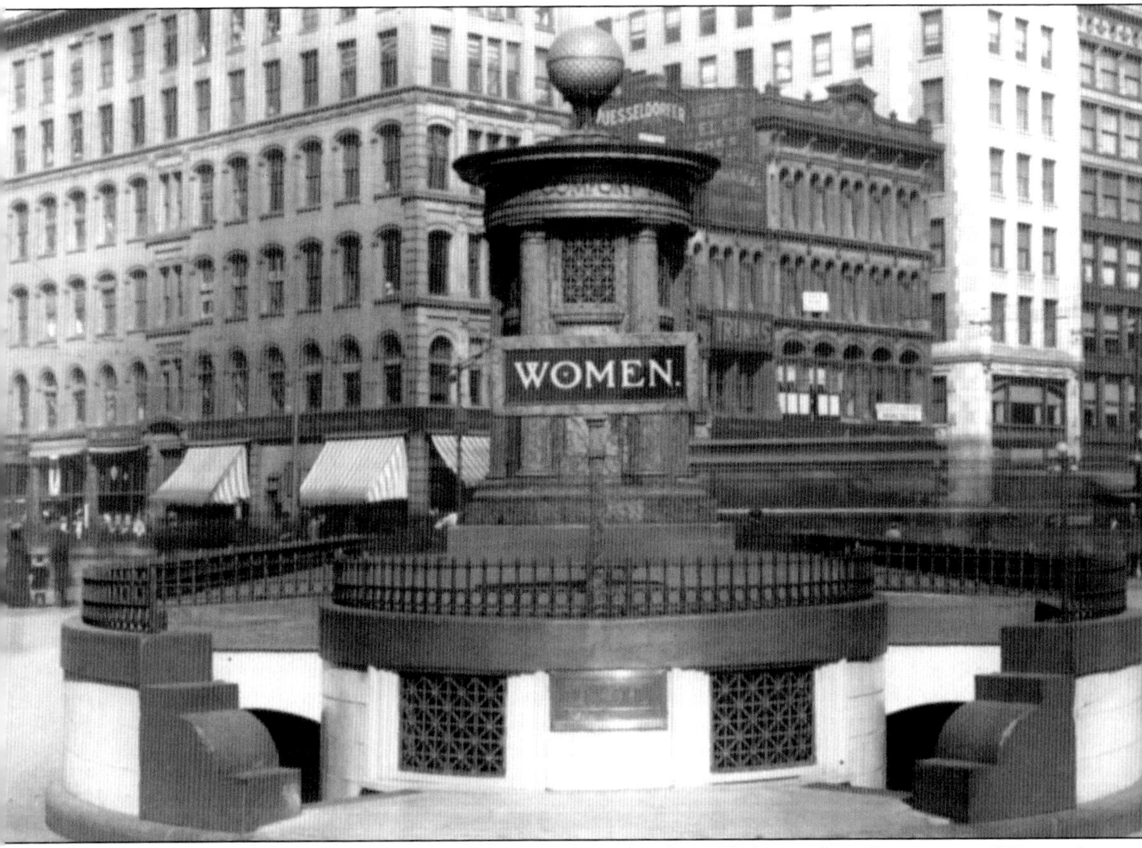

A 1911 photograph shows one of two comfort stations formerly located on the corner of Kentucky Avenue and West Washington Street in Indianapolis. The image shows the women's station, with the men's station located just a few yards away. These underground restrooms were principally used by second- and third-shift workers whose hours prohibited them from using the facilities inside stores and office buildings. Within months of their opening in 1910, women began to complain about their lack of cleanliness and terrible smell. The city council feared that they would become a haven for loafing. However, they lasted over 50 years before finally being closed in 1963. Today, the site is home to the Artsgarden outside Circle Centre Mall. (Alan E. Hunter.)

A cabinet photograph shows a woman in a horse and buggy in front of the Brinkmeyer, Kuhn & Co. store on South Meridian Street near Monument Circle. August M. Kuhn was president of the Consolidated Coal and Lime Company. George C. Brinkmeyer, born in 1865, was a partner in an Indianapolis grocery store. Brinkmeyer's wife was Catherine, and they had a daughter named Ruth. Today, this site is part of Circle Centre Mall. (April Riggle.)

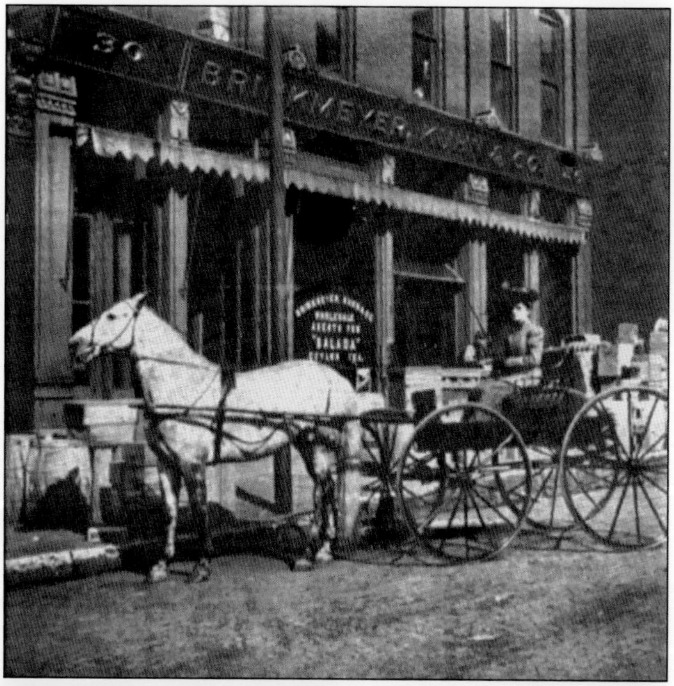

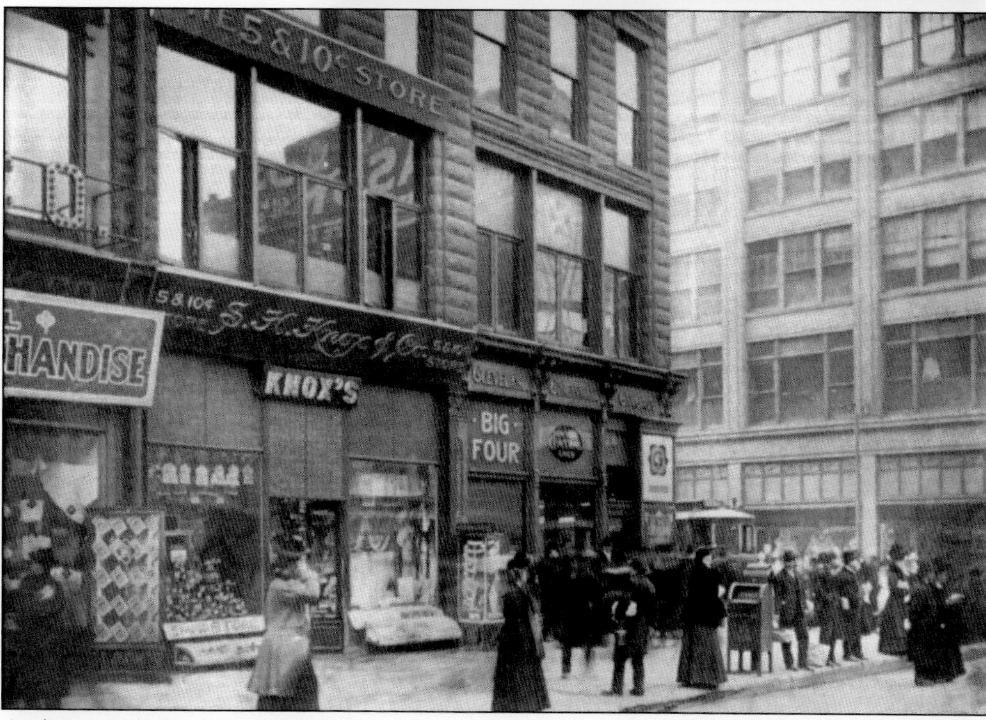

A photograph from about 1900 shows the retail district at the intersection of Washington and Meridian Streets. The offices of the Cleveland, Cincinnati & Chicago Railroad and the S.H. Knox five-and-dime store are on the corner. The well-dressed folks on the right of the photograph look as if they are jockeying for position and getting ready to board an interurban trolley (which is not in the frame). (Alan E. Hunter.)

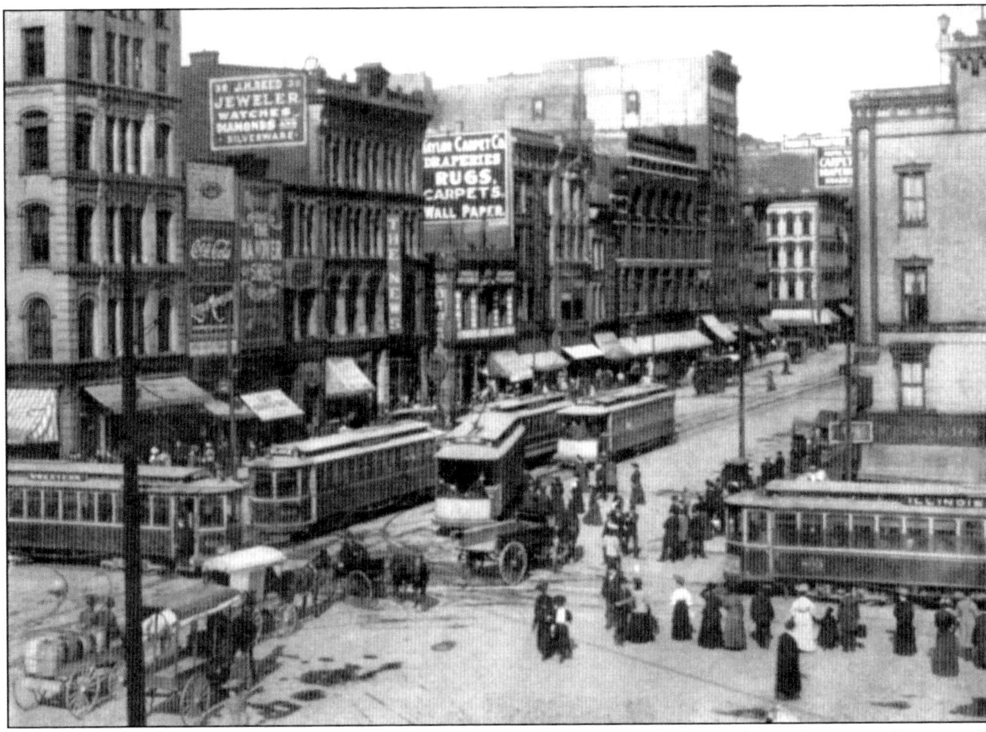

A 1900-era photograph shows a busy scene at the corner of Illinois and Washington Streets. A traffic jam of six interurban trolleys and five horses and buggies converges under Coca-Cola and Hanover Shoes signs next to the Indianapolis News Building. (Alan E. Hunter.)

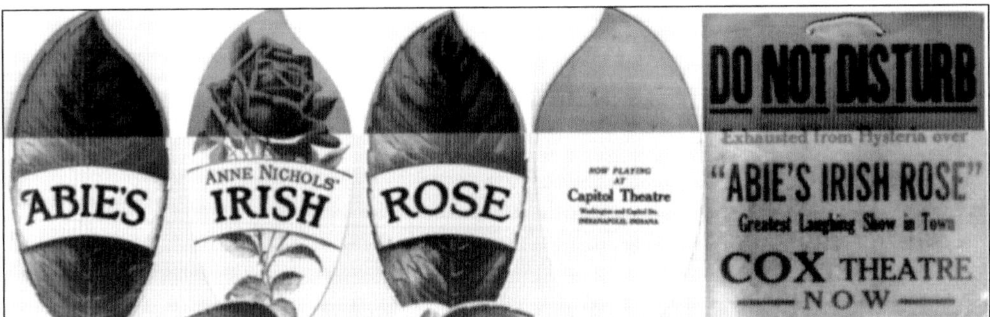

During the golden age of live theater, Washington Street in Indianapolis was *the* address for theaters and vaudeville houses, boasting no fewer than a dozen professional theaters at any given point during the era. An 1880s hand fan advertises Abie's Irish Rose at the Capitol Theater at Washington and Capitol Streets; a door hanger sign dates from the same production. Other theaters in the area included the Empire, Circle, Bijou, Colonial, Granada, Little, Lyric, Metropolitan, Ritz, Walker, Zaring Egyptian, and Indiana Theater. (Abby Allen.)

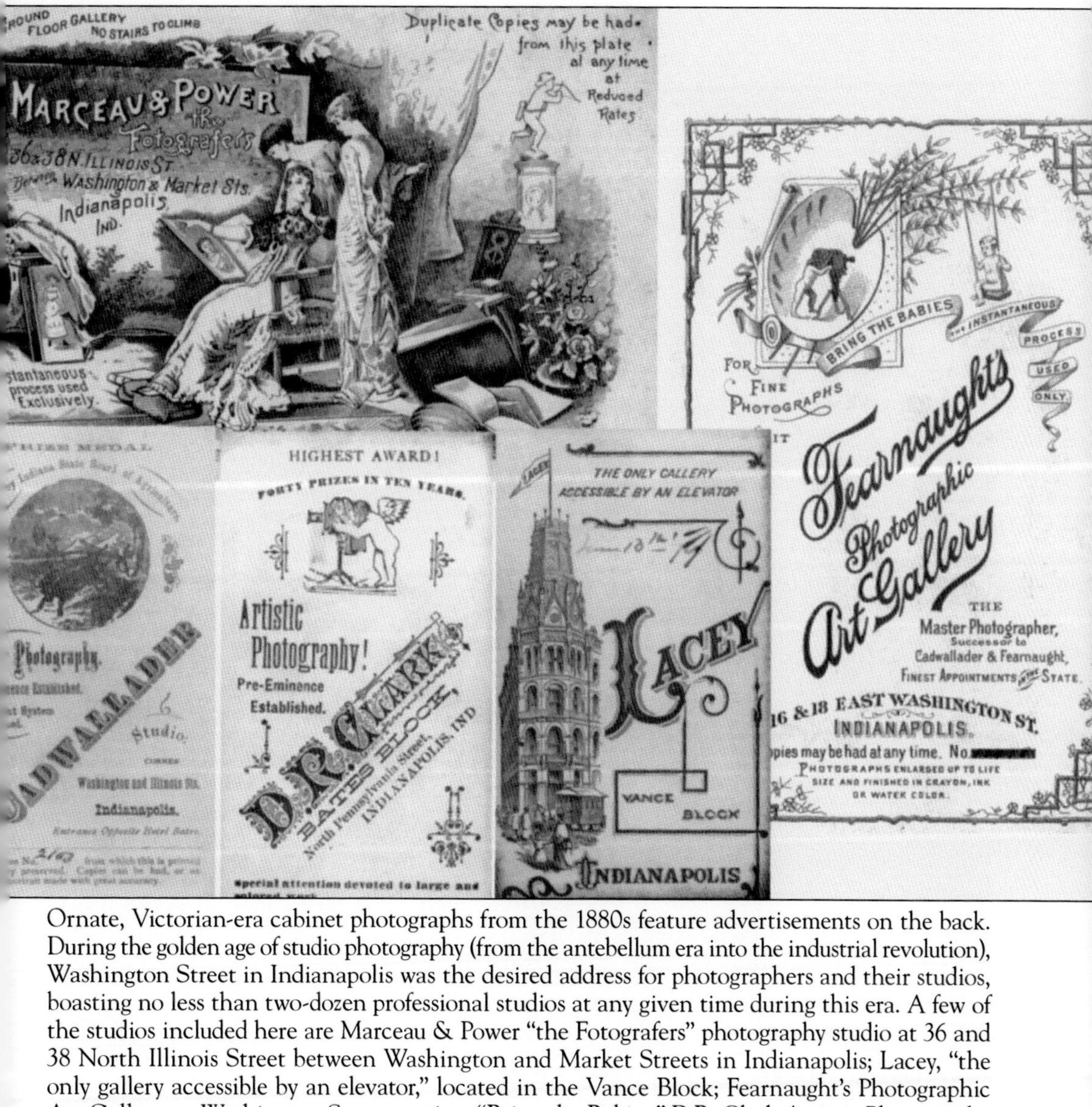

Ornate, Victorian-era cabinet photographs from the 1880s feature advertisements on the back. During the golden age of studio photography (from the antebellum era into the industrial revolution), Washington Street in Indianapolis was the desired address for photographers and their studios, boasting no less than two-dozen professional studios at any given time during this era. A few of the studios included here are Marceau & Power "the Fotografers" photography studio at 36 and 38 North Illinois Street between Washington and Market Streets in Indianapolis; Lacey, "the only gallery accessible by an elevator," located in the Vance Block; Fearnaught's Photographic Art Gallery on Washington Street, stating, "Bring the Babies;" D.R. Clark Artistic Photography in the Bates Block, stating, "Forty prizes in ten years;" and Cadwallader Studio on Washington and Illinois Streets, stating, "Prize medal awarded by Indiana State Board of Agriculture." (Alan E. Hunter.)

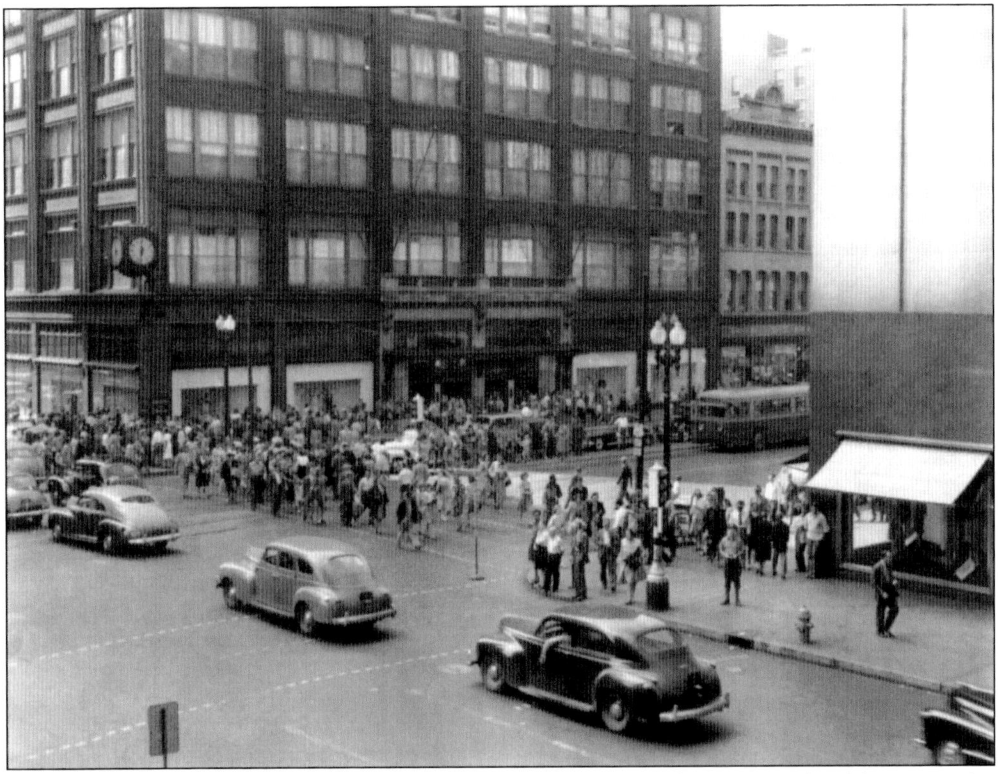

The most photographed intersection in the city and known as the Crossroads of America, the intersection of Washington and Illinois Streets is shown as it looked in the 1950s. The H.P. Wasson and Company store is at right, and the L.S. Ayres and Company department store is at left. Wasson's, the city's most prominent department store during the last century, occupied this location from 1883 until 1979. The Parisian department store currently operates on the site, now a part of Circle Centre Mall. (Indianapolis Public Library, Warren Branch.)

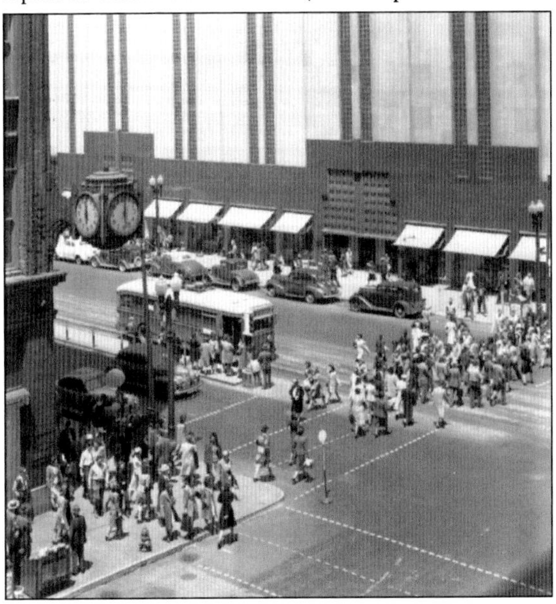

A view shows Washington and Meridian Streets in 1946. The sidewalks and intersections are bustling with shoppers during the postwar boom. The L.S. Ayres clock can be seen in the foreground at left. Ayres operated here from 1905 to 1992. (Alan E. Hunter.)

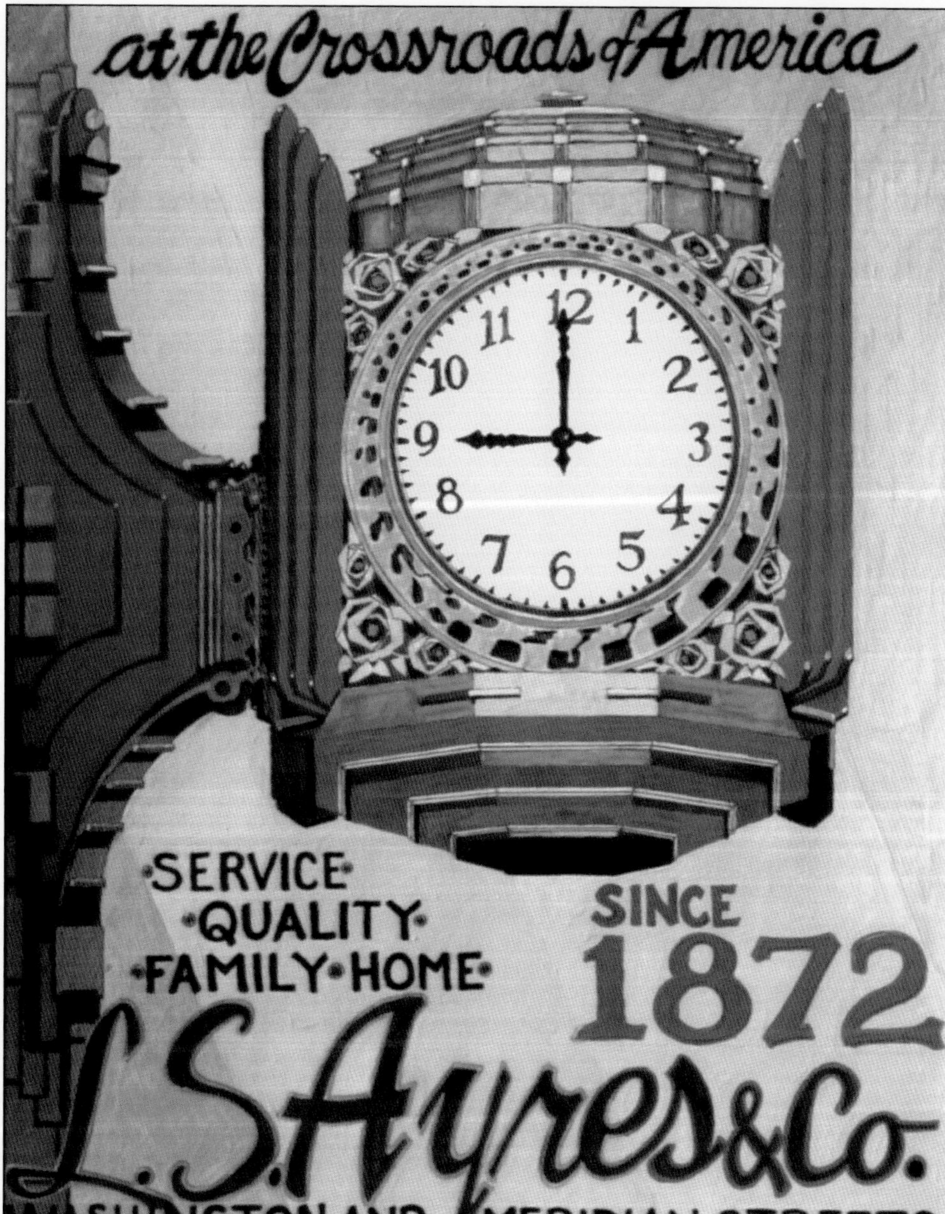

Dale Blaney painted the iconic clock on the corner of the L.S. Ayres department store at 1 West Washington Street. During the first half of the 20th century, Ayres grew to be Indianapolis's premier department store. The landmark downtown store, built in 1905, was enlarged several times, with the largest expansion after World War II. Ayres was the first department store in the United States to operate an Economy Basement Store in 1905. The L.S. Ayres Tearoom, which operated at the downtown department store from 1905 to 1990, served a clientele of fashionable shoppers in a formal setting. The painting reads: "at the Crossroads of America—Service-Quality-Family-Home—Since 1872—L.S. Ayres & Co.—Washington and Meridian Streets—Indianapolis, Indiana—Telephone-FRANKLIN 441." (Alan E. Hunter.)

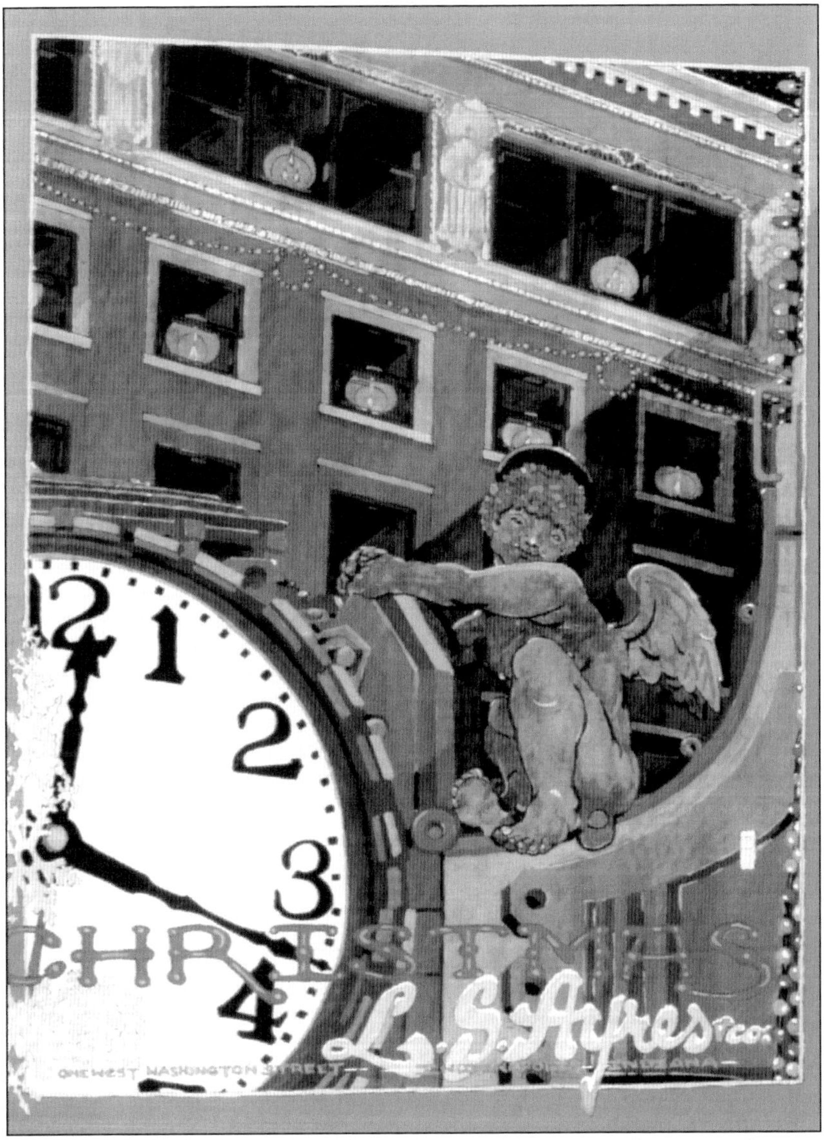

Dale Blaney painted the magical cherub that mysteriously appeared on a perch atop the L.S. Ayres clock. The cherub was one of Indianapolis's most treasured traditions. It began appearing on Thanksgiving eve in 1947. The 36-inch-tall cherub stood guard over shoppers until Santa arrived on Christmas Eve. The idea warmed the hearts of postwar shoppers of the mid-1940s, and thus, began a tradition that has had downtown shoppers on the lookout for the cherub every holiday season since. The angel arrives without pomp and circumstance, unseen when the sun sets at night, but in full view the following morning. The cherub was the brainchild of Virginia Holmes, an Ayres commercial artist who filled the empty spaces in advertisements—caused by war rationing and shortages—with sketches of cherubs. Customers loved it, and on the store's 75th anniversary, Ayres commissioned David Rubins, an Indianapolis sculptor and an instructor at the Herron School of Art, to create a bronze rendering of the cherub to adorn its outdoor clock. When Ayres was sold to the May Department Stores Company in 1986, they decided to move the cherub to their St. Louis headquarters. The people of Indianapolis were crushed, and in 1994, the May Company returned the cherub to its original home. (Alan E. Hunter.)

A December 1873 photograph shows the original L.S. Ayres building at 33–37 West Washington Street. The Charles Mayer Company is next door at 31 West Washington Street, decorated for the Christmas season. L.S. Ayres was a popular, innovative businessman who called every employee by name (all 175 of them) and greeted every customer at the door. Ayres was the first store in Indianapolis to install electric lights and an elevator and use glass display cases. (Alan E. Hunter.)

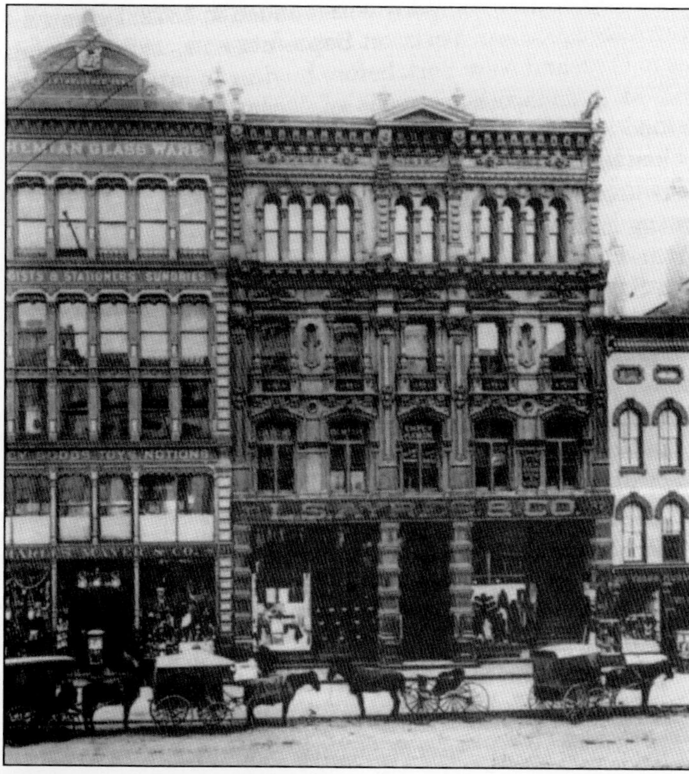

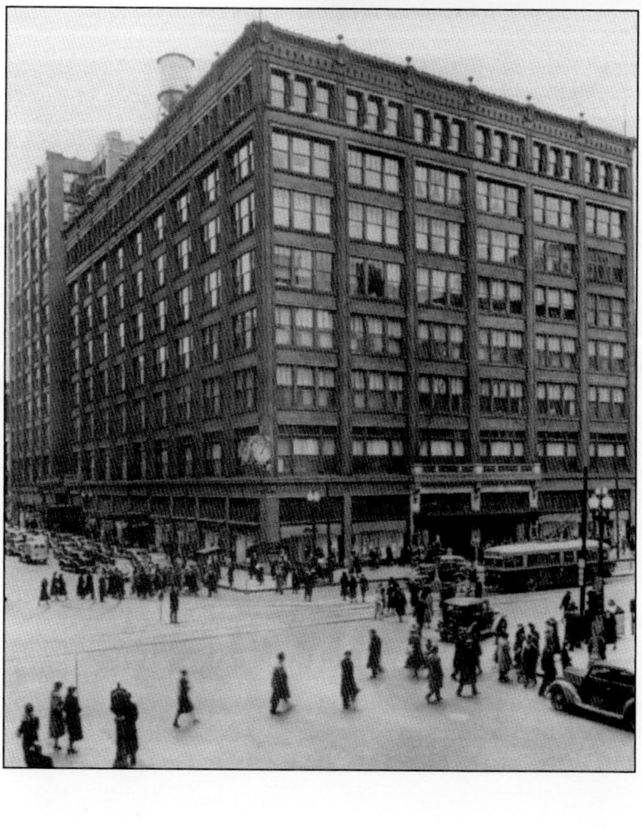

A 1936 photograph shows the second L.S. Ayres building located at Washington and Meridian Streets. Built in 1905, it was considered the city's first modern department store. The image shows one of the city's new trackless trolleys, or trolleybuses, which ran on rubber tires instead of wheels and had been introduced four years before in 1932. (Alan E. Hunter.)

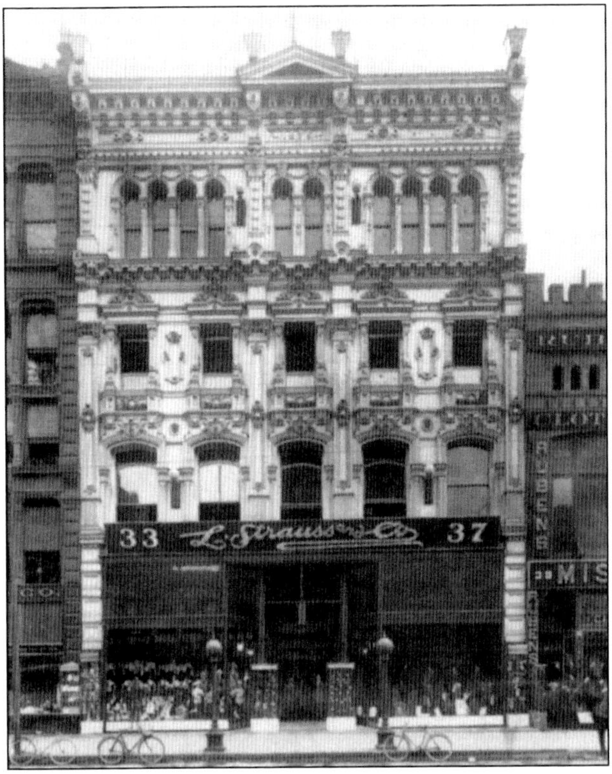

A 1906 photograph shows the L. Strauss and Co. department store on the southeast corner of Washington and Illinois Streets. L. Strauss and Co. was an upscale chain headquartered in Indianapolis. The store was originally named the Eagle Clothing Company. Eagle Clothing became a retail leader and pioneered the use of fixed prices for customers. In 1879, Leopold Strauss acquired the store, later changing the name to L. Strauss and Company. (Alan E. Hunter.)

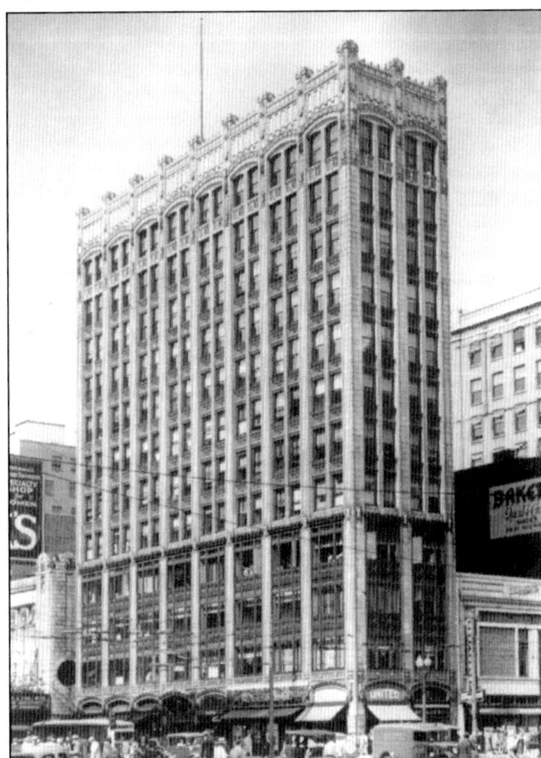

The largest building in Indianapolis to be demolished intentionally and not because of fire or structural damage, the Roosevelt Building is shown as it looked in 1938. The distinctive, narrow skyscraper was only 30 feet wide and designed by the architecture firm of Vonnegut, Bohn, and Mueller. Opened in 1923 on the northeast corner of Washington and Illinois Streets, the building was imploded by the city on August 12, 1990, to make way for a Saks Fifth Avenue. Saks pulled out, and the lot remained vacant for years. The luxurious Conrad Hotel was built on the spot in 2006. (Indianapolis Public Library, Warren Branch.)

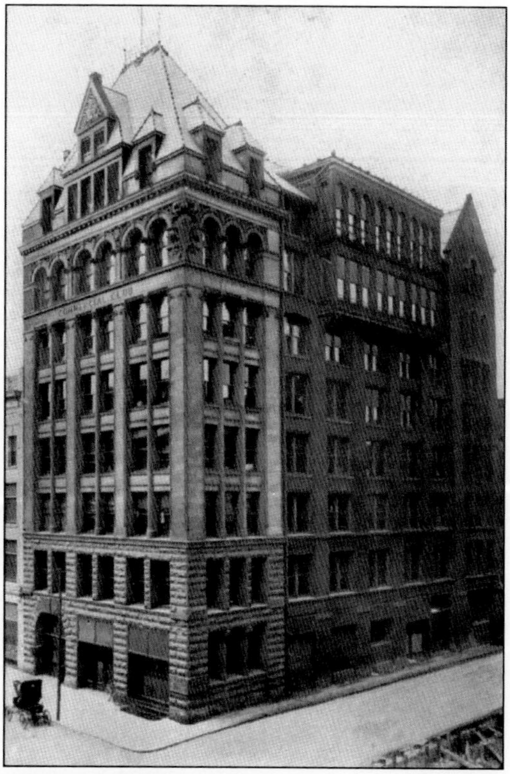

A view shows the Indianapolis Commercial Club at Washington and Meridian Streets in 1914. The club was created by several prominent Indianapolis businessmen, and Eli Lilly was its first president. In 1914, the commercial club had an estimated 1,100 members. The building was constructed in 1891 with the Commercial Club occupying the sixth, seventh, and eighth floors. (Alan E. Hunter.)

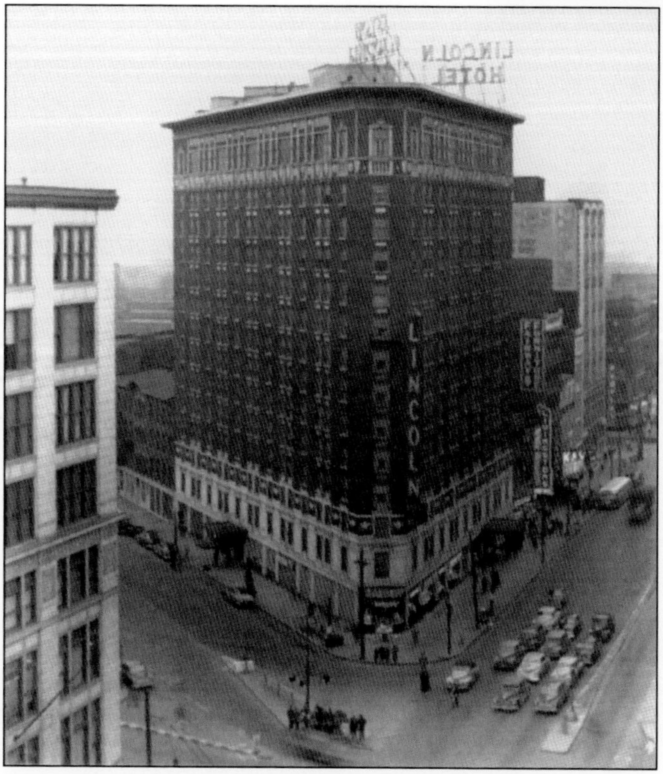

The Lincoln Hotel is pictured as it appeared in the early 1950s. The 14-story flatiron building located at the corner of Washington and Illinois Streets and Kentucky Avenue was designed by Rubush and Hunter, Indianapolis's premier architectural firm. The Rubush and Hunter firm is widely acknowledged for changing the Indianapolis streetscape in the early 20th century. The building was razed in 1973, and the site is now home to Merchants Plaza and the Hyatt Regency Hotel. The entire intersection is now gone. (Indianapolis Public Library, Warren Branch.)

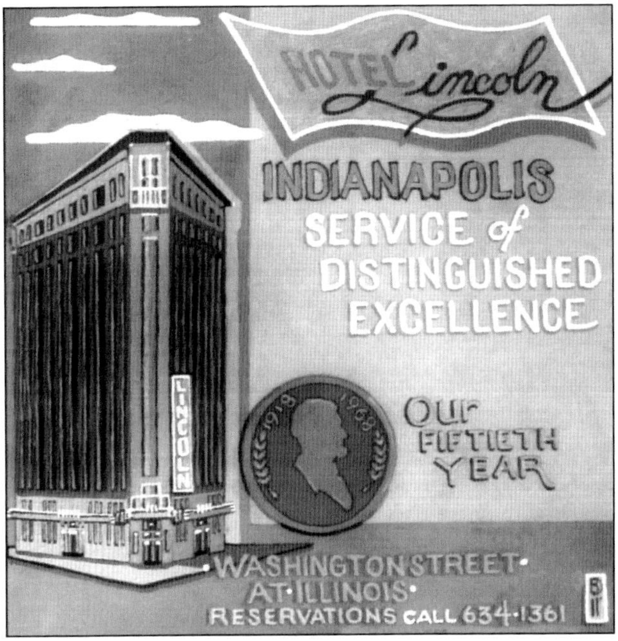

Dale Blaney created a painting of the Lincoln Hotel from a colorized vintage advertisement. The painting reads, "Hotel Lincoln—Indianapolis Service of Distinguished Excellence—Our Fiftieth Year—Washington Street at Illinois—Reservations Call 634-1361." (Alan E. Hunter.)

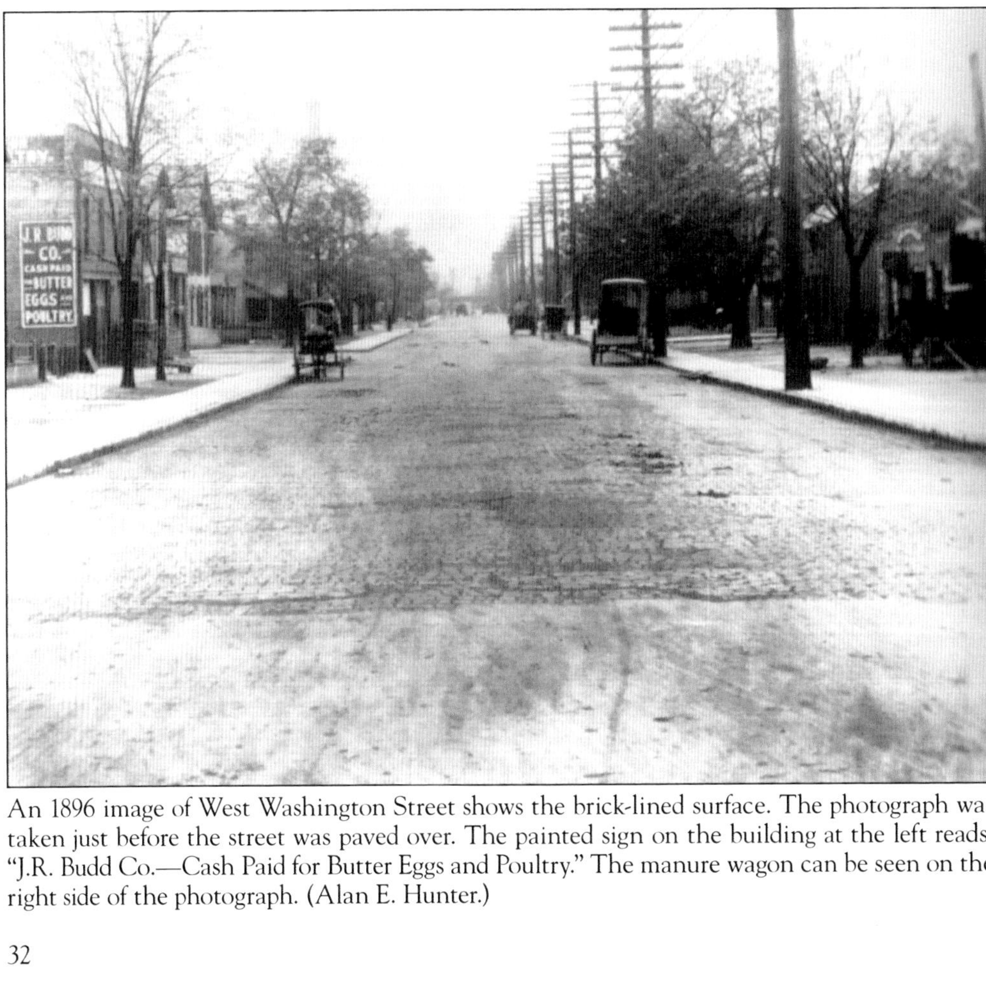

An 1896 image of West Washington Street shows the brick-lined surface. The photograph was taken just before the street was paved over. The painted sign on the building at the left reads, "J.R. Budd Co.—Cash Paid for Butter Eggs and Poultry." The manure wagon can be seen on the right side of the photograph. (Alan E. Hunter.)

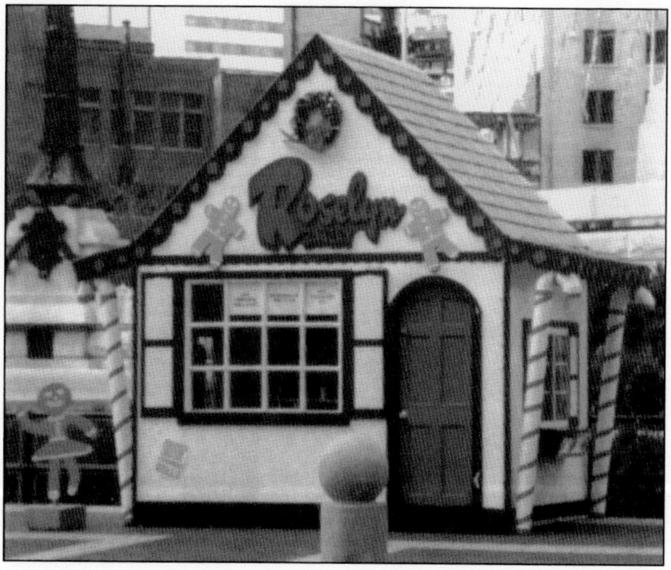

Every year, starting in 1974, on the night after Thanksgiving, Roselyn Bakery set up a special Christmas Hut to celebrate the lighting of the "World's Largest Christmas Tree" at the Indiana Soldiers and Sailors Monument. Guests received free cookies. In the quarter century that Roselyn set up on the west side of the circle, an estimated 1.2 million gingerbread men were given away. For 25 years, it was a treasured Christmas tradition. (Alan E. Hunter.)

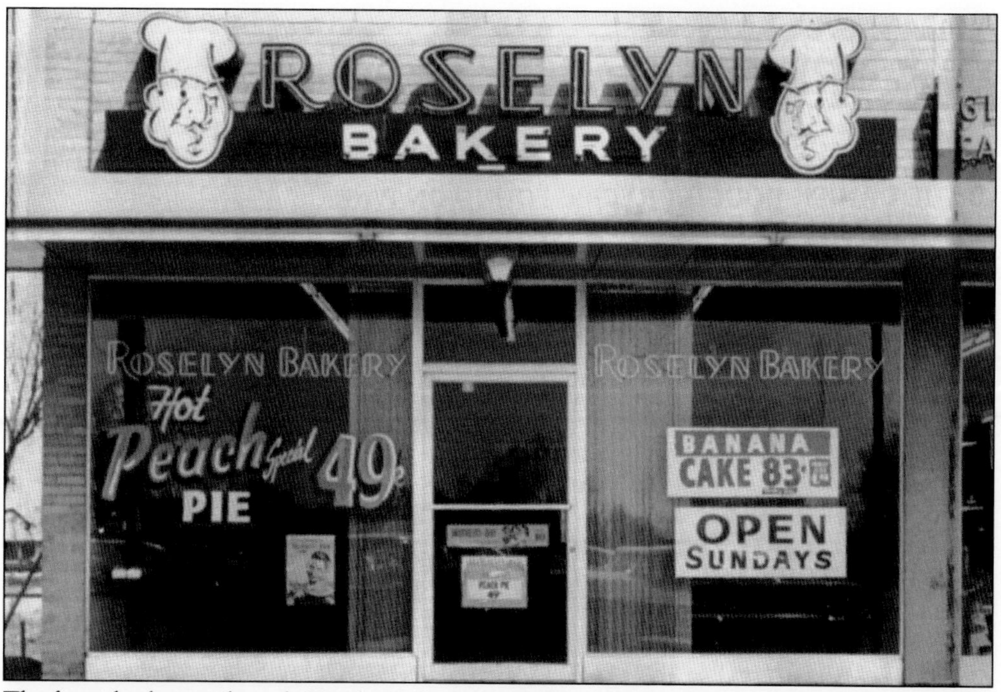

The front display window of a Roselyn Bakery store is shown around 1960. The Indianapolis-based chain was founded in 1943 on the corner of Twenty-second and Meridian Streets in Indianapolis. By the early 1950s, there were several Roselyn stores, and Roselyn's donuts, cakes, and cookies began appearing in local grocery stores. The first Roselyn logo (1943–1955) was a carbonized chef known as Mr. Henry. (Alan E. Hunter.)

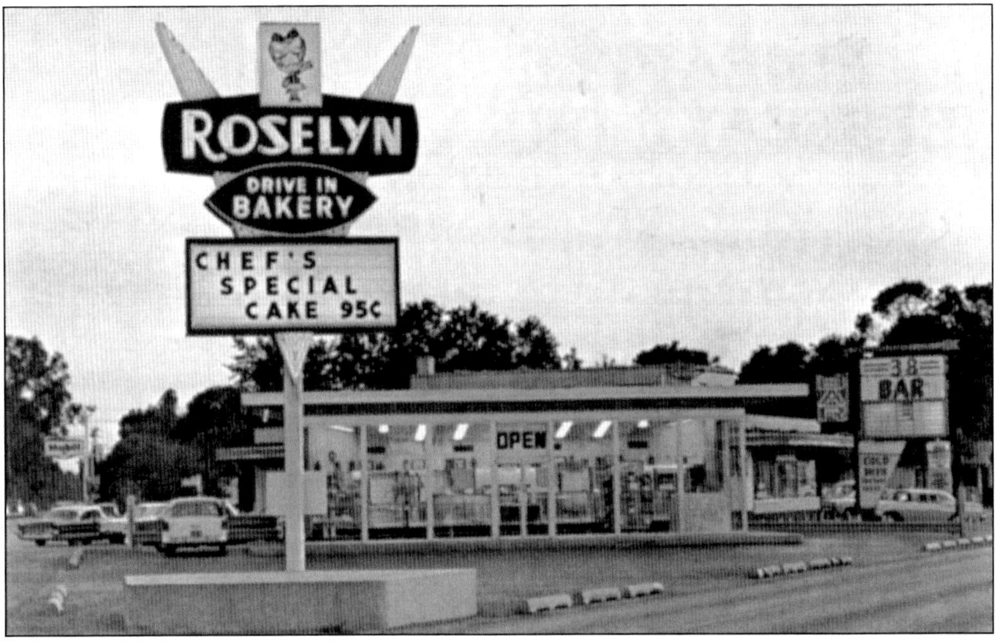

A 1960s-era Roselyn Bakery store was located at Thirty-eighth Street and Massachusetts Avenue. Roselyn founder John S. Clark Jr. and his wife, Mildred, struggled through World War II while John was away serving in the Army. Clark described the Roselyn Bakery business boom: "We always felt that if we made something very, very good, people would buy it and pay extra for a higher quality product. We have grown from one store to 18 freestanding stores and 16 bakeshops in shopping centers." (Alan E. Hunter.)

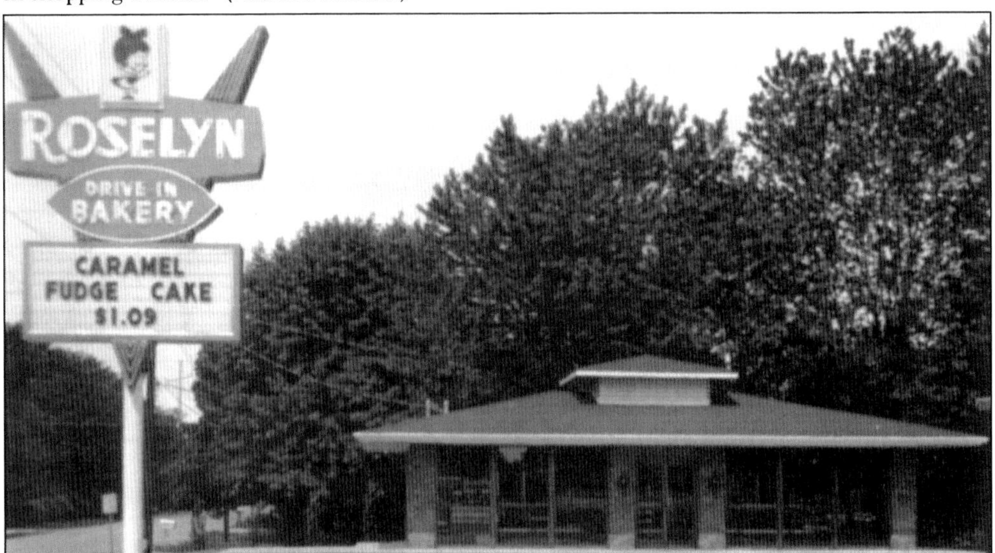

A Roselyn Bakery store is shown in the 1970s. The freestanding stores with their flying V signs became a familiar sight all around Indianapolis. As customers drove by, they could look to signage in the windows and the marquee to see what items were featured that week. The smiling little mascot, known as Rosie Roselyn, became a Hoosier city icon, making her debut in 1955. (Alan E. Hunter.)

A 1950s automobile window decal souvenir from the golden age of travel touts the "Old National Trail U.S. 40" with a tip of the cap to the pioneers who forged the trail before them. (Alan E. Hunter.)

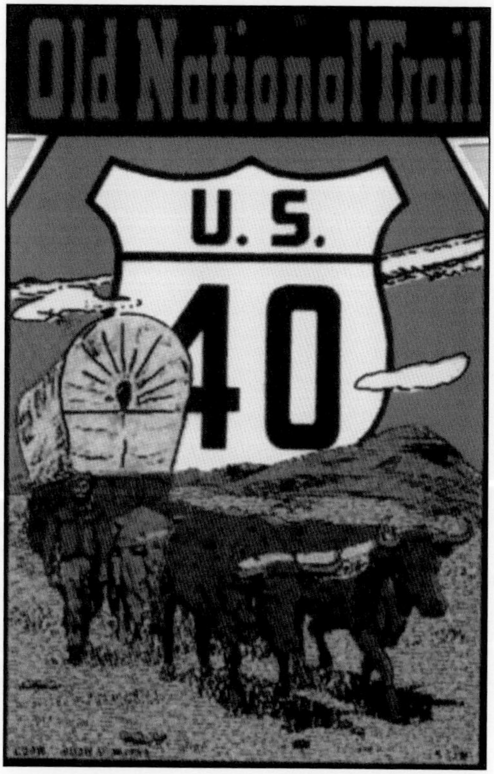

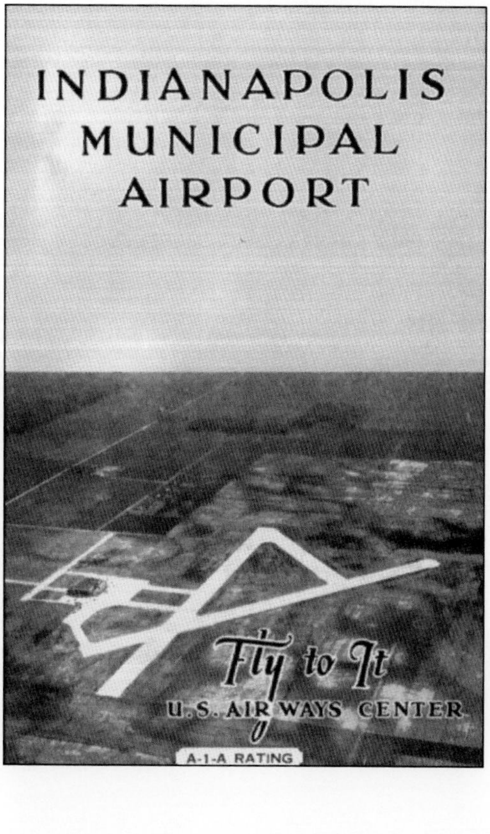

A booklet promotes the proposed Indianapolis Municipal Airport in August 1931, the year the airport opened. It states, "Fly to It U.S. Air Ways Center—A-1-A Rating." The airport was to be located on the west side of the city between Banner Avenue and High School Road. The name was changed to Weir-Cook Municipal Airport in 1944, after Col. Harvey Weir-Cook of Wilkinson, Indiana. A US Army Air Force pilot in World War I and World War II, Weir-Cook became an ace during World War I, with seven victories. He was killed during World War II while flying a P-39 over New Caledonia. Indianapolis's primary, commercial air, passenger and cargo facility received its international designation in 1975. (Alan E. Hunter.)

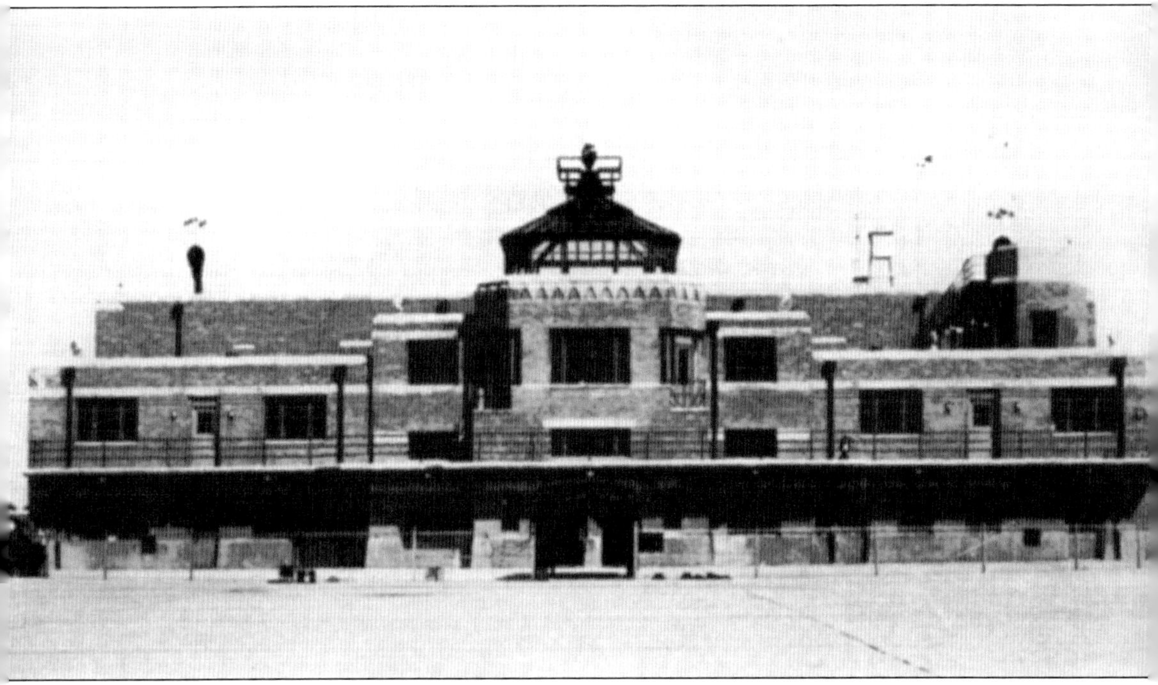

An August 1931 official Indianapolis Municipal Airport booklet was titled *Field View of Administration-Hangar Building.* According to the booklet, "The building is 156 by 136 feet in dimensions over all. It contains a hangar 100 feet in width with a 20-foot clearance, administrative offices, restaurant, United States Weather Bureau, pilot's rooms, shops, rest room, check room and offices of the transport companies operating off the field. A feature of the building is a U-shaped ramp which runs through the basement of the structure which must be used by automobiles coming to the field to discharge plane passengers. The passengers are unloaded on a waiting platform from where they walk up a short flight of stairs to the main waiting room." (Alan E. Hunter.)

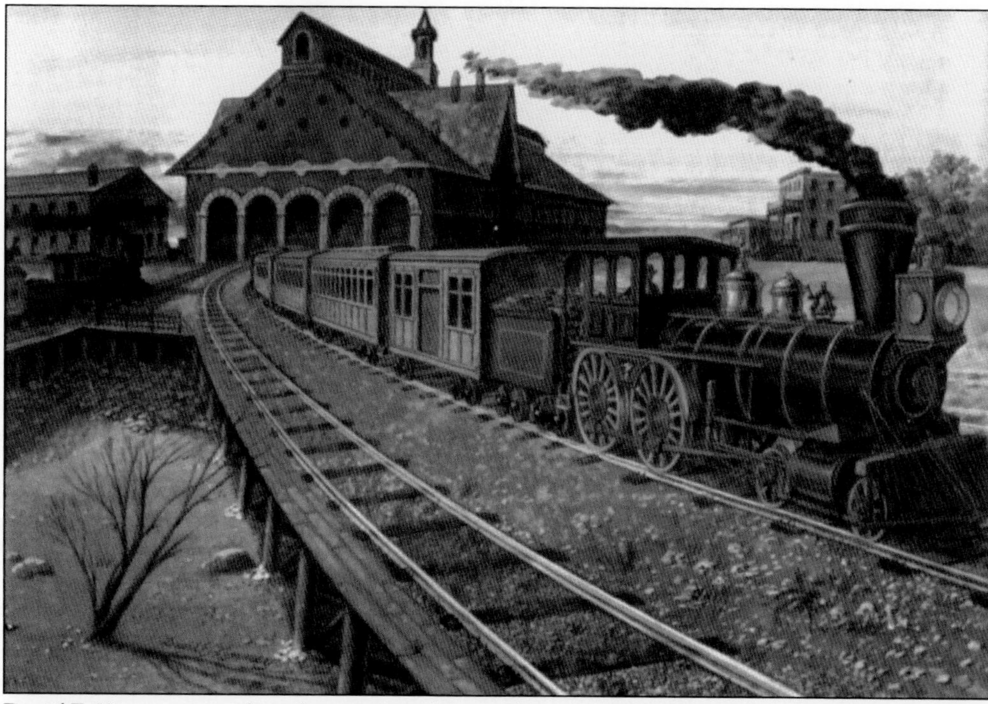

David E. Kinney created a color painting from a Christian Schrader woodcut for the Indianapolis sesquicentennial celebration in 1971. The artwork depicts Indianapolis's original Union Station as candidate Abraham Lincoln would have known it. The Indianapolis Union Station was the first of its kind in the world, opening on September 20, 1853, by the Indianapolis Union Railway in the Wholesale District of Indianapolis at 39 Jackson Place. (Alan E. Hunter.)

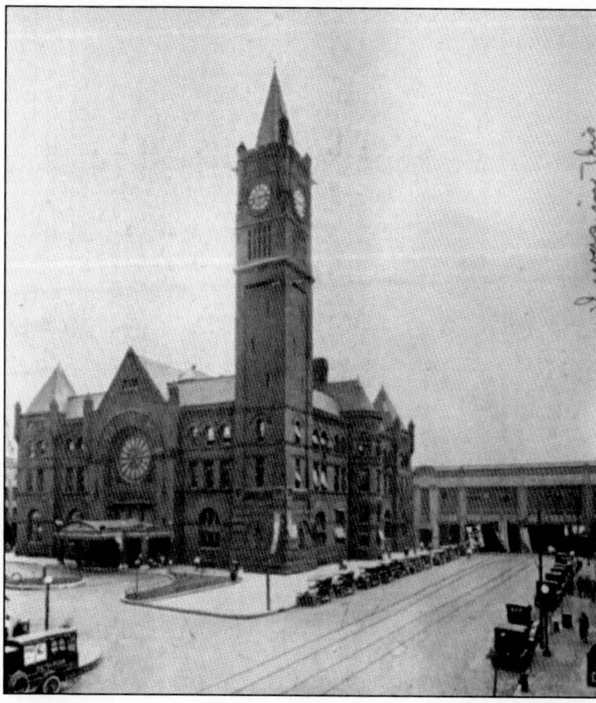

A 1920s image shows the Thomas Rodd–designed Union Station built in 1888. It is the oldest, still standing Union Rail terminal in the country—the distinctive head house and clock tower stand out. In 1888, the station featured a large, street-level iron train shed. By 1900, over 200 trains a day were serviced; the station built an expansive elevated platform. Thomas Edison got his start as a telegraph operator in this building but was fired for spending too much time tinkering with his inventions. The owner of this photograph wrote, "I was in this." (Alan E. Hunter.)

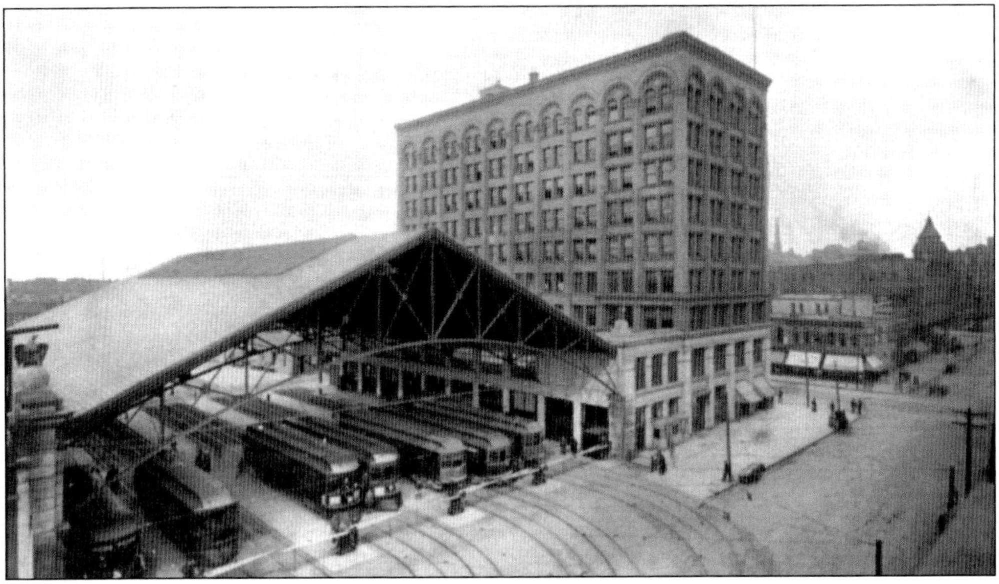

The Indianapolis Traction Terminal building is shown in 1914. Opened in 1904 in the heart of the downtown area, the great Traction Terminal in Indianapolis, Indiana, grew to become the largest interurban railway terminal in the world. In its heyday, this terminal hosted seven million passengers a year and 500 interurban trains a day, from as far away as Louisville, Kentucky. Indianapolis was a major transportation center; 13 lines fed into the city from other cities around the state. (Alan E. Hunter.)

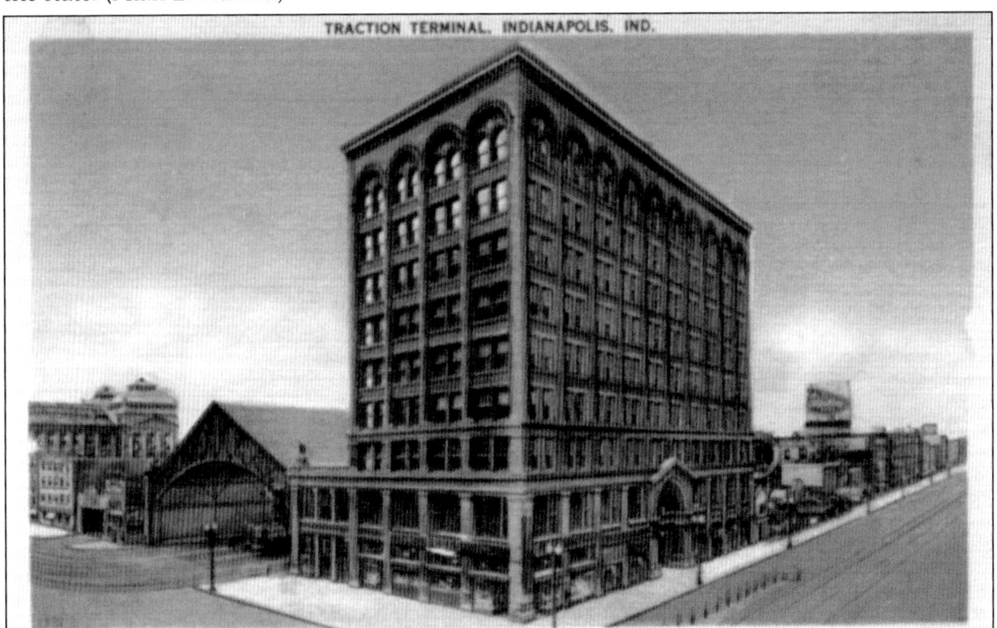

A 1940s linen postcard shows the Indianapolis Traction Terminal building after it was retooled for bus use. Several factors, including service-disrupting floods in 1937 and a fatal accident in 1941, put an end to the Indianapolis interurbans. The tracks in the Traction Terminal were paved over. The train shed was torn down in 1968, and the terminal's office building was razed in 1972. The Indianapolis Hilton hotel stands in its place today. (Alan E. Hunter.)

Three

The Interurban
The Forgotten Progress in Public Transportation

Before the automobile, a thread of railroad lines brought people, goods, and services from one end of the country to the other. Light rail connected small towns to big cities and linked small downtowns, encouraging local commerce. Locally owned shops, restaurants, law firms, and businesses served customers who came into town, and community focused around the town center.

Three types of streetcars provided service on the streets of Indianapolis. The first public transportation available in Indianapolis, the mule car, served passengers between 1864 and 1894. Typically, one or two mules pulled a 14-passenger car along iron rails in the middle of the dirt streets. Beginning in 1890, a streetcar with an electric motor drawing power from an overhead wire ran on rails. The electric streetcar usually seated 40 passengers. The last trolley car ran in January 1953 on the Broad Ripple line. A third type of streetcar with 40 passenger seats, the trackless trolley, or trolleybus, ran on rubber tires instead of rails; it was also powered by an electric motor connected to overhead wires. In 1932, Indianapolis Railways became the first transit company to operate the trolleybus in downtown traffic. Use continued until 1957, when it was replaced by the gasoline-powered bus, which was more maneuverable and had no wires to maintain.

Service on intercity electric railways, or interurbans, began in Indianapolis in 1900. By 1910, a total of 12 companies operated routes to all major towns within 120 miles of Indianapolis. Interurbans offered convenient schedules and cheaper fares than steam railroad.

In 1904, the Indianapolis Traction Terminal opened on Market Street between the Indiana Statehouse and Monument Circle—a single station to serve 12 lines, which would relieve congestion from loading on the streets. The nine-story terminal housed 250 offices, nine baggage storerooms, a ticket office, and a large waiting room. The complex featured a nine-track train shed remembered for its high-peaked roof. During the first week of operation, coinciding with the state fair, the terminal handled an average of 10,000 passengers per day.

By the dawn of the Great Depression, interurban usage had declined by almost 40 percent because of the popularity of the automobile. The tracks in the Traction Terminal were paved over. The train shed was torn down in 1968 after construction of a new bus station, and the office building was razed in 1972. Today, the Indianapolis Hilton occupies the site. The only architectural remains are two stone eagles now located in front of the Indiana State Museum.

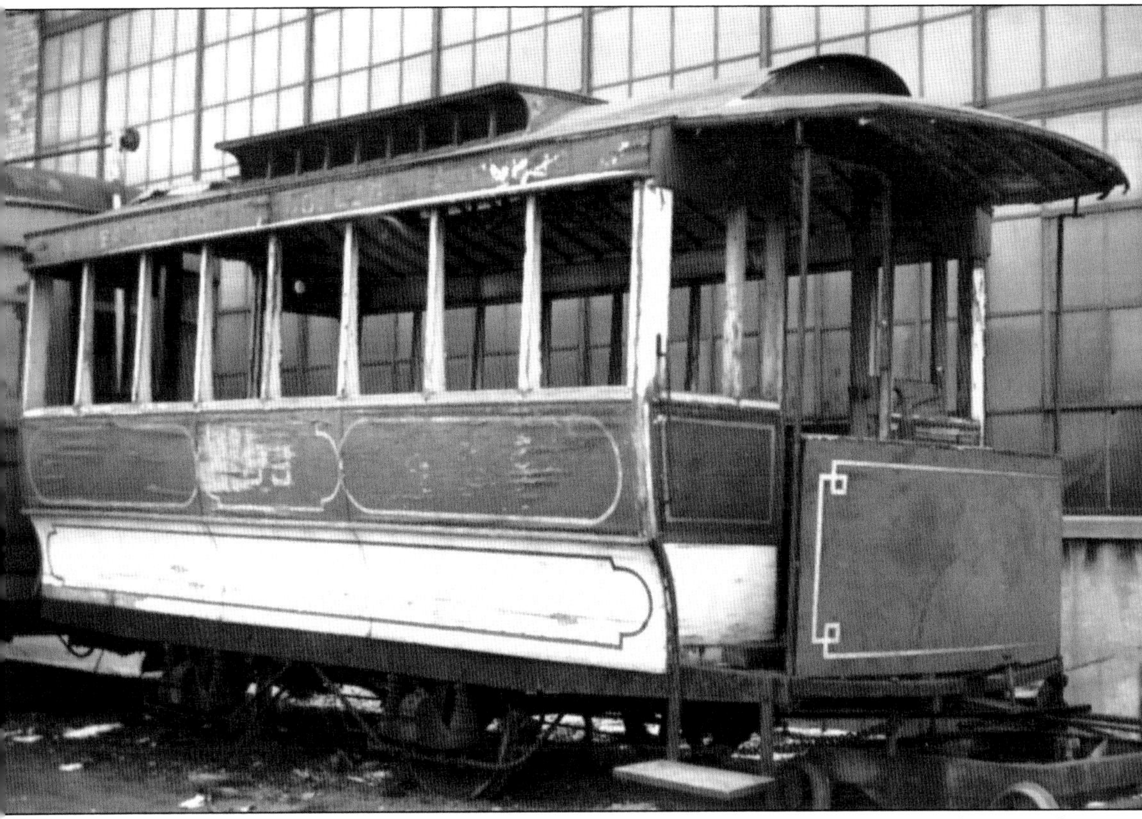

In 1891, the first electric streetcar clanged and rumbled through the city. Known as the interurban, the electric railway cars were widely used in the early 1900s. Low on comfort and frills, early interurbans used converted lightweight wooden railway passenger cars with a small express or freight motor. It was not uncommon for passengers to have to get off the car and walk as teams of horses pulled the underpowered machines up a steep grade. Here, a decommissioned mule car-turned-interurban waits for the scrap heap behind the terminal in 1947. (Alan E. Hunter.)

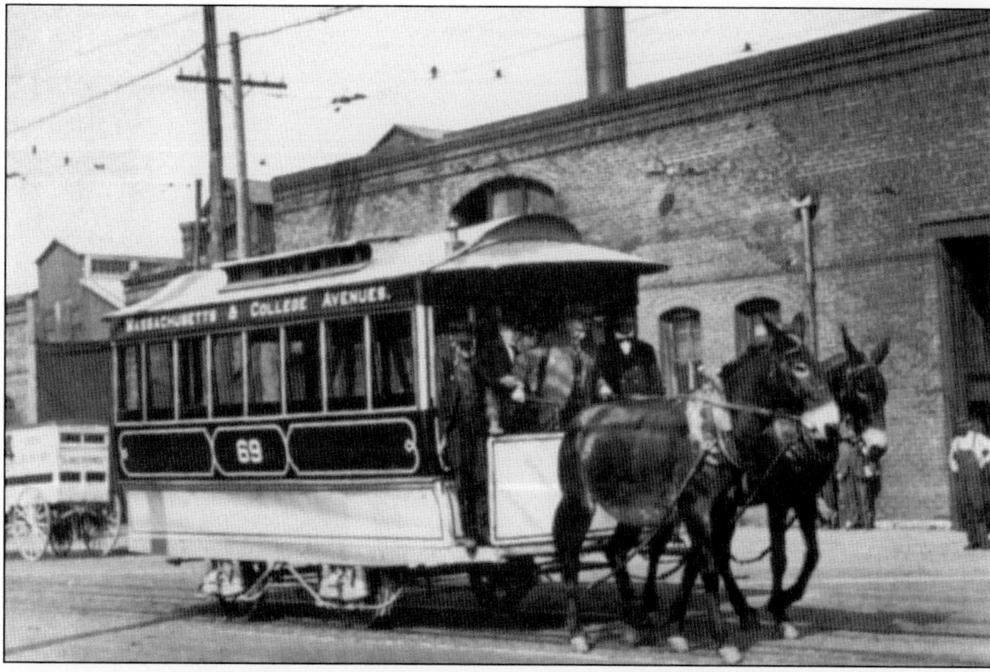

An image from the 1890s shows a mule-drawn streetcar on Washington Street in Indianapolis. In 1864, the first mule-drawn car began on the rails here. This is car No. 69, which serviced Massachusetts and College Avenues. The uniformed conductor stands on the side as a distinguished-looking gentleman in a suit and hat tries his hand at steering the car and leading the team. (Indianapolis Public Library, Warren Branch.)

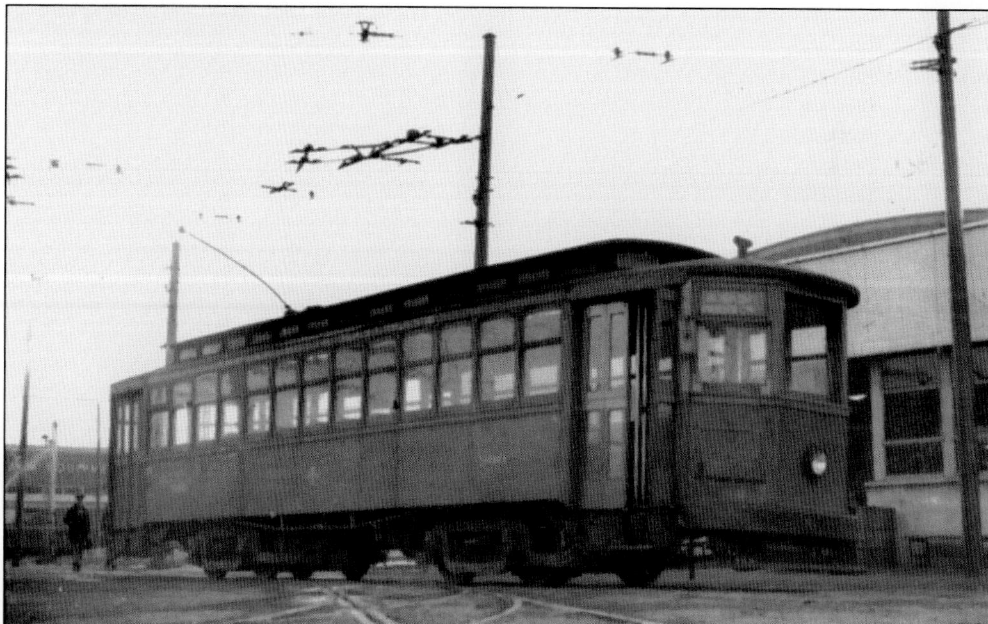

A photograph taken in 1940 shows two Indianapolis Railways interurban drivers chatting behind car No. 900 in the haze of an Indianapolis morning. The destination sign above the windshield reads, "West Wash. 900 Block Only." (Alan E. Hunter.)

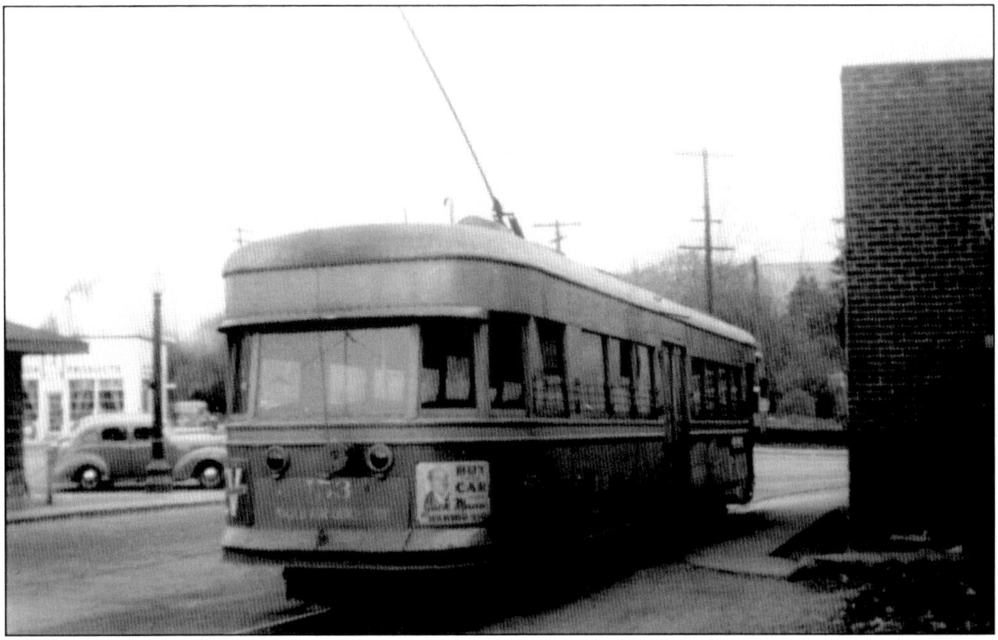

A photograph from around the 1940s shows the modernized, lightweight Indianapolis Railways interurban car No. 153 at the West Washington Loop. The sign on the front tempts the pedestrians to "buy your car from Jack Maurer," whose dealership was located on North Meridian Street. (Alan E. Hunter.)

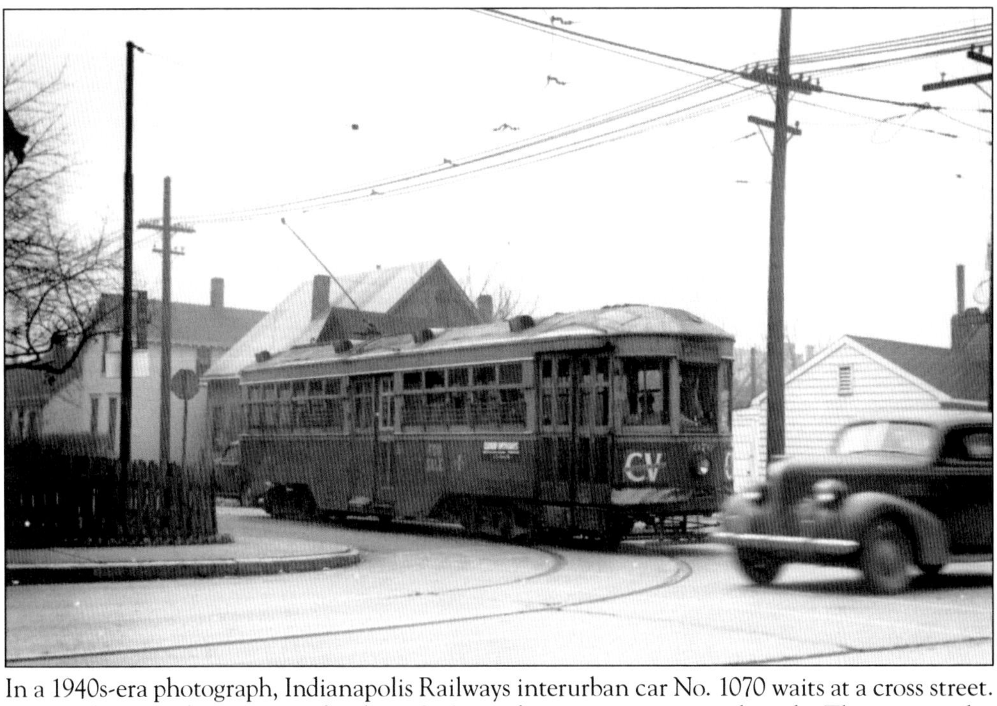

In a 1940s-era photograph, Indianapolis Railways interurban car No. 1070 waits at a cross street. The car has an advertisement for the L.S. Ayres department store on the side. The rectangular sign posted high on the telephone pole at left reads, "Car Stop," and "Michigan Street" appears in the destination sign above the driver's open windshield. (Alan E. Hunter.)

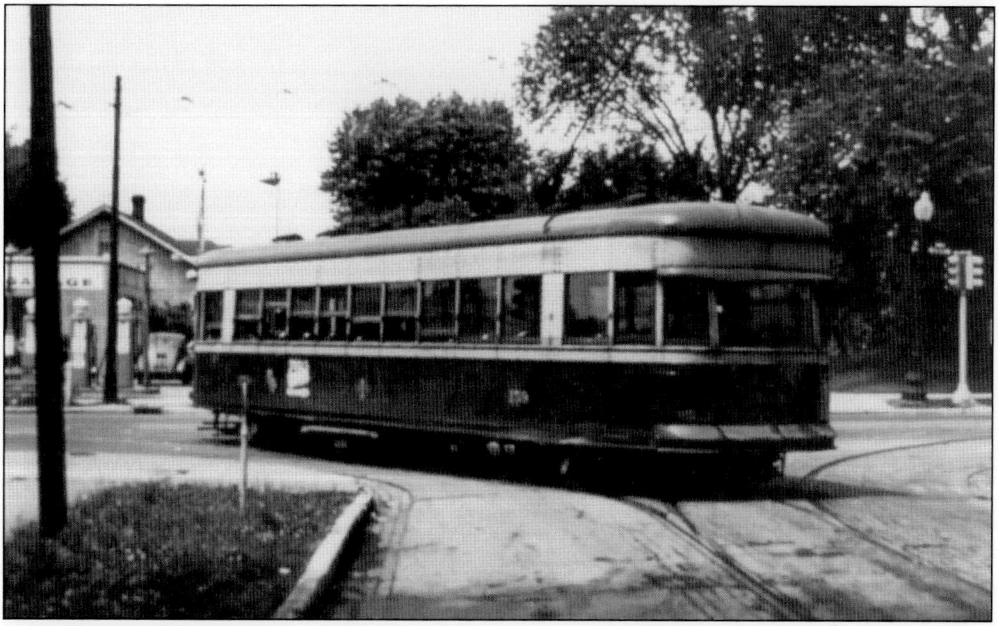

In a 1950s-era photograph, Indianapolis Railway System interurban car No. 159 rounds a corner. A Standard Oil gas and service station featuring three pumps with the ornate Standard Red Crown Gasoline glass globes is in the background. (Alan E. Hunter.)

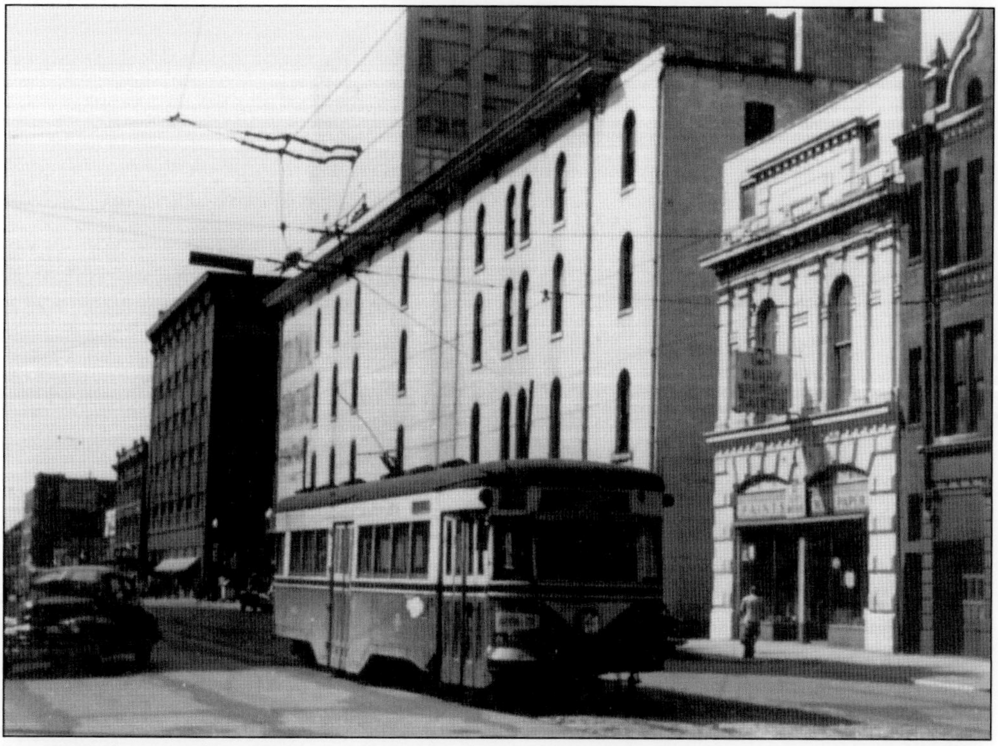

In a 1948 photograph, an Indianapolis Railway System interurban passes the Berry Brothers Paints and Wallpaper store and the Colonial Furniture Company on Washington Street in Indianapolis. (Alan E. Hunter.)

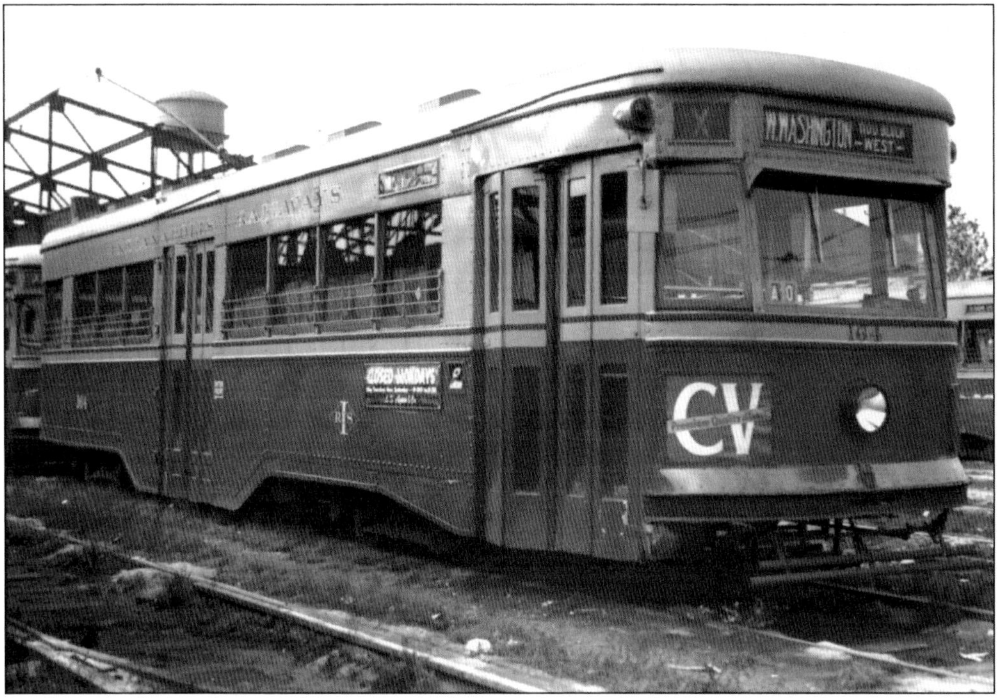

A photograph dated November 23, 1947, shows Indianapolis Railways interurban car No. 164 staged in the rail yard. The destination sign above the windshield reads, "W. Washington 1100 Block West." The car sports an advertisement for Terre Haute–made Champagne Velvet beer on front. (Alan E. Hunter.)

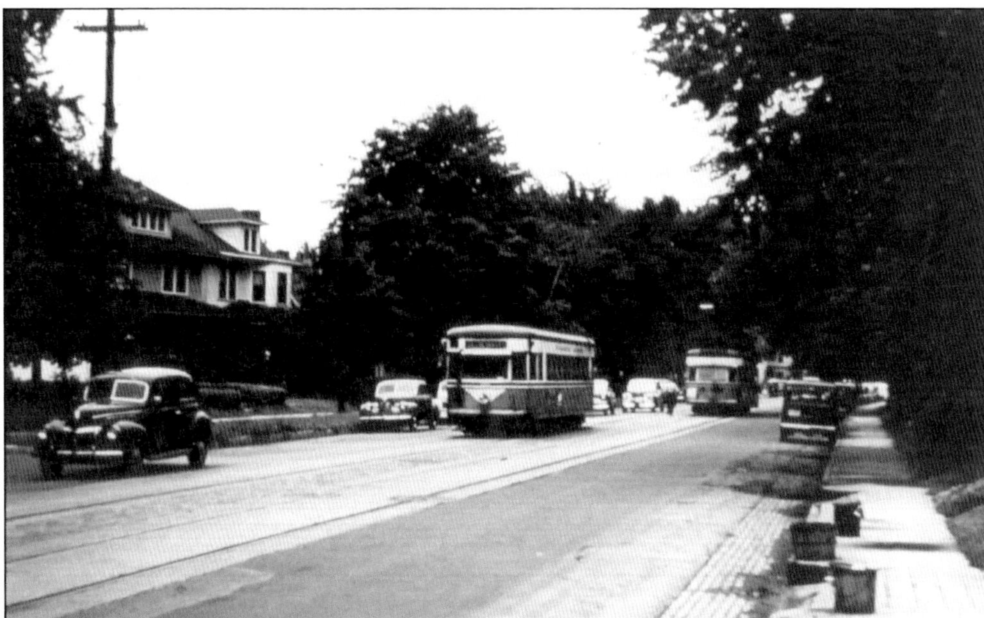

A 1940s image shows one Indianapolis Railways interurban car passing another on West Washington Street. The sidewalks have wooden ash cans placed at the curb, and brick-gutter road remnants from the old National Road are visible. (Alan E. Hunter.)

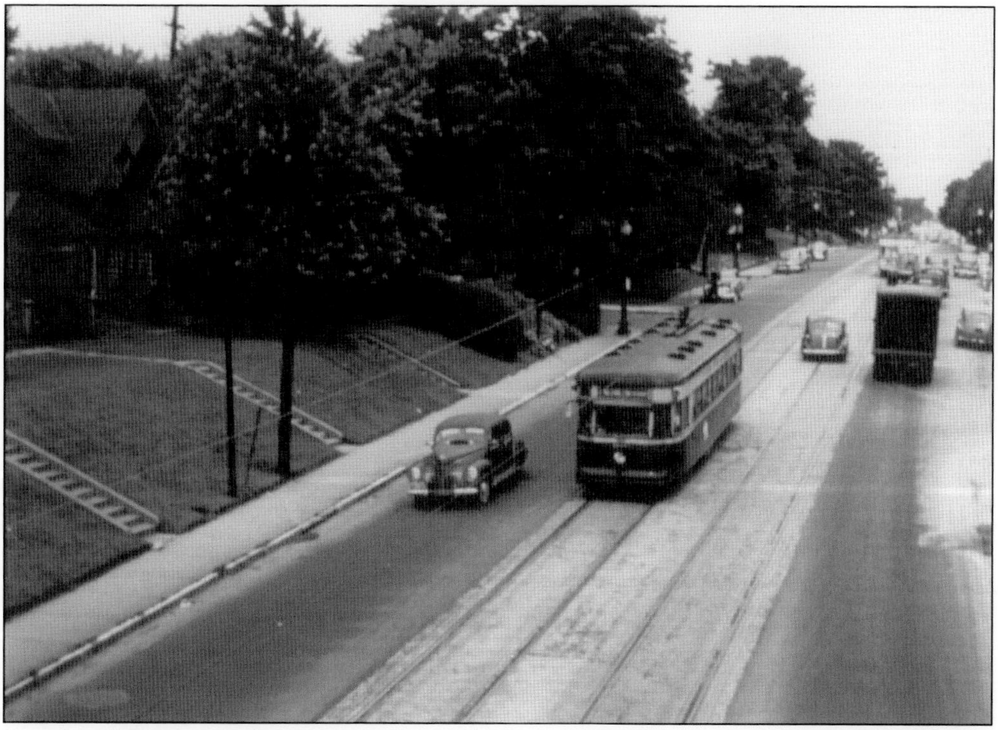

Another 1940s image shows two Indianapolis Railways interurban cars heading in opposite directions on West Washington Street as vintage sedans pass close by. (Alan E. Hunter.)

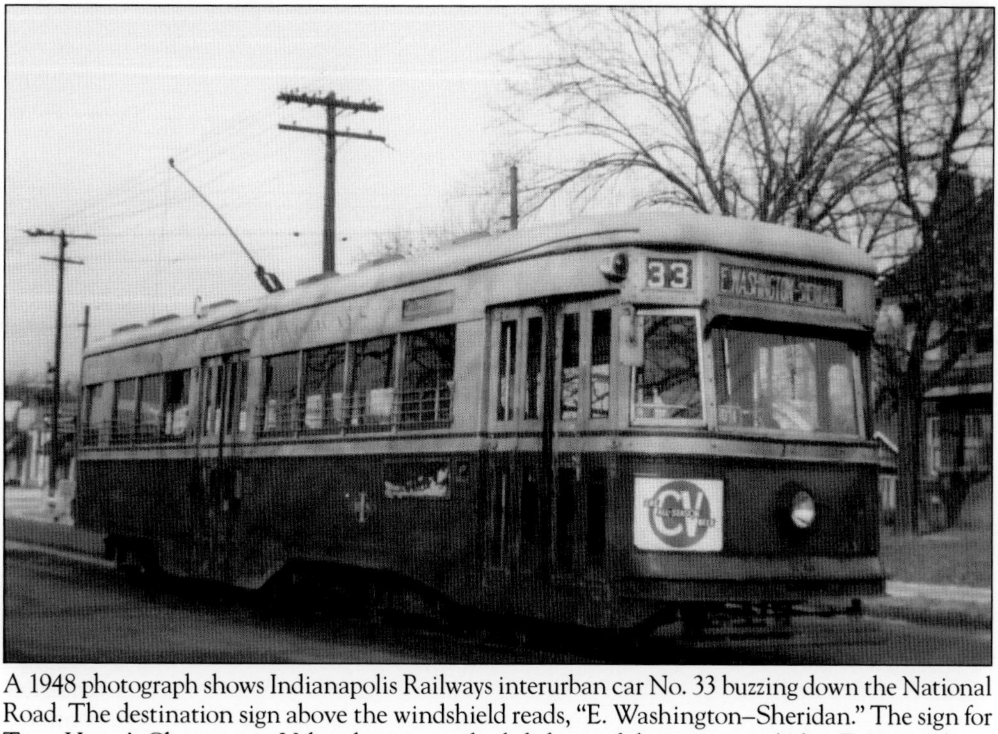

A 1948 photograph shows Indianapolis Railways interurban car No. 33 buzzing down the National Road. The destination sign above the windshield reads, "E. Washington–Sheridan." The sign for Terre Haute's Champagne Velvet beer is on the left front of the train car. (Alan E. Hunter.)

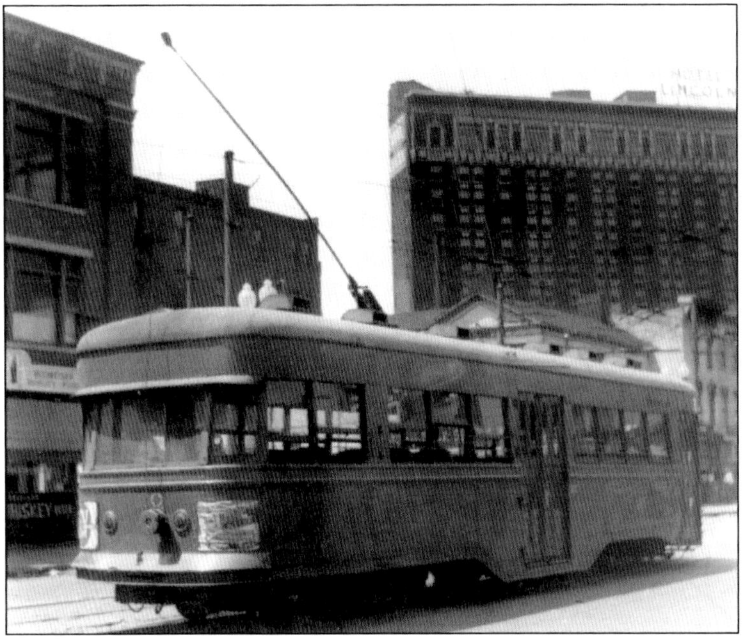

A 1940s-era photograph shows interurban car No. 167 as it passes the 14-story flatiron Hotel Lincoln at the intersection of Washington and Illinois Streets and Kentucky Avenue. The wrinkled, weather-beaten signs for Champagne Velvet beer and Jack Maurer's car dealership are visible on the back corners. A Budweiser sign hangs above the door of the bar at left. (Alan E. Hunter.)

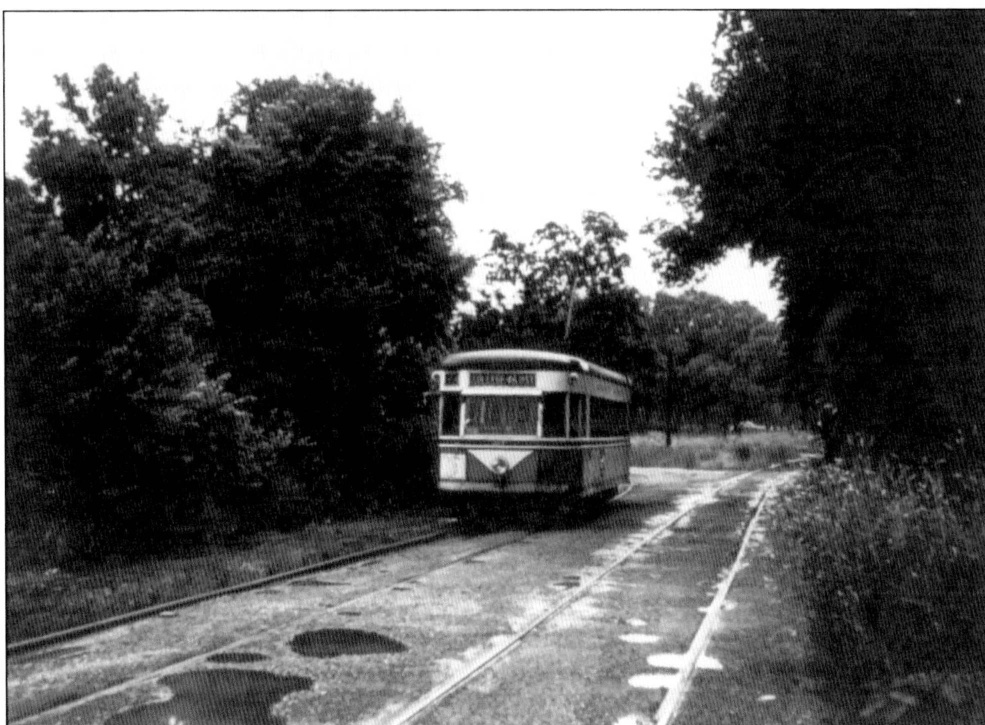

A 1940s photograph shows an Indianapolis Railways interurban car traveling through an uncharacteristic wooded area of Indianapolis. Puddles of fresh rain can be seen around the tracks and on the ground. The destination sign above the windscreen reads, "College–46th St." (Alan E. Hunter.)

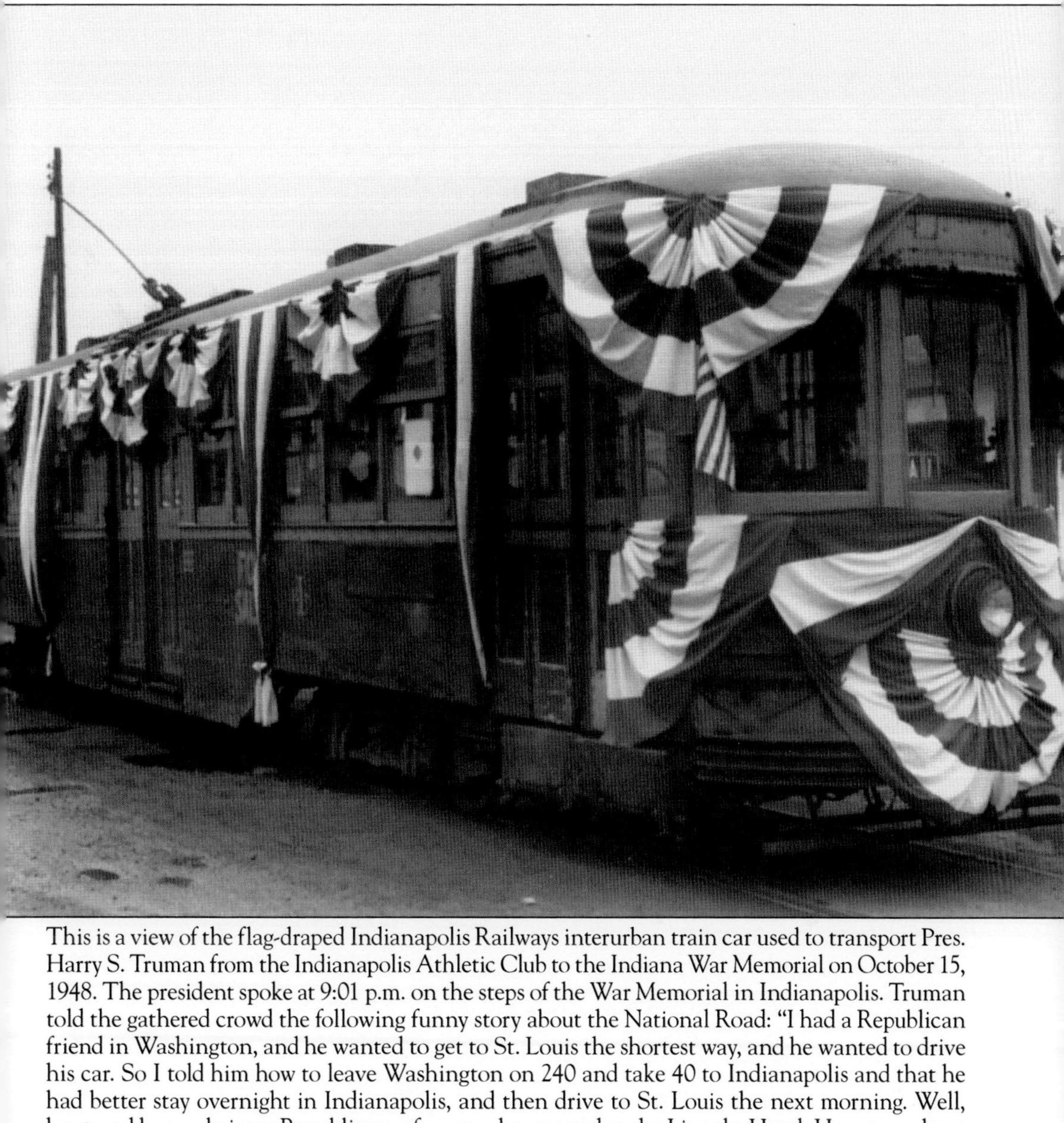

This is a view of the flag-draped Indianapolis Railways interurban train car used to transport Pres. Harry S. Truman from the Indianapolis Athletic Club to the Indiana War Memorial on October 15, 1948. The president spoke at 9:01 p.m. on the steps of the War Memorial in Indianapolis. Truman told the gathered crowd the following funny story about the National Road: "I had a Republican friend in Washington, and he wanted to get to St. Louis the shortest way, and he wanted to drive his car. So I told him how to leave Washington on 240 and take 40 to Indianapolis and that he had better stay overnight in Indianapolis, and then drive to St. Louis the next morning. Well, he stayed here—being a Republican, of course, he stopped at the Lincoln Hotel. He got up about 5:30 the next morning and they gave him his car out on that diagonal street that's on the east side of the Lincoln Hotel; and he inquired the way to 40, and they pointed out Washington Street to him, and he drove down the diagonal street and started on 40 toward what he thought was St. Louis—and about two hours after that he found out he was in Richmond, Indiana. Now, I think that's rather typical of the way the Republicans go most of the time." (Alan E. Hunter.)

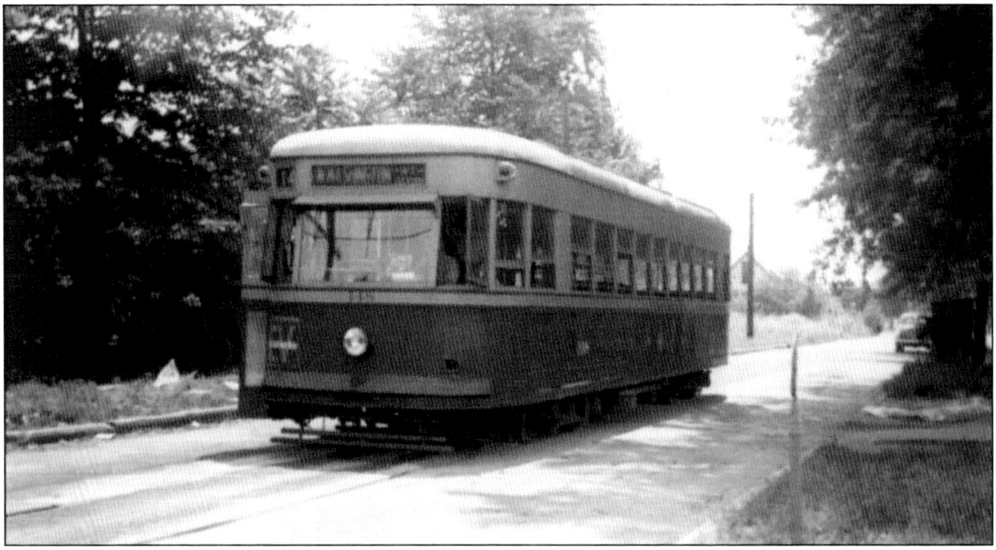

This September 8, 1946, photograph shows Indianapolis Railways interurban car No. 148 stopped, door open, waiting to pick up passengers in a wooded area of Indianapolis. The destination sign above the windscreen reads, "W. Washington–Mt. Jackson." The Mt. Jackson area of Indianapolis, now known as Hawthorne, is located on Highway 40, just three blocks south of the Indianapolis Motor Speedway. (Alan E. Hunter.)

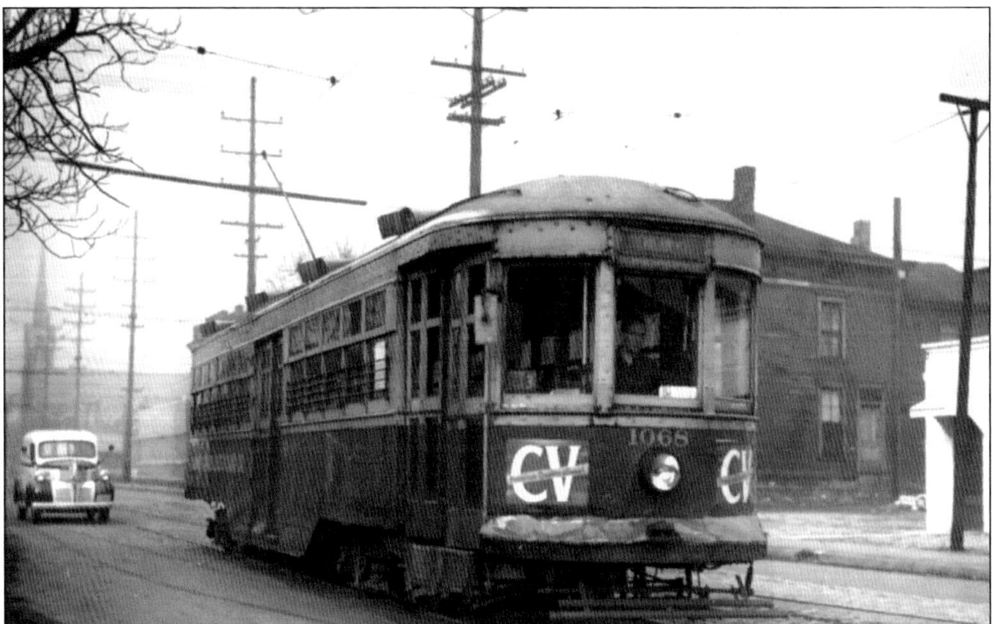

A World War II–era photograph shows Indianapolis Railways interurban car No. 1068 traveling down Washington Street in Indianapolis in the early-morning hours. The destination sign reads, "Michigan–West Wash." The World War II years were busy for interurban trolley lines because of rationing of gasoline and tires and the scarcity of new automobiles. Interurban lines enjoyed passenger counts not seen since the early 1900s before the rise of the automobile. (Alan E. Hunter.)

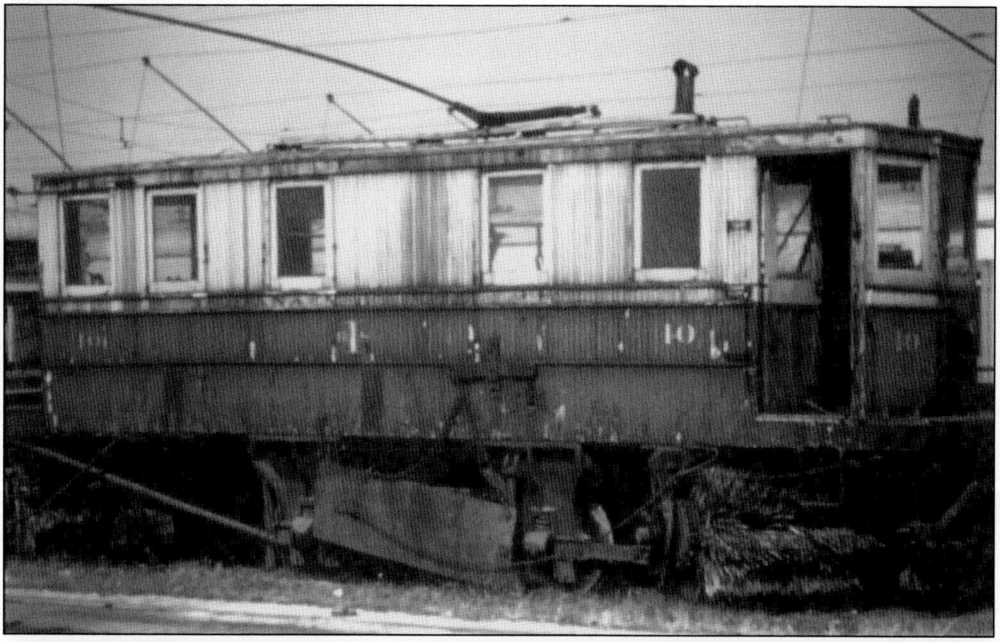

A March 28, 1948, photograph shows abandoned wooden Indianapolis Railways car No. 40 staged in the scrap yard of the Washington Street train shed in Indianapolis. The car had been retooled, with a large brush attached to the front, for use as a street sweeper. This was the last stop before the junkyard. (Alan E. Hunter.)

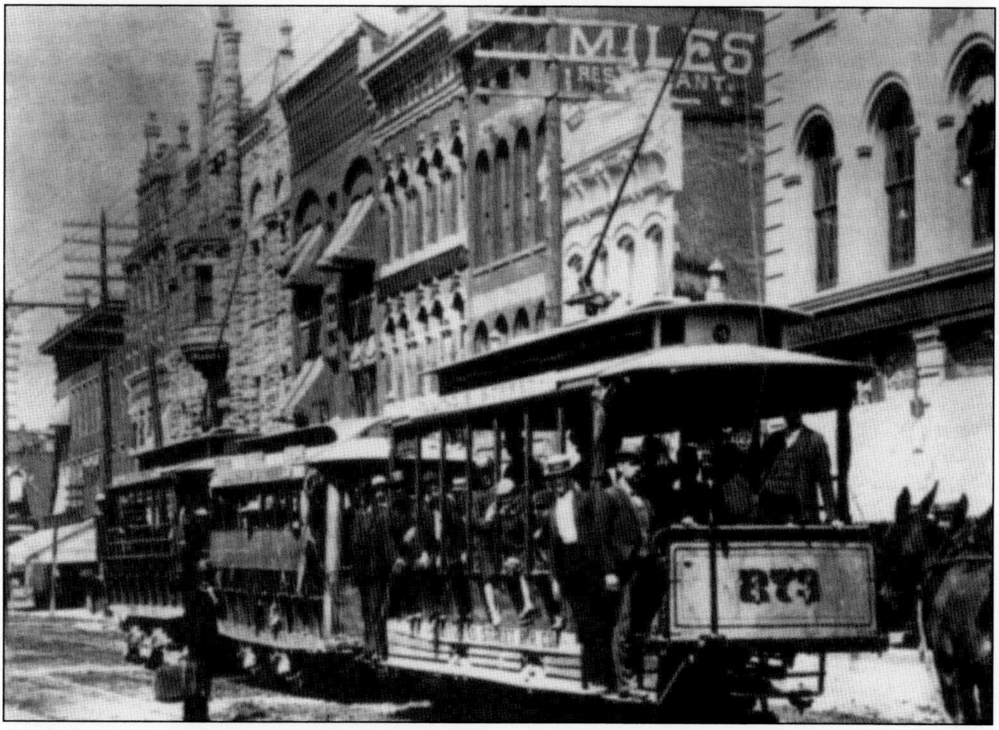

An 1873 photograph shows Indianapolis Railways mule-drawn streetcar No. 873 on Washington Street. The image shows a triple piggyback set of cars full of passengers. (Alan E. Hunter.)

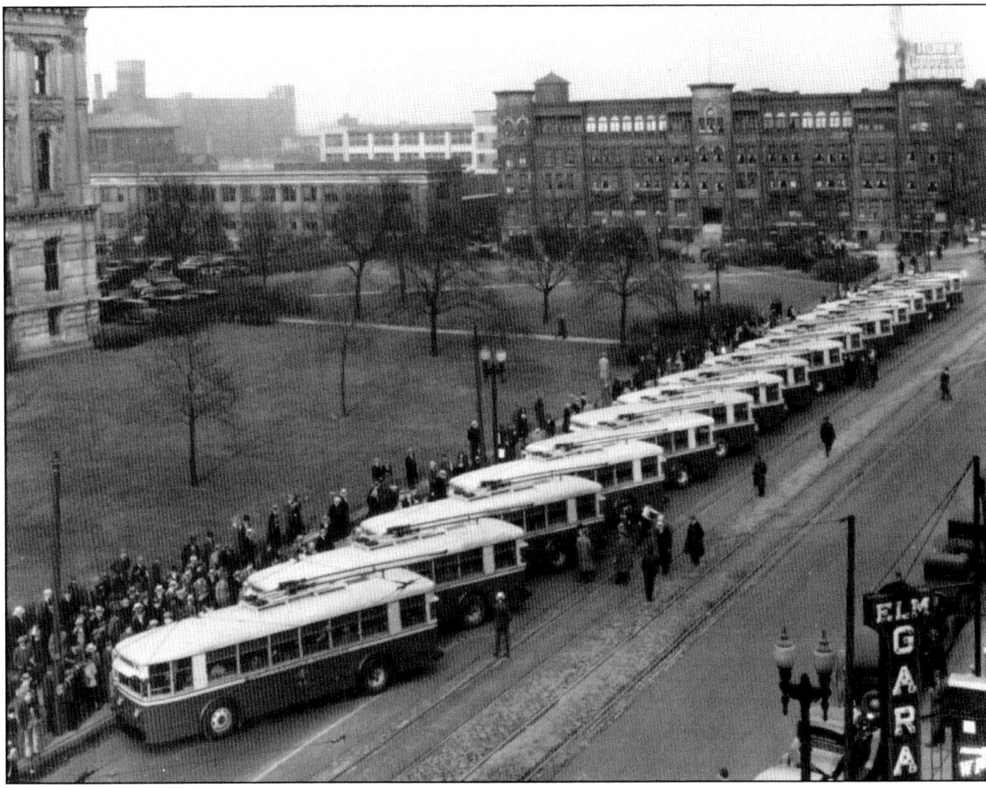

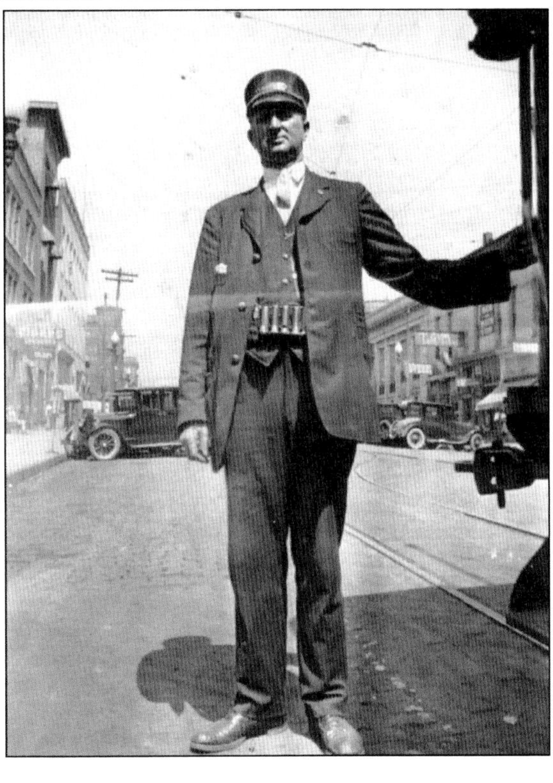

A December 1932 photograph shows a line of new Indianapolis Railway trackless trolleys lined up in front of the Indiana Statehouse prior to the start of a christening parade. By 1937, Indianapolis had the largest fleet of trackless trolleys in the country. The Hotel Roosevelt can be seen in the background. (Alan E. Hunter.)

A photograph from around the 1920s shows an unidentified Indianapolis Railways interurban train conductor with his token taker/change maker clipped onto the front of his belt and his hand firmly gripping the back of the railcar. This photograph was taken from the inside of an automobile; there is a half-open window in the center of the image. (Alan E. Hunter.)

A 1940 map and timetable from the Indianapolis Railways–Peoples Motor Coach Company is titled A *Map for Going Anywhere in Indianapolis.* (Alan E. Hunter.)

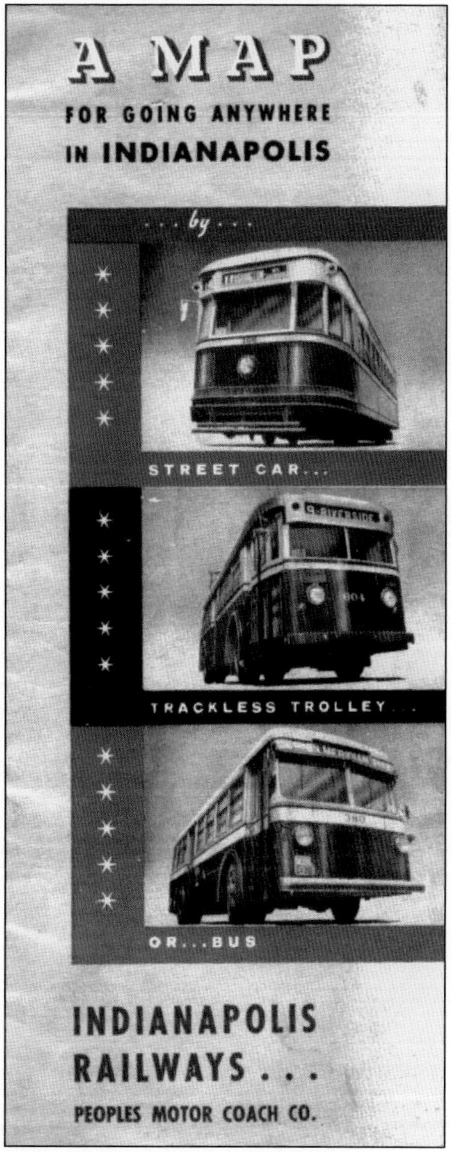

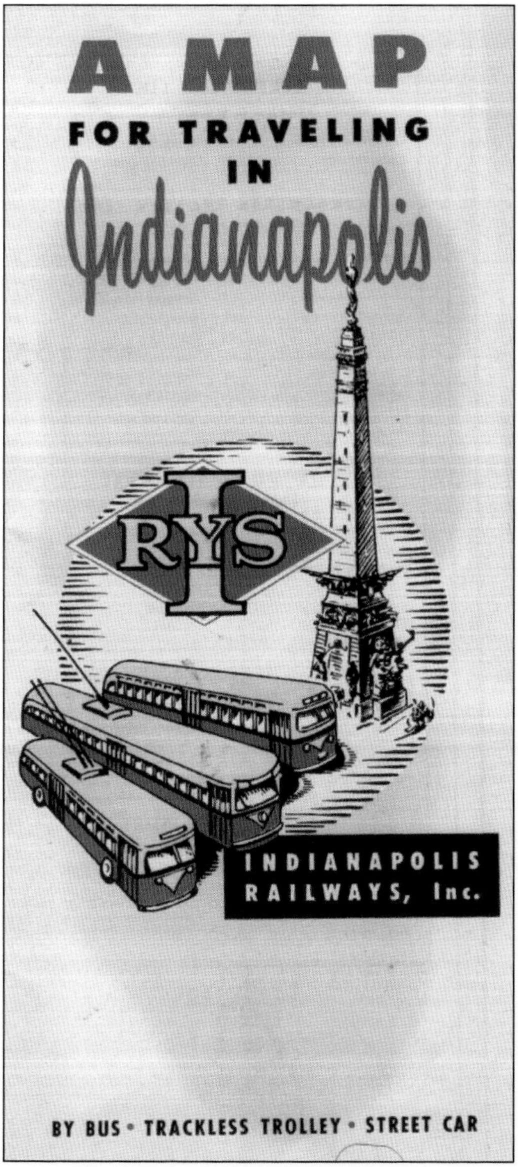

A May 1, 1948, map and timetable from the Indianapolis Railways' electric bus system is titled *A Map for Traveling in Indianapolis.* The Indianapolis Transit System bought Indianapolis Railways in 1955, and in 1974, the city bought the company and formed the Indianapolis Public Transportation Corporation, which operated as the Metro until 1998 when it became IndyGo. (Alan E. Hunter.)

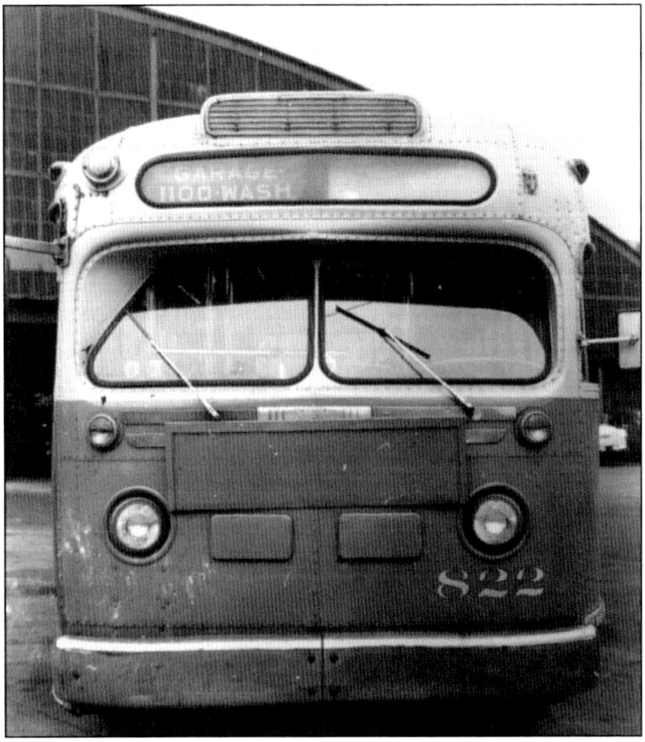

A late-1950s–era photograph of an Indianapolis Transit System motorized bus is captioned, "W. Washington # 822" and refers to the new express lights and flag holders. The destination sign reads, "Garage–1100 Wash." The distinctive, curved roof of the massive train shed can be seen in the background. (Alan E. Hunter.)

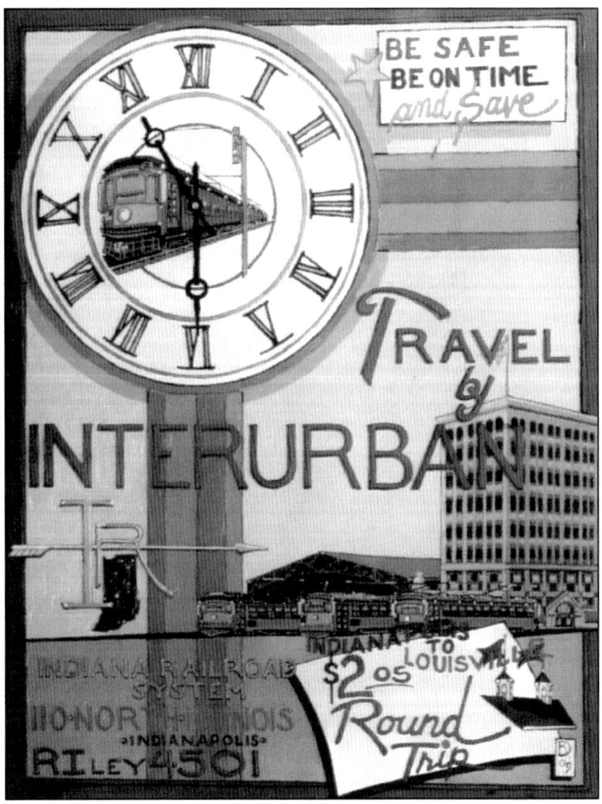

Dale Blaney created an Indianapolis Union Station travel poster by painting and colorizing a vintage item. The massive Union traction building and attached shed are filled with streetcars. The poster reads, "Be Safe—Be On Time—and Save—Travel by Interurban—Indianapolis to Louisville $2.05 Round Trip—Indiana Railroad System 110 North Illinois—Indianapolis—RILEY 4501." (Alan E. Hunter.)

Four

INDIANAPOLIS TO PLAINFIELD

QUAKERS AND PRESIDENTIAL PRATFALLS

Leaving Indianapolis and heading into the western region, the Historic National Road experience changes from the journey experienced in the eastern region of the state. This evolution from pioneer history into the 20th-century-automobile heritage becomes apparent right away as the road enters Plainfield and passes the original 1940s Bridgeport Diner. Once in the smaller community of Bridgeport, the diner is part of the heritage of Plainfield and offers a glimpse into the important automobile culture in which the National Road had a part.

In 1822, a tract of land west of Indianapolis, which included the area now known as Plainfield, was obtained by Jeremiah Hadley of Preble County, Ohio. Jeremiah Hadley sold it to his son Elias Hadley 10 years later. Levi Jessup and Elias Hadley laid out the town in 1839, and Plainfield was incorporated in that same year. The town got its name from the early Friends, or Quakers, who settled around the area and established several meetinghouses throughout the county, including the important Western Yearly Meeting of Friends in Plainfield. The Friends were plain people, thus, the name *Plainfield*. The high school continues to honor the Quakers, using the name for the school's mascot.

Plainfield has long been associated with the National Road US Route 40, which goes through town as Main Street. An incident that brought Plainfield national attention occurred in 1842 when Pres. Martin Van Buren was spilled (perhaps deliberately) from his stagecoach into the thick mud of the highway. The alleged practical joke came because Van Buren vetoed a bill from Congress to improve the highway, a move that angered western settlers. When Van Buren came through Plainfield on a swing to shore up his popularity for the 1844 election, it is rumored that a group of perpetrators set up the incident. The elm tree whose roots caused the president's carriage to topple became known as the Van Buren Elm. Today, an elementary school near this site is named Van Buren Elementary School.

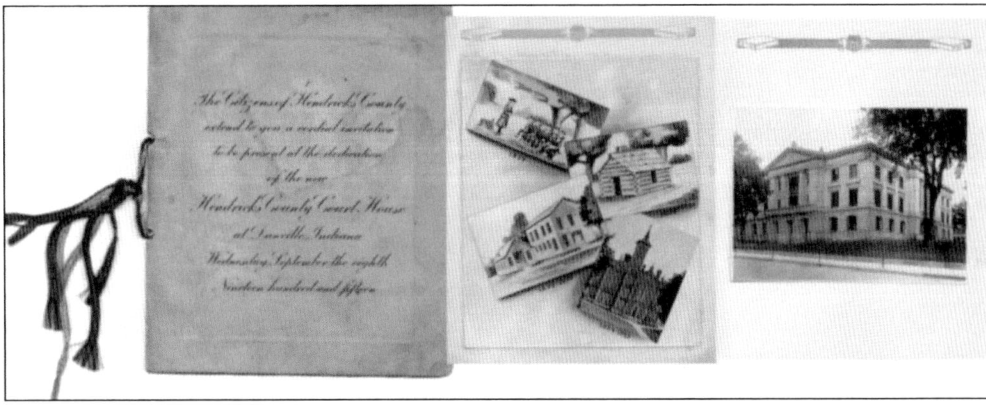

This program was handed out at the dedication of the Hendricks County Courthouse. Interior pages feature Hendricks County historical scenes from 1824 to 1913. The schedule started at 9:30 a.m. with a "Formal Opening of Building," followed by an "Automobile Parade" at 10:30 a.m., lunch at noon, then the "Dedication Exercise" with Judge John V. Hadley as master of ceremonies, and finally culminated with an address by Vice Pres. Thomas R. Marshall at 2:00 p.m. (Alan E. Hunter.)

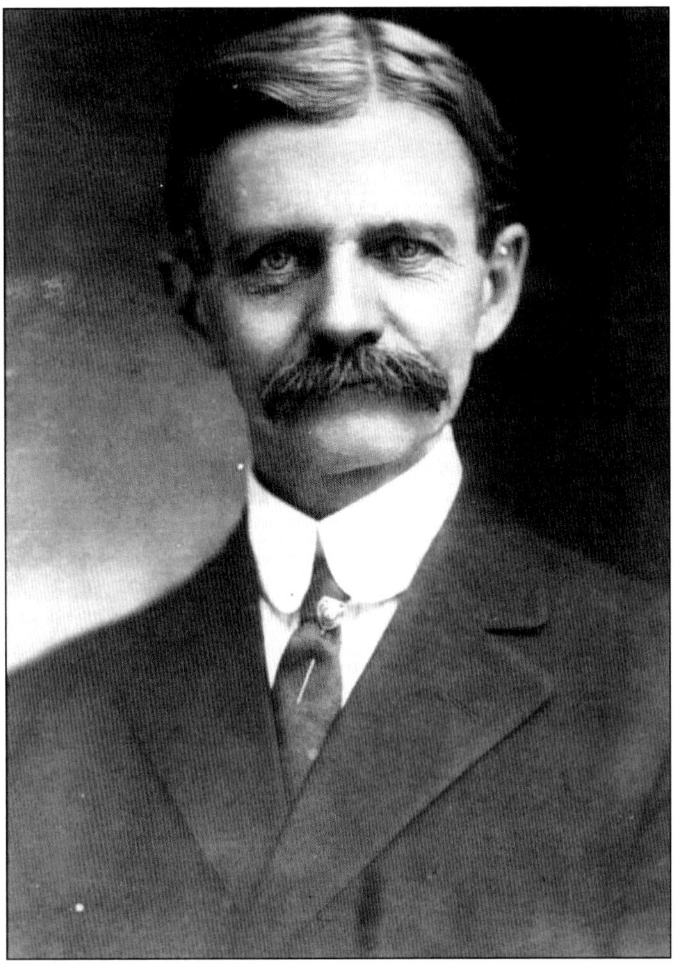

Thomas R. Marshall, Pres. Woodrow Wilson's vice president, was the featured speaker at the dedication of the Hendricks County Courthouse on September 8, 1915. A prominent lawyer in Indiana, he became the state's 27th governor in 1908. His popularity as governor in a critical swing state helped him secure the Democratic vice presidential nomination in 1912. Known for his sense of humor, Marshall is remembered for saying, "What this country needs is a really good five-cent cigar." (Indiana State Library.)

An 1870s-era *carte de visite* photograph portrays Pres. Martin Van Buren, who is credited for improvements eventually made to the dilapidated National Road. Although Van Buren had vetoed a congressional bill to improve the poor conditions along the road, he changed his mind after he was unceremoniously dumped from his carriage onto the road while traveling near Plainfield. (Alan E. Hunter.)

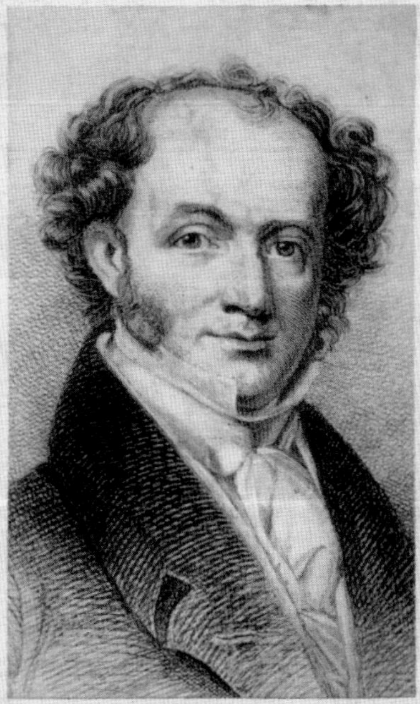

MARTIN VAN BUREN.

A postcard from about 1910 shows "Main Street, Looking West, Showing Van Buren Elm," and an X marks the place where President Van Buren's stagecoach was overturned by tree roots in 1842. Rumors circulated, suggesting that he was deliberately dumped as a joke in response to his veto of the road improvement bill. Allegedly, the coach driver received a new silk hat for his part in the plot. (Alan E. Hunter.)

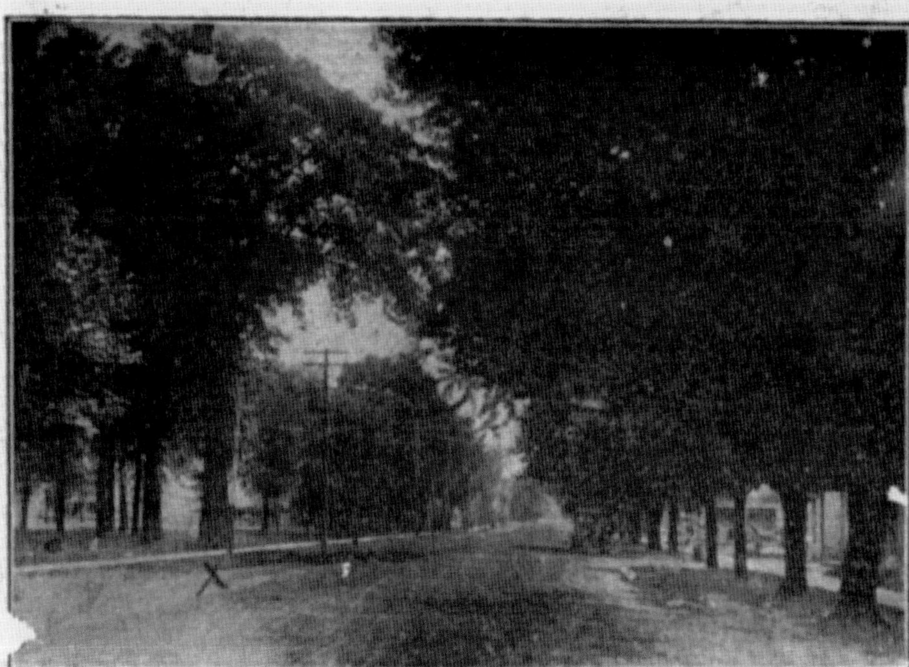

MAIN STREET, LOOKING WEST, SHOWING VAN BUREN ELM.

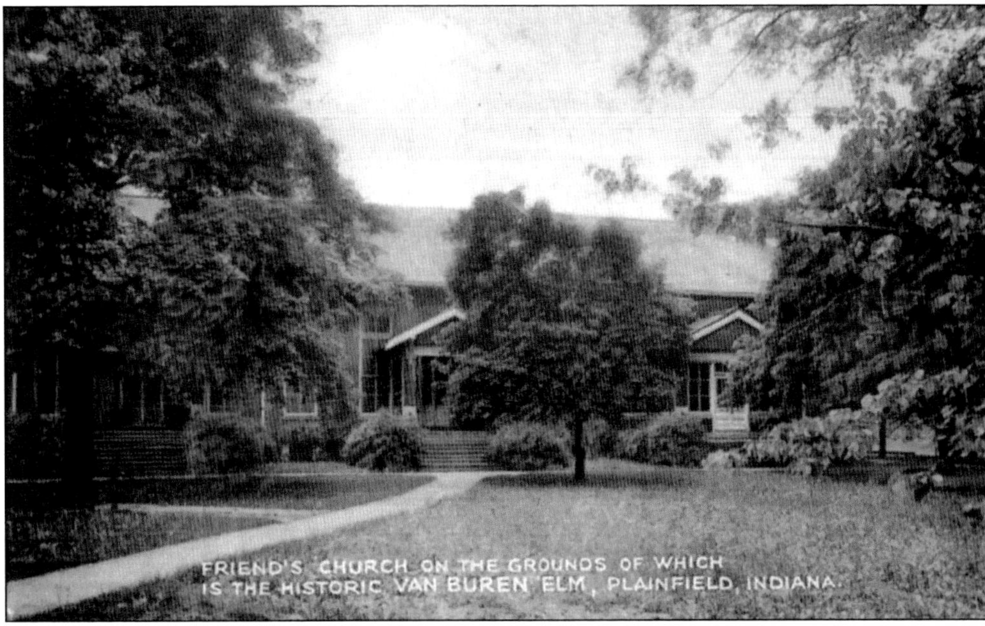

A postcard from around 1915 shows the Plainfield Friends Quaker Church in Plainfield and is captioned, "Friend's Church on the grounds of which is the historic Van Buren Elm, Plainfield, Indiana." (Hendricks County Historical Society.)

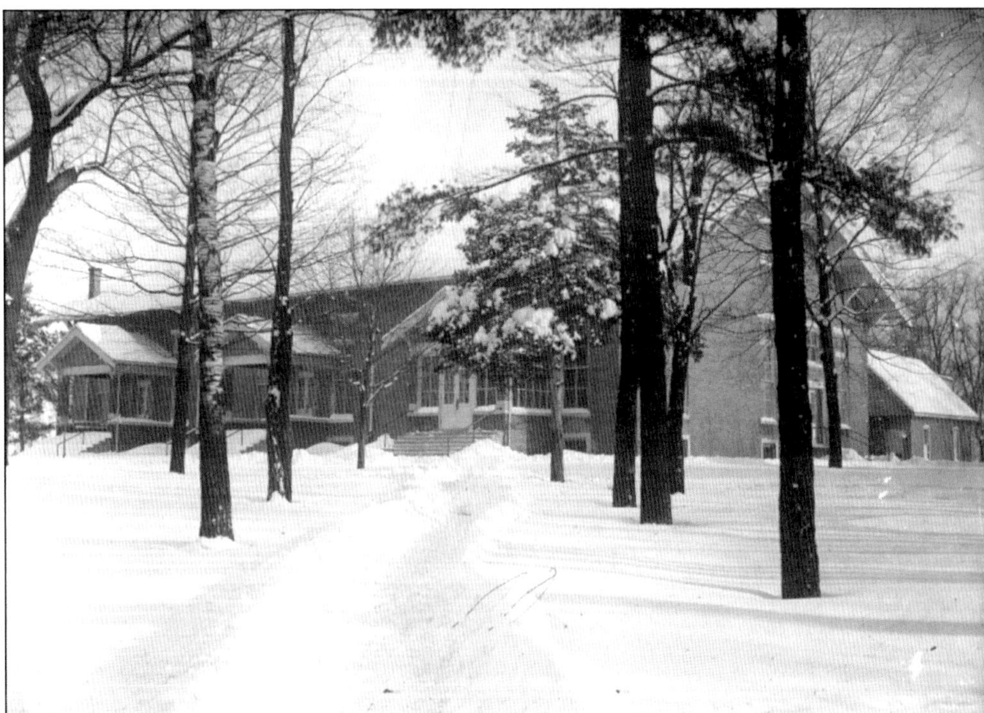

A photograph from around the 1950s shows the Plainfield Friends Quaker Church in winter with snow covering the grounds. (Hendricks County Historical Society.)

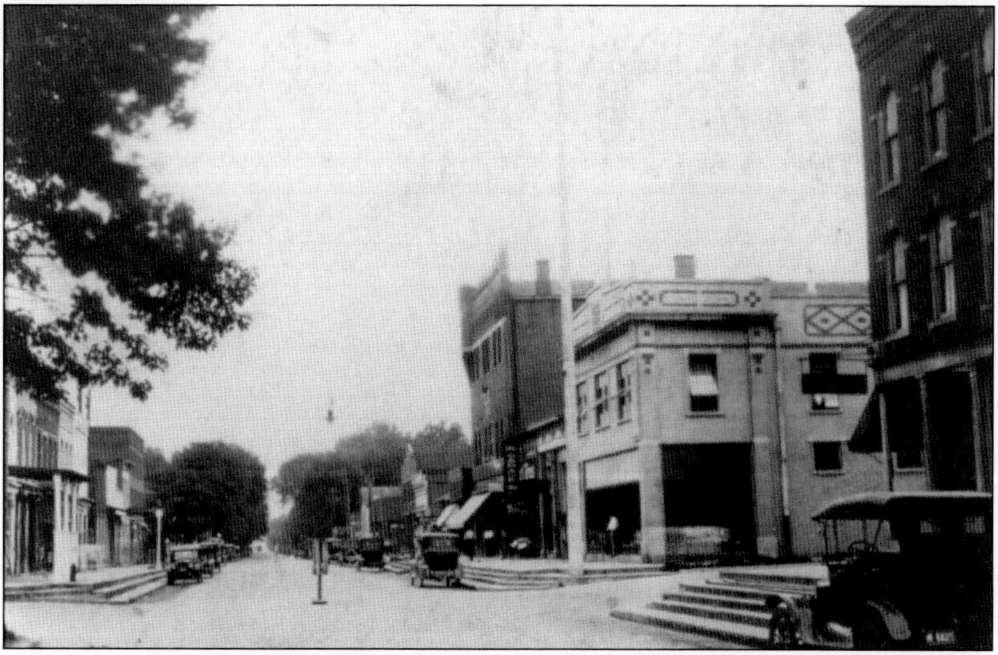

A 1920s-era postcard provides a Main Street view and is captioned, "Business Section, Plainfield, Ind." (Hendricks County Historical Society.)

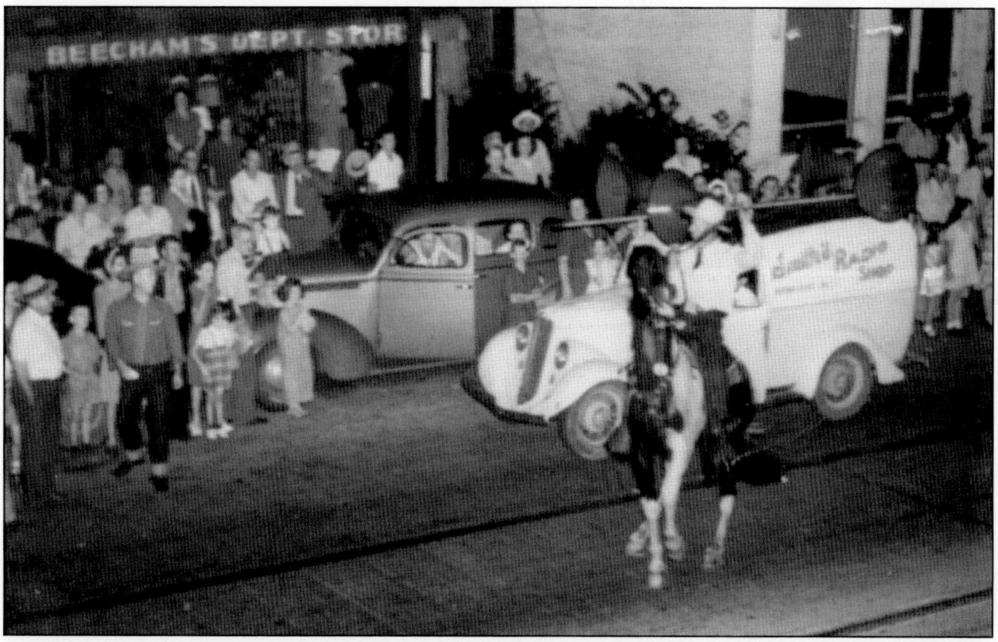

A photograph from around the 1950s shows a Hopalong Cassidy look-alike cowboy in a parade passing Beecham's department store on US 40 in Plainfield. The interurban tracks can be seen in the foreground. (Clay County Historical Society.)

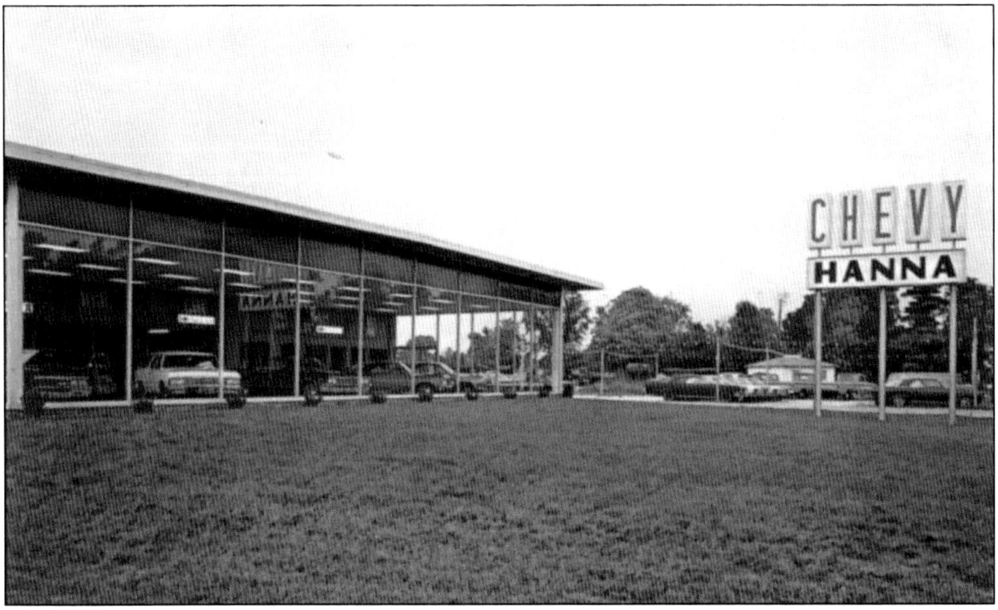

A 1960s-era postcard view is captioned, "Hanna Chevrolet 704 W. Main St. Plainfield." The postcard shows several bright, shiny new cars in the showroom at left, with a used car lot full of classics on the right. (Bill Raney.)

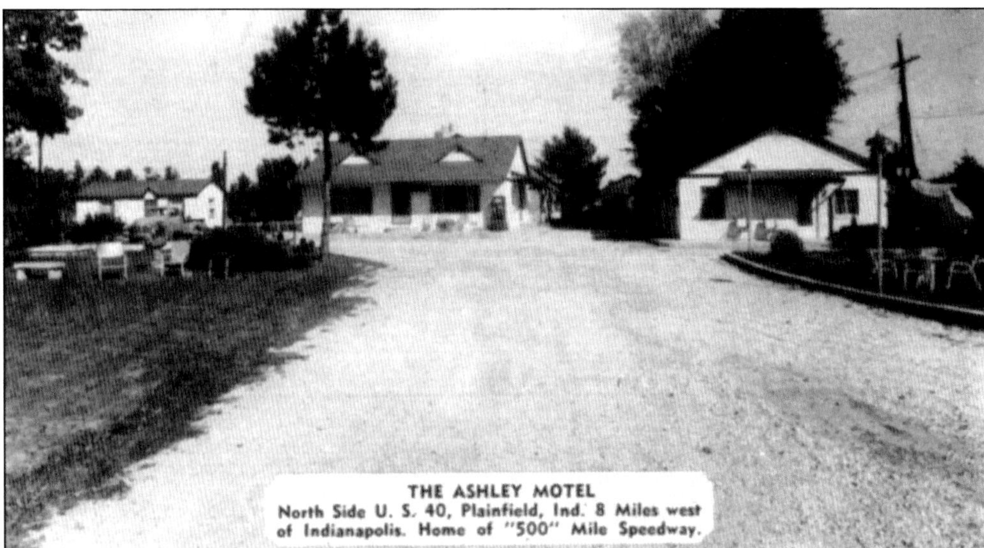

A 1940s-era postcard view is captioned, "The Ashley Motel—North Side U. S. 40, Plainfield, Ind. 8 Miles west of Indianapolis. Home of '500' Mile Speedway." According to the back of the postcard, "The Ashley Motel Elbert and Lelia Plainfield Ind. Air conditioned by refrigeration 21 inch TV Kitchenettes family rooms baby cribs." (Bill Raney.)

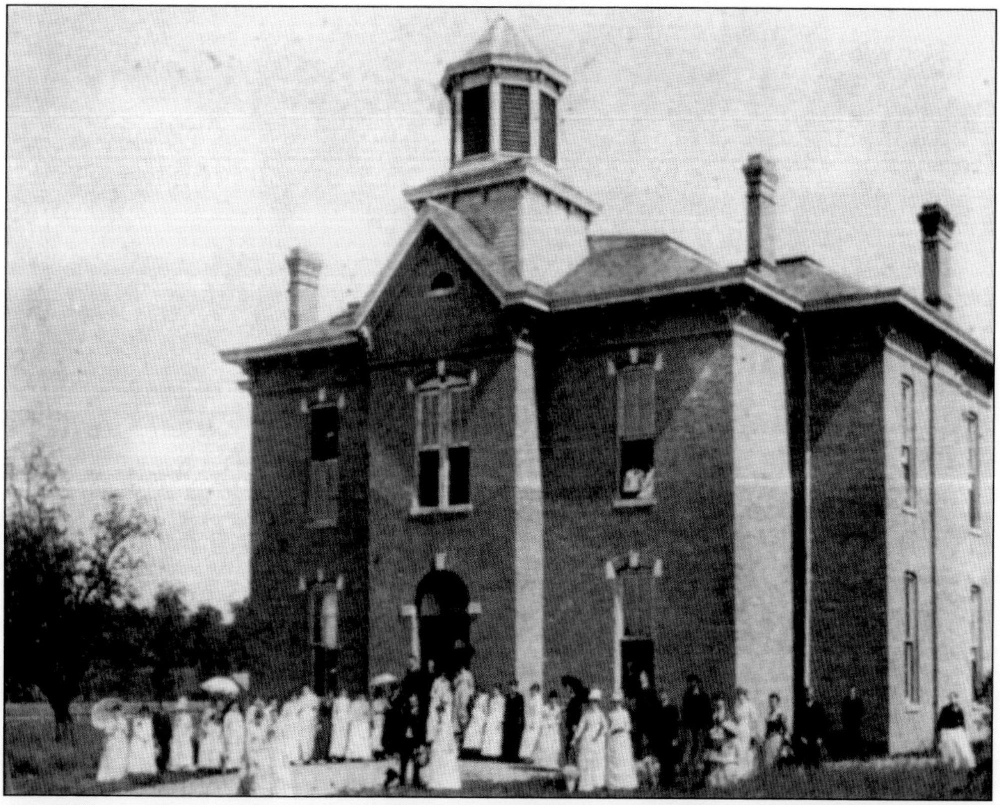

An 1880s-era photograph shows the Central Academy School in Plainfield with a gathering in front. (Indianapolis Public Library, Warren Branch.)

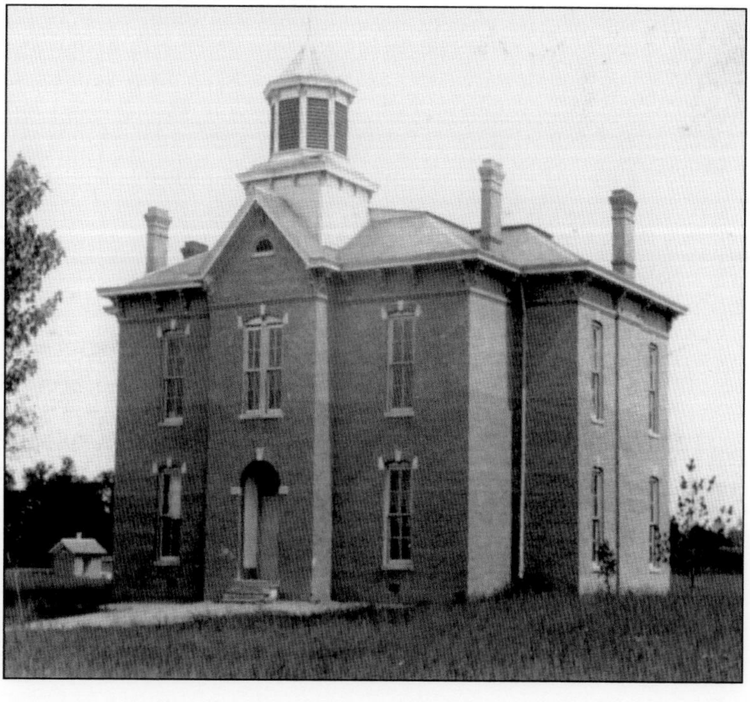

A photograph from about 1900 shows another view of the Central Academy School in Plainfield. (Hendricks County Historical Society.)

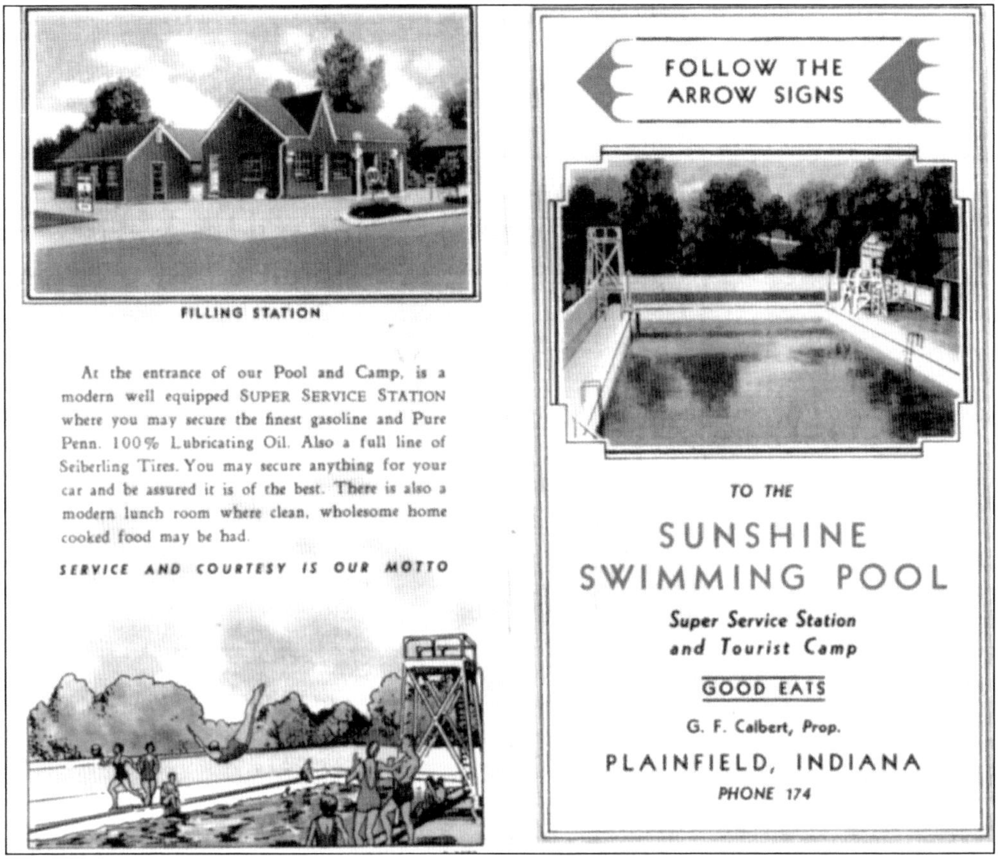

The front of an advertising brochure from around the 1940s promotes Plainfield's Sunshine Swimming Pool on US 40. The complex featured a Pure Penn Gas and Oil service station and tourist cabins for National Road travelers. (Hendricks County Historical Society.)

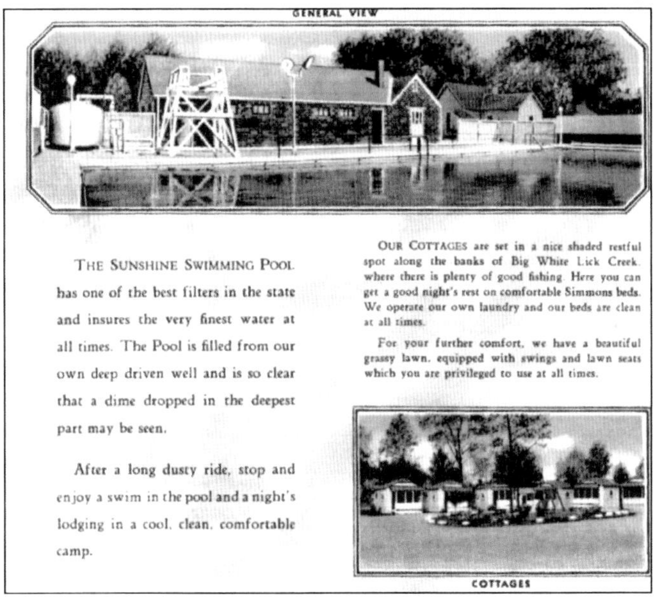

The inside of a 1940s-era advertising brochure describes Plainfield's Sunshine Swimming Pool on US 40. The flyer claims, "the Sunshine swimming pool has one of the best filters in the state and insures the very finest water at all times. The pool is filled from our own deep driven well and is so clear that a dime dropped in the deepest part may be seen." (Hendricks County Historical Society.)

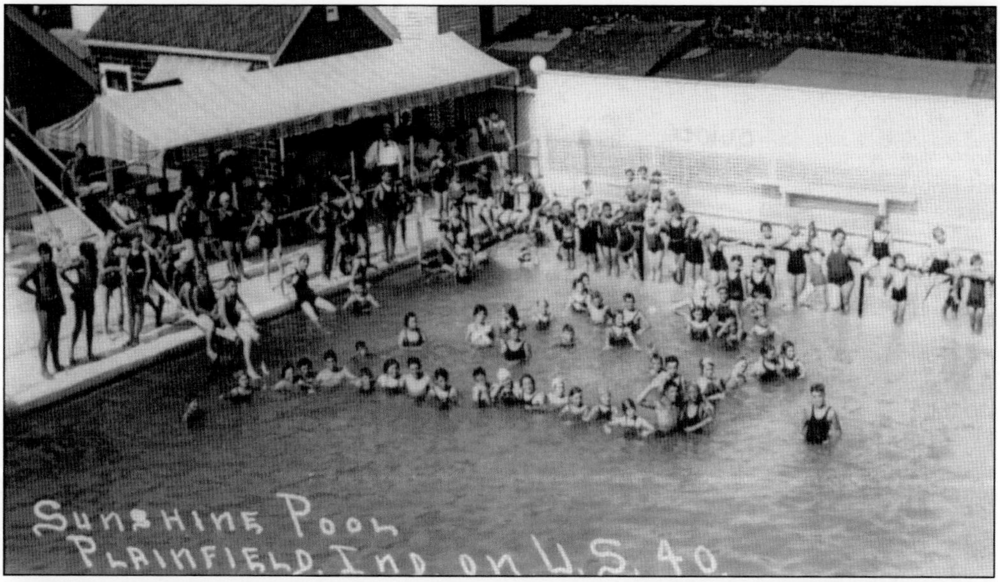

A 1940s real-photo postcard shows Plainfield's Sunshine Swimming Pool full of children and lounging poolside at left. Gen. Forest Calbert, the pool's owner, can be seen in hat, bow tie, and suspenders under the awning. The postcard is captioned, "Sunshine Pool—Plainfield, Ind. on U.S. 40." (Hendricks County Historical Society.)

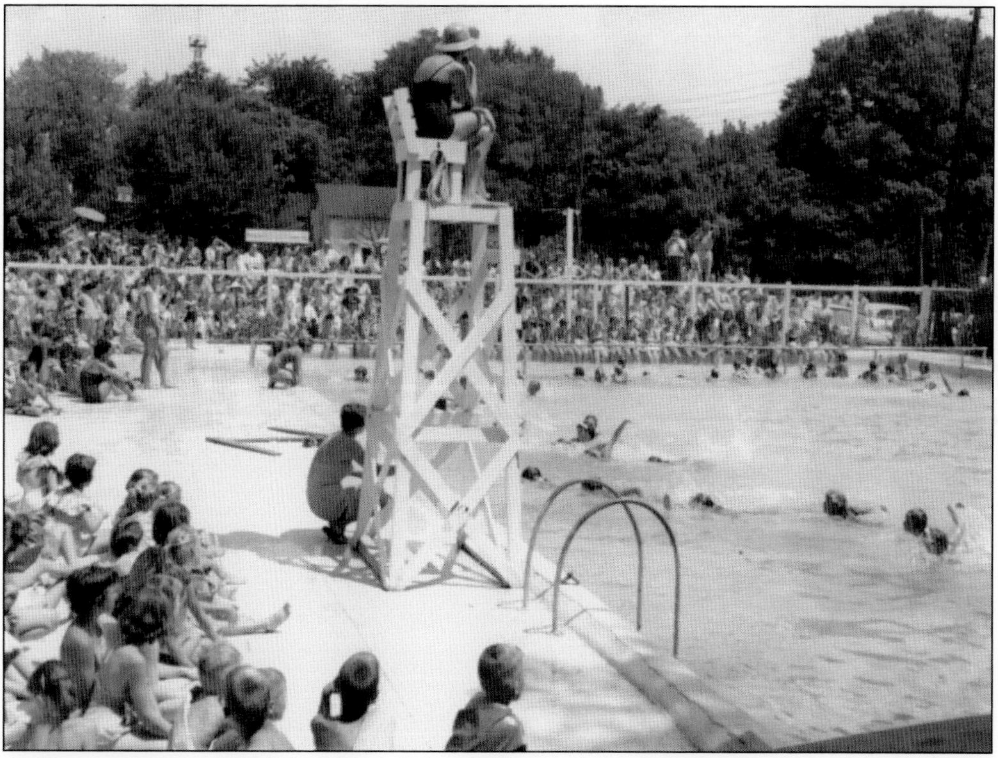

A photograph from around the 1960s of Plainfield's Sunshine Swimming Pool pictures children in the midst of a race under the watchful eye of the lifeguard perched high above them and wearing a pith helmet. (Hendricks County Historical Society.)

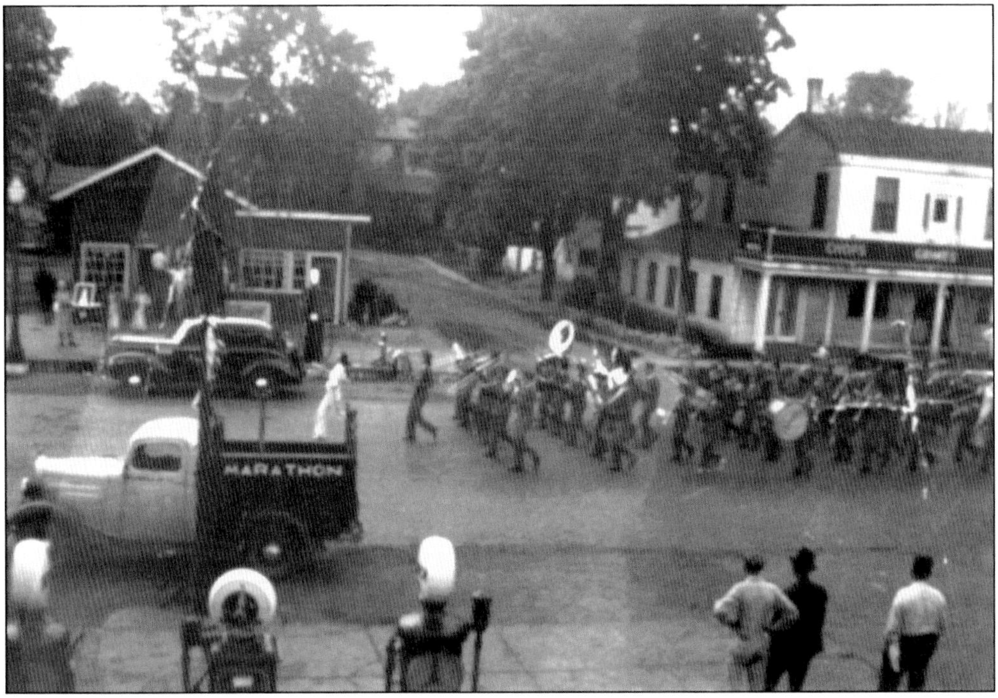

A 1930s-era photograph shows a parade passing in front of the Marathon gas station on the brick-paved National Road in Plainfield. The parade was organized to celebrate the last day of the original brick-lined National Road through town. The next day, road crews came in to remove the bricks and repave the road with concrete. (Hendricks County Historical Society.)

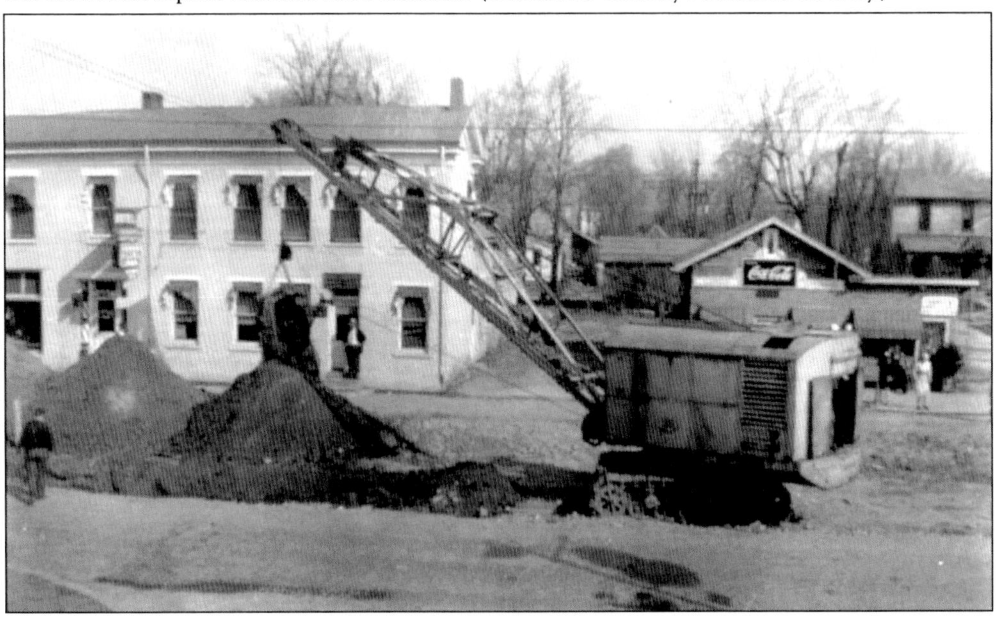

First in a series of 1930s-era photographs of the digging, grading, and laying of cement along the National Road in Plainfield, this image was taken from the upstairs window of a business and offers an excellent example of how the early stages of the road came together. (Hendricks County Historical Society.)

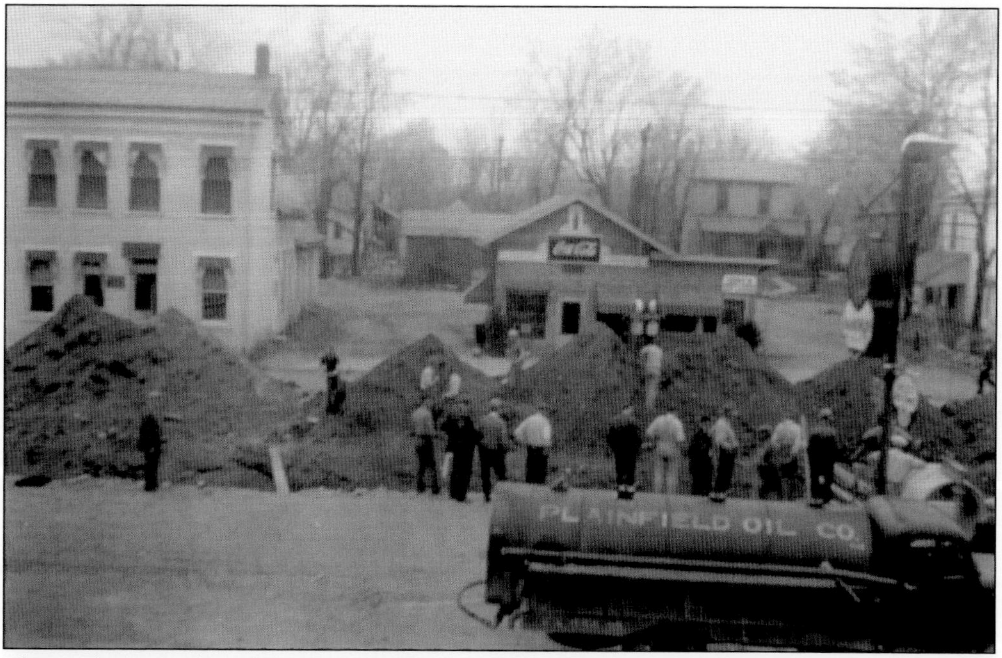

This is the second in the series of 1930s-era photographs showing the digging, grading, and laying of cement along the National Road in Plainfield. It shows the piles of dirt awaiting the arrival of the road graders. Soon, the road will be smoothed in preparation of laying the concrete. (Hendricks County Historical Society.)

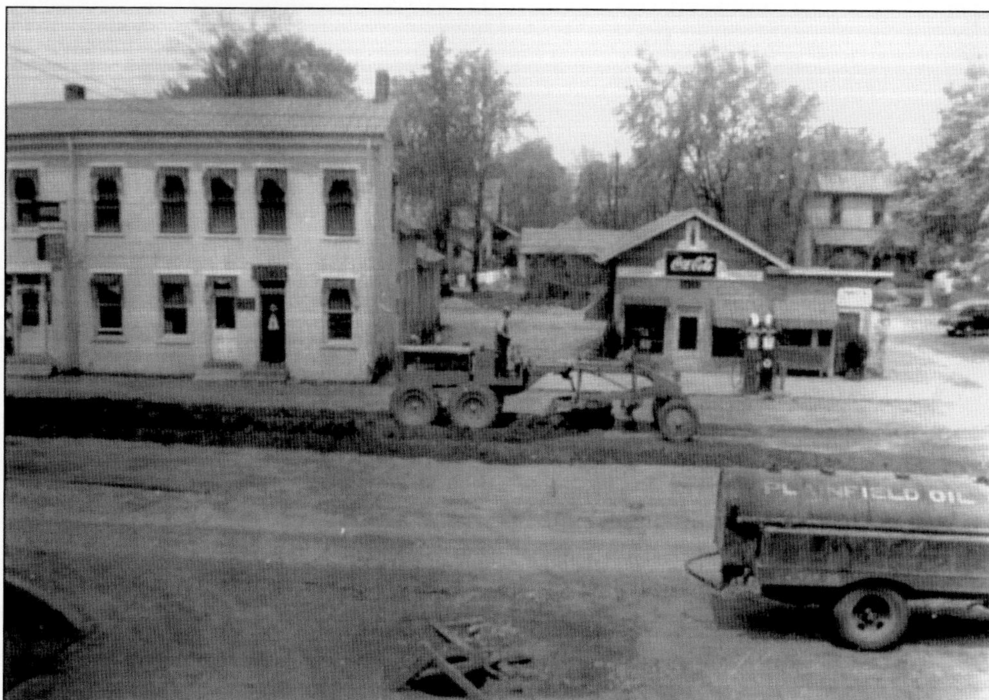

Third in the series of 1930s-era photographs, this image shows the arrival of the road graders to smooth the bed of the National Road in Plainfield. (Hendricks County Historical Society.)

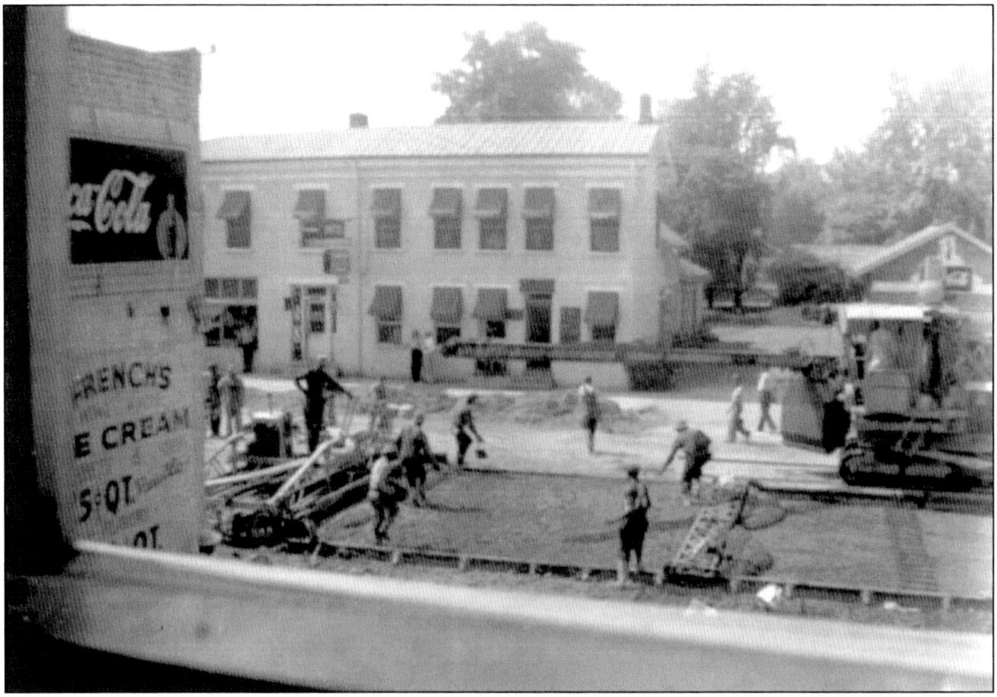

Fourth in the series of 1930s-era photographs of the digging, grading, and laying of cement along the National Road in Plainfield, this image shows the concrete workers smoothing the westbound lanes of the new National Road. (Hendricks County Historical Society.)

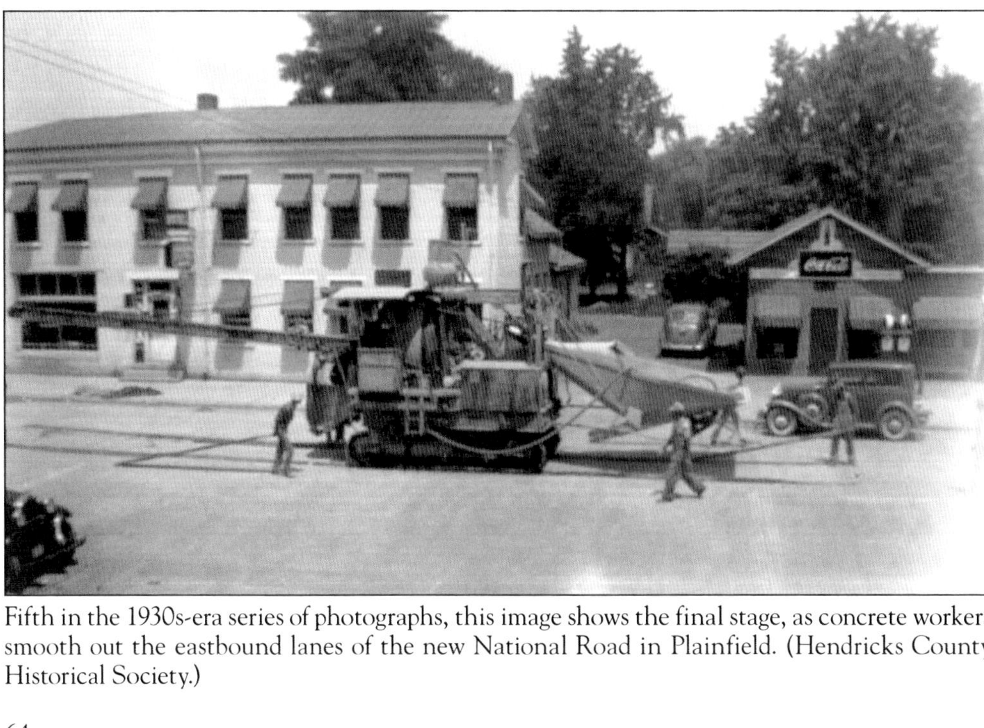

Fifth in the 1930s-era series of photographs, this image shows the final stage, as concrete workers smooth out the eastbound lanes of the new National Road in Plainfield. (Hendricks County Historical Society.)

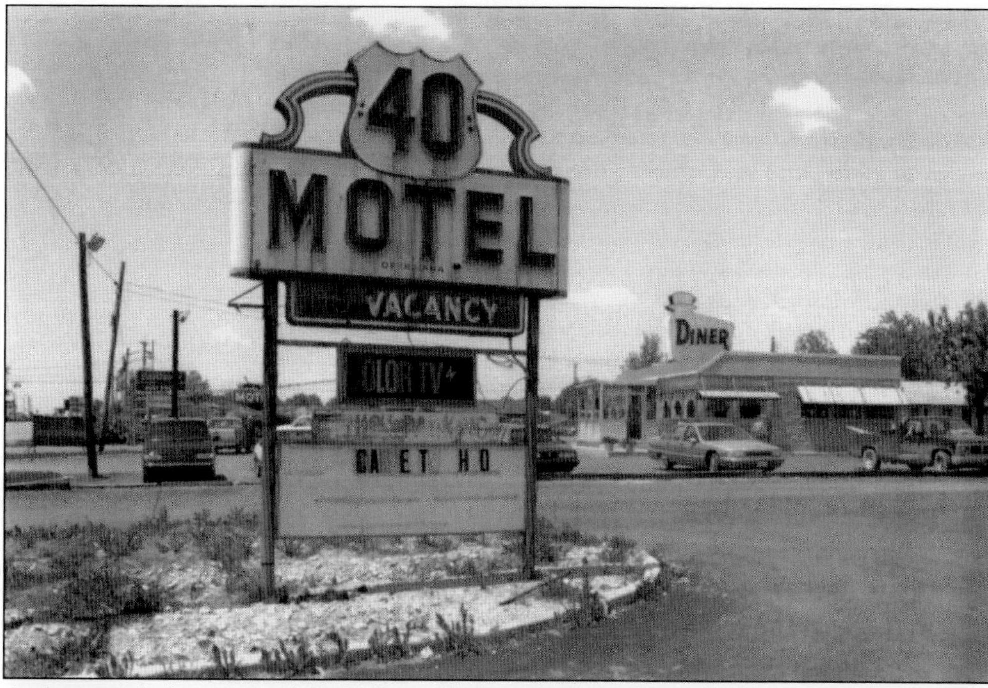

A photograph from around 2010 shows the Plainfield Diner at 3122 East Main Street. This beautifully preserved diner is an excellent example of the type of eateries that dotted the landscape along the National Road (US 40) during the automobile touring days of the mid-20th century. The diner closed in the summer of 2009. Sands Motel is in the background. (Jan Davis.)

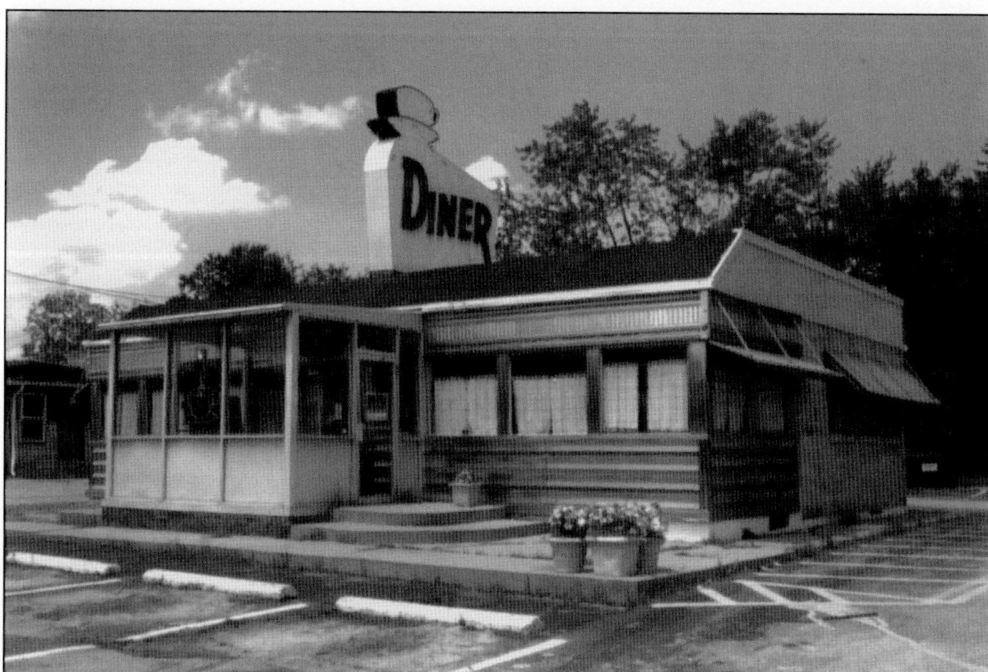

A photograph from around 1990 shows the Plainfield Diner. (Jan Davis.)

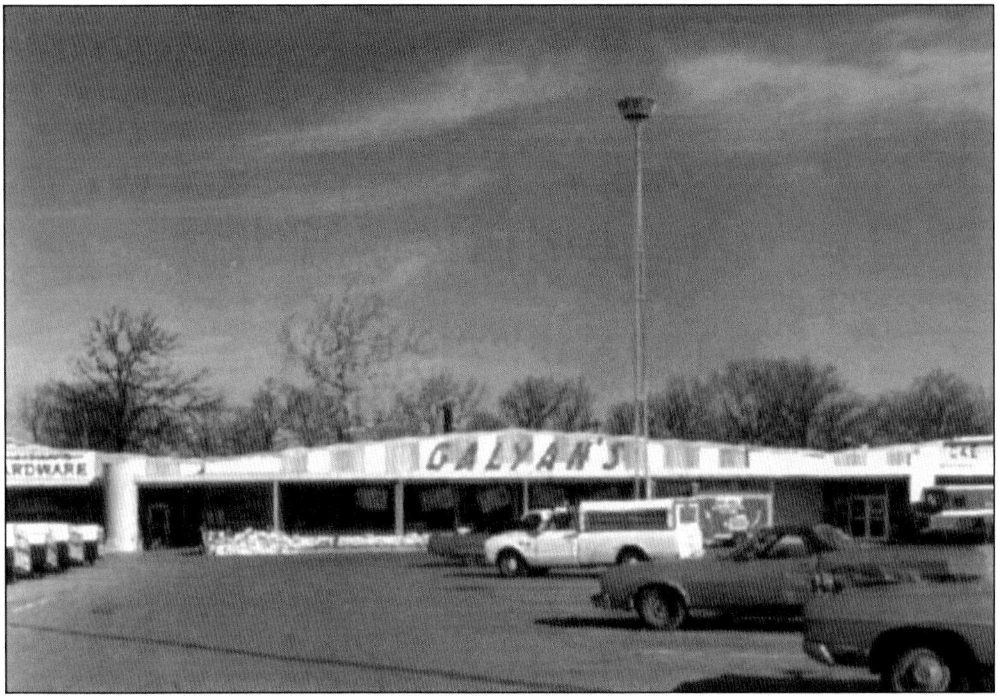

The original Galyan's store in Plainfield is shown in the mid-1970s. Albert Galyan and his wife, Naomi, founded Galyan's Trading Company in 1946. Galyan's was originally a grocery that also sold hunting and fishing supplies. It evolved into a small, successful sporting goods store. Albert Galyan died in 1975, and management passed to his son Pat, who built Galyan's into a sporting goods giant in the Midwest. It eventually was sold to the Dick's Sporting Goods chain. (Plainfield Library.)

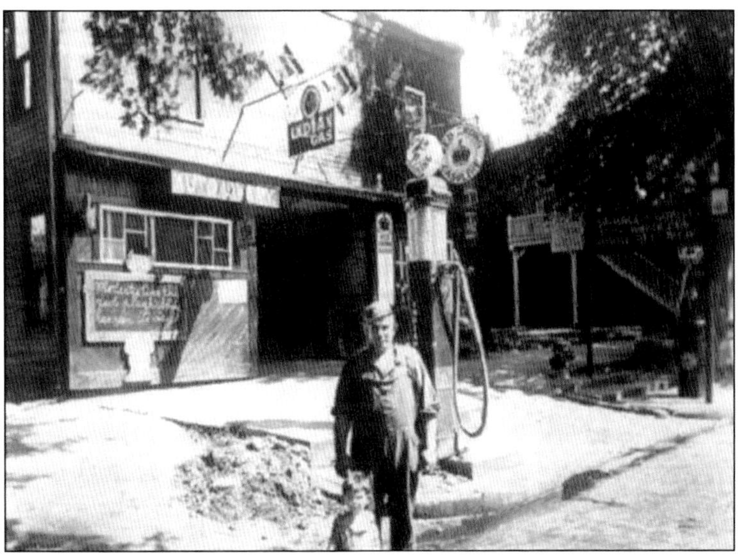

Howard Christopher's gas station was located on West Main Street (US 40) in Plainfield, as seen in this photograph taken sometime in the 1940s. The site was previously a livery stable. (Plainfield Library.)

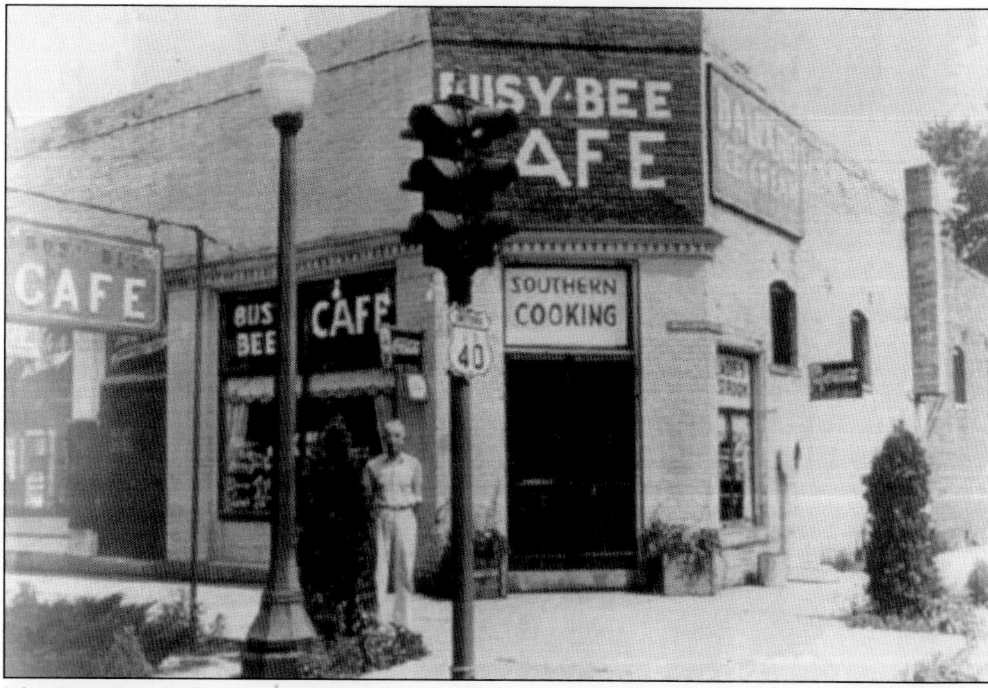

The Busy Bee Café was located at the southeast corner of Vine Street and US 40/Main Street in Plainfield. The building was formerly home to Stacey's Restaurant and is currently home to Floor Fashions. (Plainfield Library.)

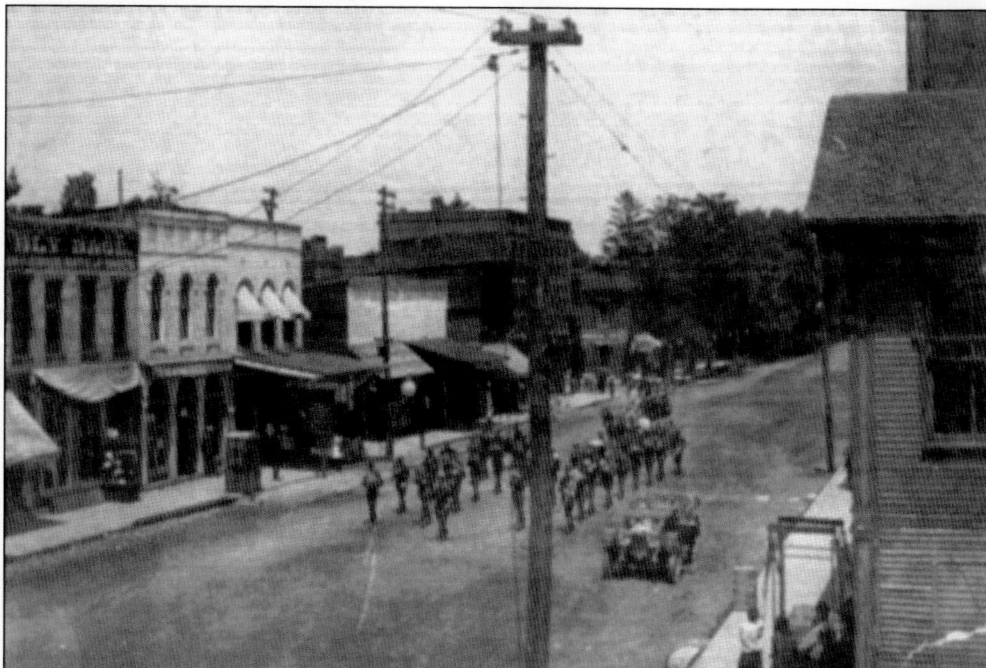

A parade from about 1910 in downtown Plainfield, Indiana, is shown in a view that looks east on US 40/Main Street, with the Bly Brothers dry goods store in the background and an open roadster parked in the street. (Plainfield Library.)

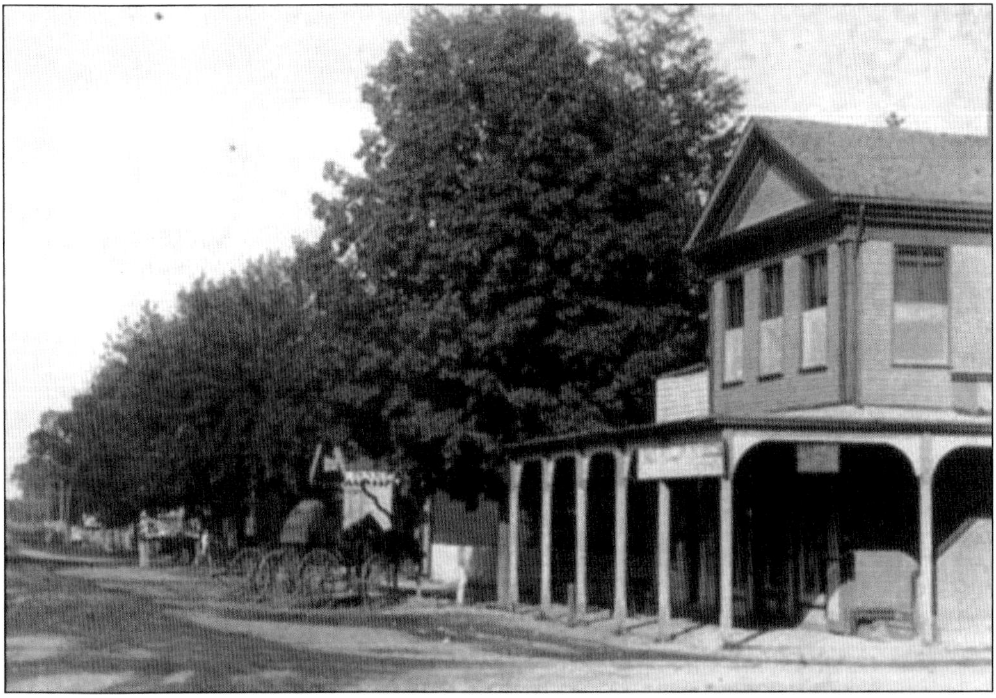

A photograph from around 1900 was taken at the corner of Main and Center Streets. The Village Theater, Shirt Tales, and the Masonic Lodge are currently located on this spot in downtown Plainfield. In the distance, the hill on US 40 going east out of town (toward Duke Energy today) is visible. (Plainfield Library.)

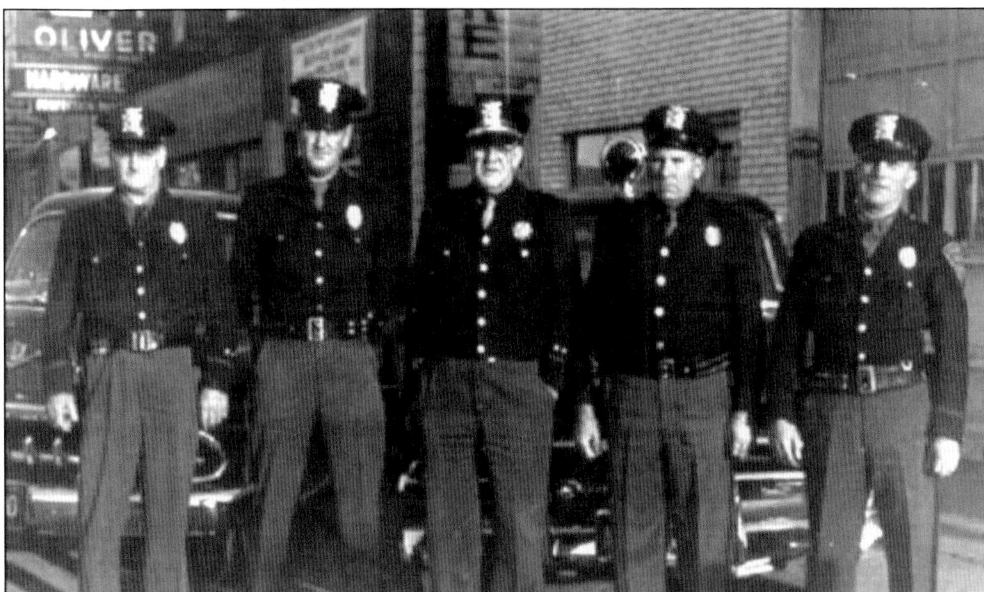

The 1954 Plainfield Police Department includes, from left to right, Joe Chandler, Gene Gray, Charles "Sap" Franklin, Everett Crowe, and Paul Clifford "Red" Smith. This picture was taken when the department added a second police car, a Ford, to its fleet. Both cars can be seen behind them, as well as the facade of the Oliver hardware store. (Plainfield Library.)

Five

Plainfield to Terre Haute

Remnants of a 20th-Century Automobile Culture

Replacing the inns and pike towns, the next generation of architecture to line the road included motels, gas stations, and drive-in movie theaters. In Terre Haute, travelers will find the Indiana National Road Association's first preservation success: the Coffee Cottage/Gas Station now located on the campus of the Rose-Hulman Institute of Technology. Across the street, a historical billboard showcases the Clabber Girl Flour Company, recalling the 1930s experience along the road.

Along this stretch in the western region, travelers have the opportunity to steer off modern US 40 onto the original 1920s sections of the road. There are few places in the country where motorists can drive on original concrete alignments of historic roads; here, travelers may drive on the early roadbed, passing over original concrete arch bridges. On the Deer Creek bridge, travelers can stop to look over and view the creek bed pioneers once forged. Standing on the 1920s route, a visitor might also see bridge abutments from the steel truss bridge that was moved to a nearby location and hear the roar of the current US Route 40—experiencing four generations of the National Road in one place.

Farther on, near Stilesville, travelers will see Rising Hall Estate, arguably the most impressive home along the Historic National Road. Famous for its connection to the Civil War (mules were raised there for the Grand Army of the Republic), the mansion was saved and restored by longtime National Road supporter Walt Prosser and his wife, June. Walt and June led preservation efforts in Indiana through active involvement in the Indiana National Road Association; and they assisted the Indiana Landmarks advocate for the Indiana Homeowners Tax Credit to encourage owners to restore their homes.

From the speedway in Indianapolis to Clabber Girl Flour Company in Terre Haute, this stretch of the road continues the story of the Historic National Road from Indiana's eastern region, beginning in Richmond. In Indiana, the road retains much of its integrity, but the full significance of the byway can only be comprehended by travelers when they drive the road between Baltimore and East St. Louis. The road reaches back 200 years and spans over 900 miles from the Chesapeake Bay to the Mississippi River, from the Appalachian Mountains to the Midwest farmlands. Indiana's Historic National Road is only part of a larger story, the unique heritage of the "Road that Built the Nation."

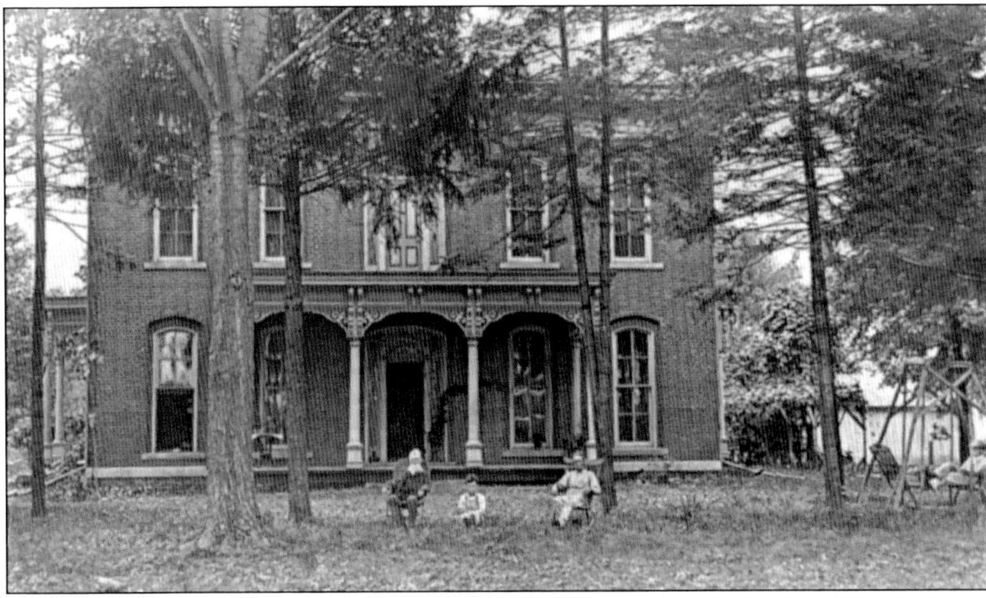

A photograph from about 1900 shows Rising Hall Estate, located on the border of Hendricks and Putnam Counties near Stilesville. This extraordinary Italianate-style home was built in 1872 by Melville F. McHaffie at a cost of $2,500. It was the home of Indiana National Road Association founding member Walt Prosser. (Walt and June Prosser.)

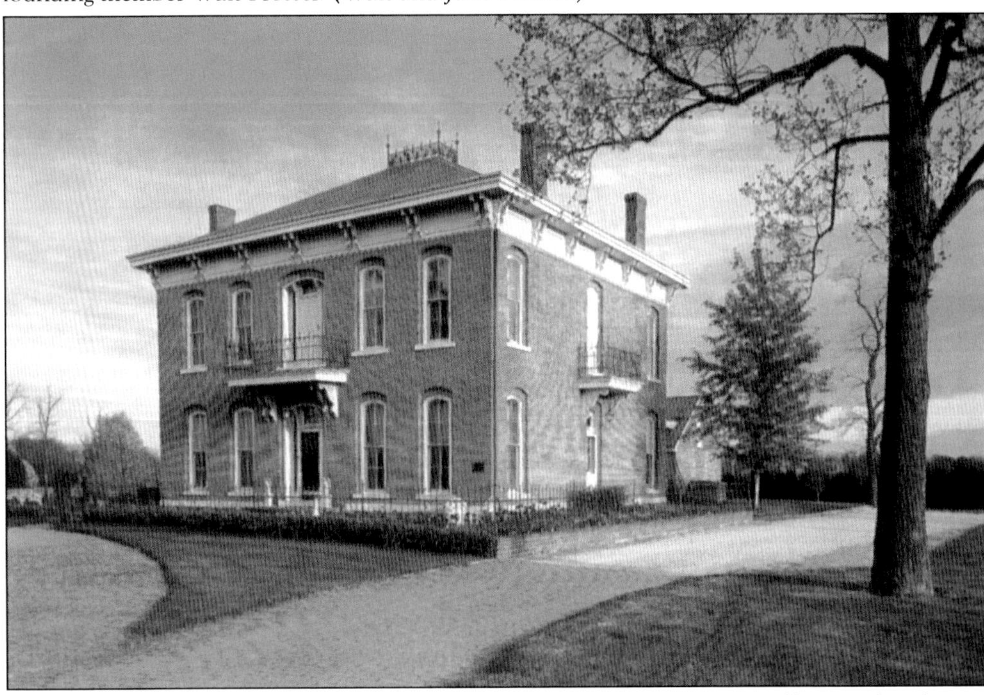

A photograph from around 2010 shows Rising Hall Estate. Melville McHaffie raised mules and received a commendation from President Lincoln for providing the Union army with the largest number of mules of anyone in the state during the Civil War. McHaffie's son Ernest later ran the farm as a breeding-and-training facility for racehorses. Famous trotter Dan Patch trained on the farm at the turn of the 20th century. (Indiana Landmarks.)

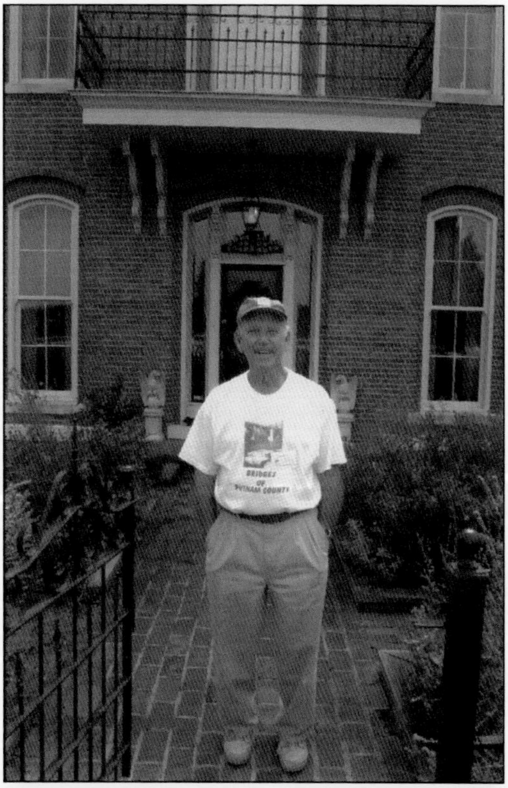

Walt Prosser was a founding member of the Indiana National Road Association and owner of Rising Hall Estate. Prosser was a great leader in Indiana's preservation movement, saving bridges, promoting the heritage of the National Road, lobbying (successfully) for preservation legislation, and serving as a board member of Indiana Landmarks. Walt's devotion was never more evident than in the heroic restoration of his beloved Rising Hall Estate. (Ron Sanders.)

A 1930s-era photograph of the National Road looks west from Plainfield. The rails of the fence along the road has a hand-painted sign for a local dry goods store in town. (Hendricks County Historical Society.)

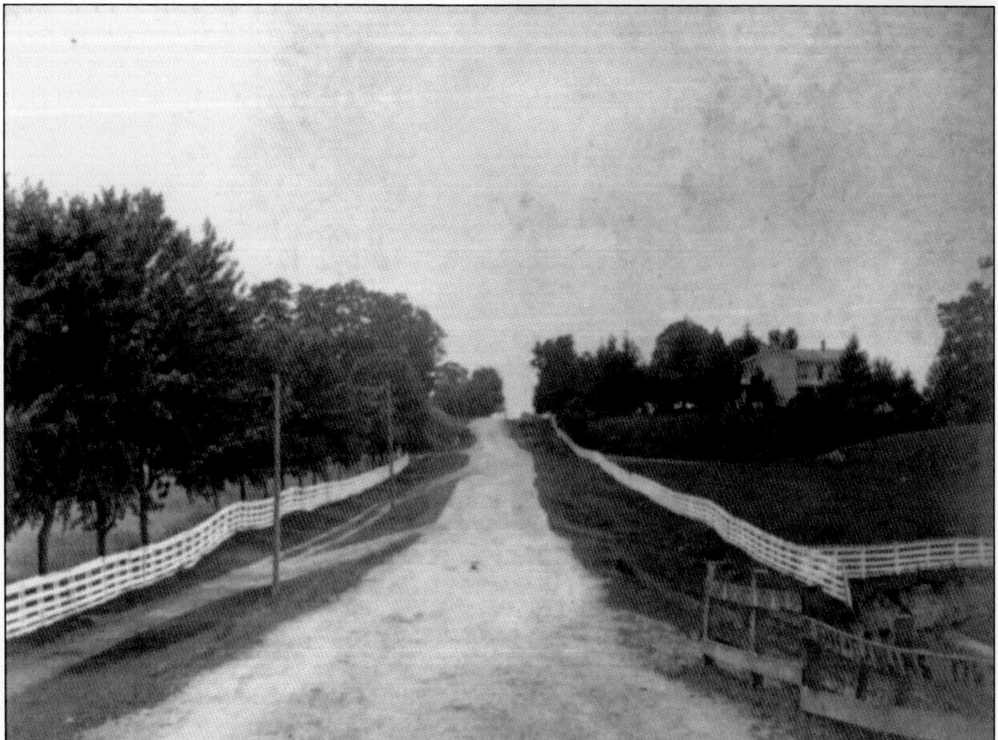

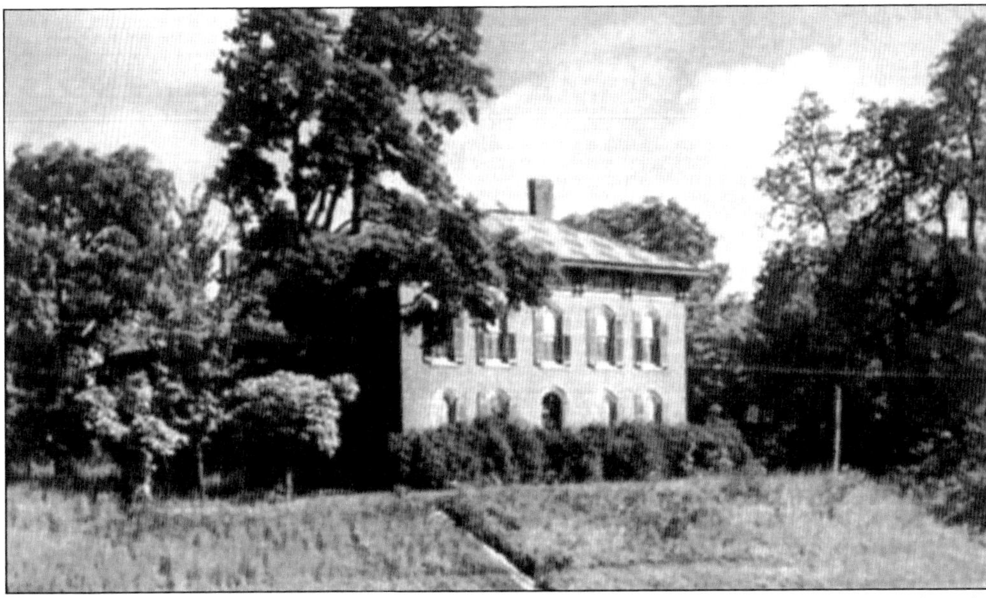

This landmark house is perched atop a hill along the road east of Brazil just before it reaches the little town of Harmony. It was erected in 1872 by Dr. George Green McKinley, one of the original contractors who helped build the National Road. Dr. McKinley built a 14-room, Italianate-style house of red brick made on-site from clay dug at nearby Croy Creek. Today, the home is known as the McKinley Bed and Breakfast. (Plainfield Library.)

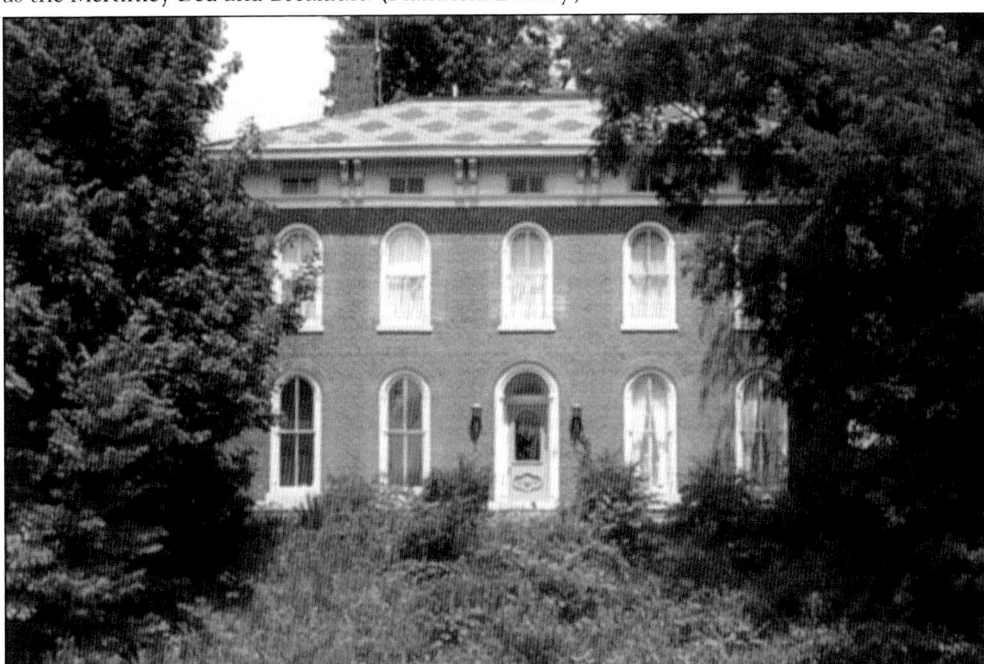

The home's front yard now resembles a jungle. When the house was built just after the Civil War, the National Road was a narrow path much farther south from the front door and was level with the front stoop. Today, the house sits atop a rise that was probably cut out when the road was widened and leveled around 1940. (Plainfield Library.)

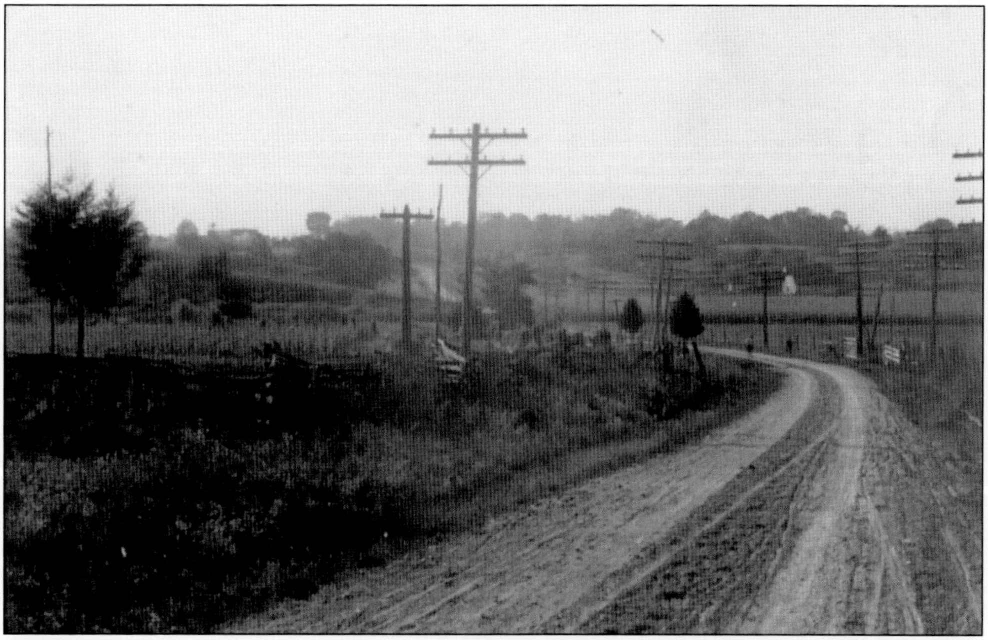

A 1916 view shows the National Road at Reelsville. A child can be seen walking around the bend of the road, probably on his way home from school. (Vigo County Historical Society.)

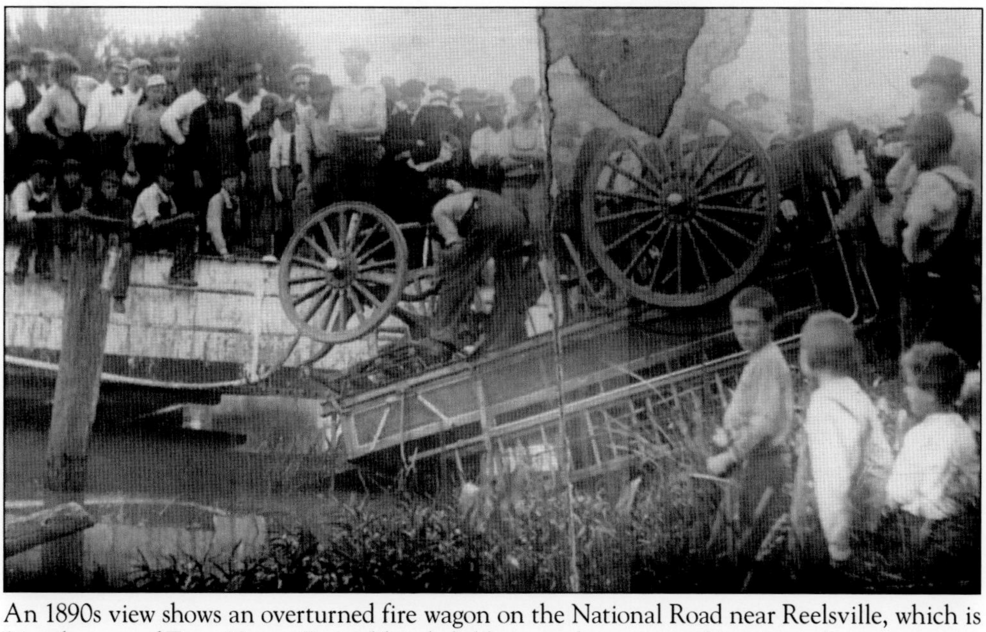

An 1890s view shows an overturned fire wagon on the National Road near Reelsville, which is 24 miles east of Terre Haute. Several local children can be seen watching intently as men try to pull the horse-drawn wagon out of Big Walnut Creek. The head of one of those men can be seen rising from the water under the wagon. (Alan E. Hunter.)

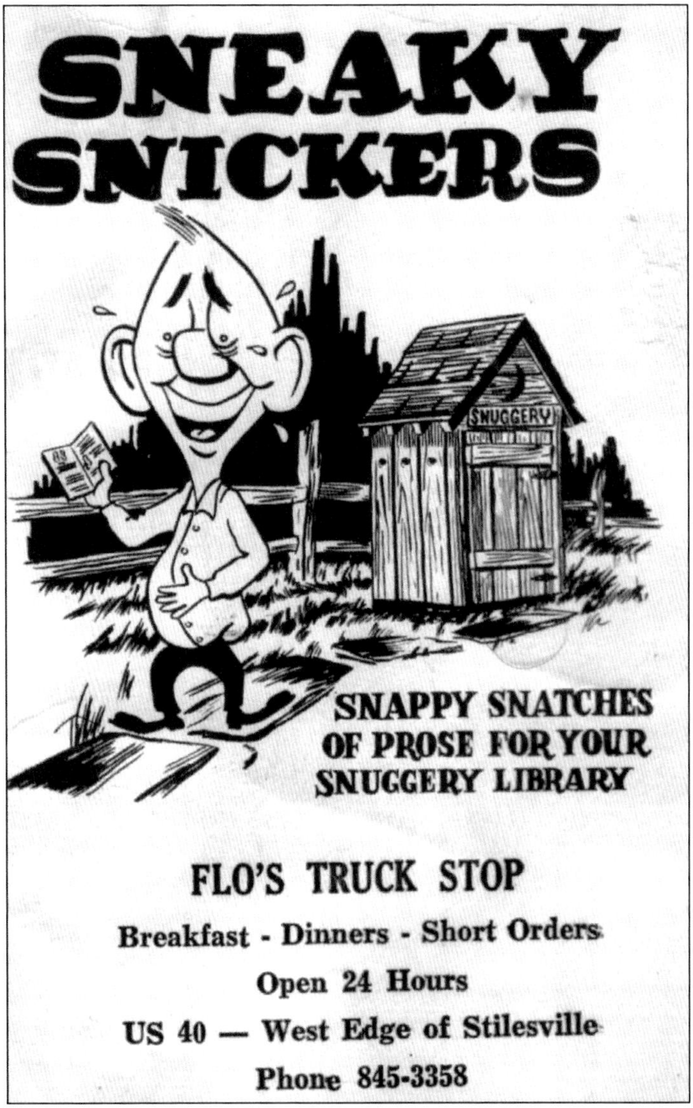

A 1960s-era souvenir joke book comes from a truck stop on Highway 40 in Stilesville. This little outhouse joke booklet is called *Sneaky Snickers—Snappy Snatches of Prose for Your Snuggery Library* and has advertising at the bottom for Flo's Truck Stop, which offered breakfast, dinner, and short orders; was open 24 hours a day; and was located on US 40 at the west edge of Stilesville. (Alan E. Hunter.)

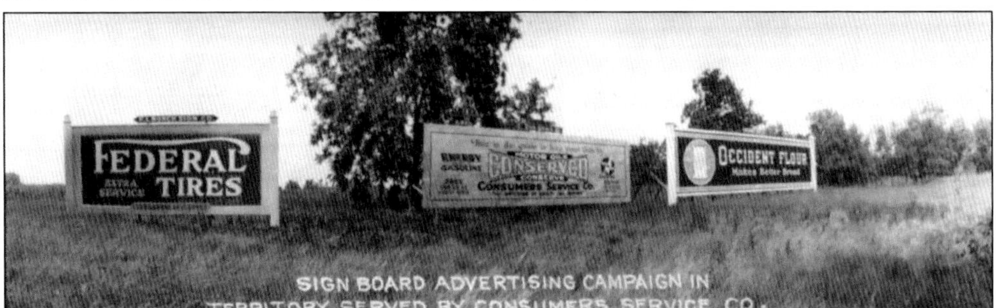

A 1930s view of three road signs on the National Road east of Reelsville is captioned, "Sign Board Advertising Campaign in Territory Served by Consumers Service Co." The signs advertise Federal Tires, Conservco Motor Oil, and Occident Flour. Judging by the haphazard, flimsy construction, they are temporary structures. (Alan E. Hunter.)

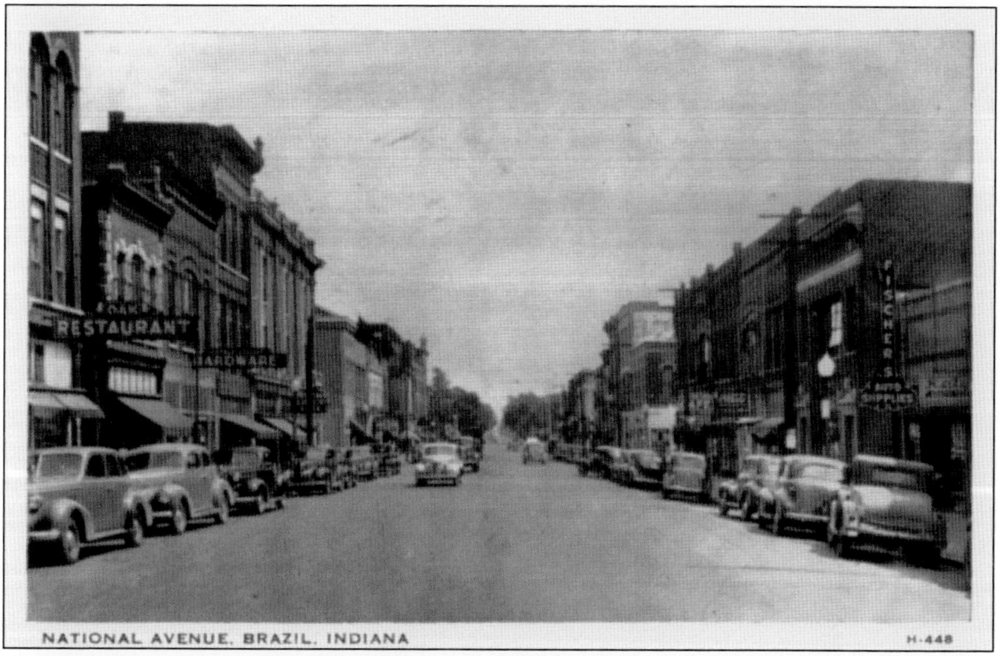

A postcard view from around the 1940s is captioned, "National Avenue, Brazil, Indiana." The Oak Restaurant is pictured on the left side of the street, and Fischer's Auto Supplies store can be seen directly across the street from the eatery. (Bill Raney.)

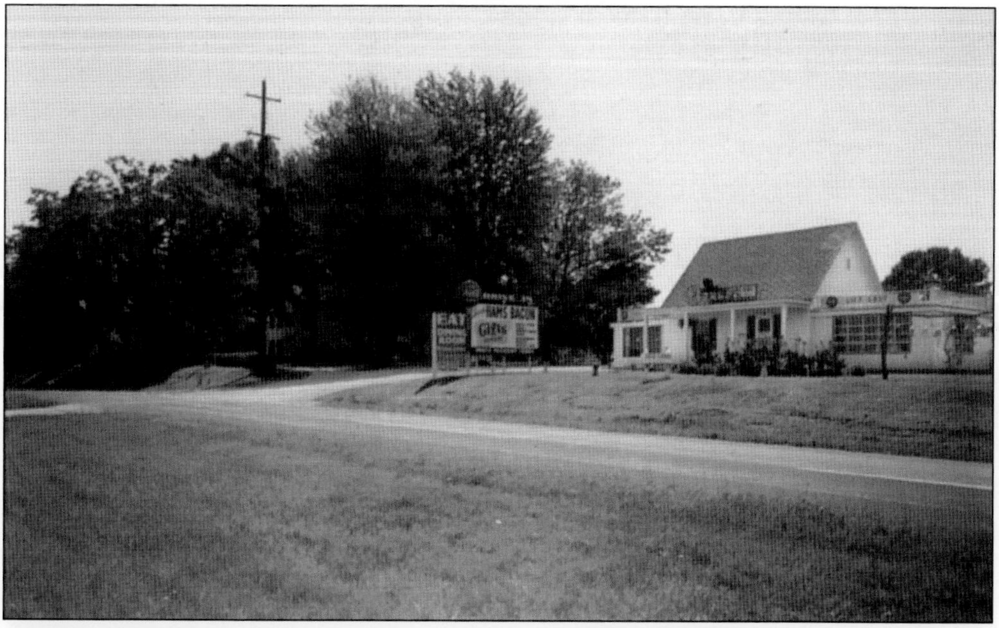

A 1950s–1960s Dexter Press color postcard shows the Hunt's Pleasant Acres motel located six miles east of Brazil on US 40. The motel featured a gift shop specializing in country hams and smoked bacon. The sign over the door includes an old-fashioned horse and buggy—a tip of the cap to its location on the National Road. (Steve and Kim Hunt.)

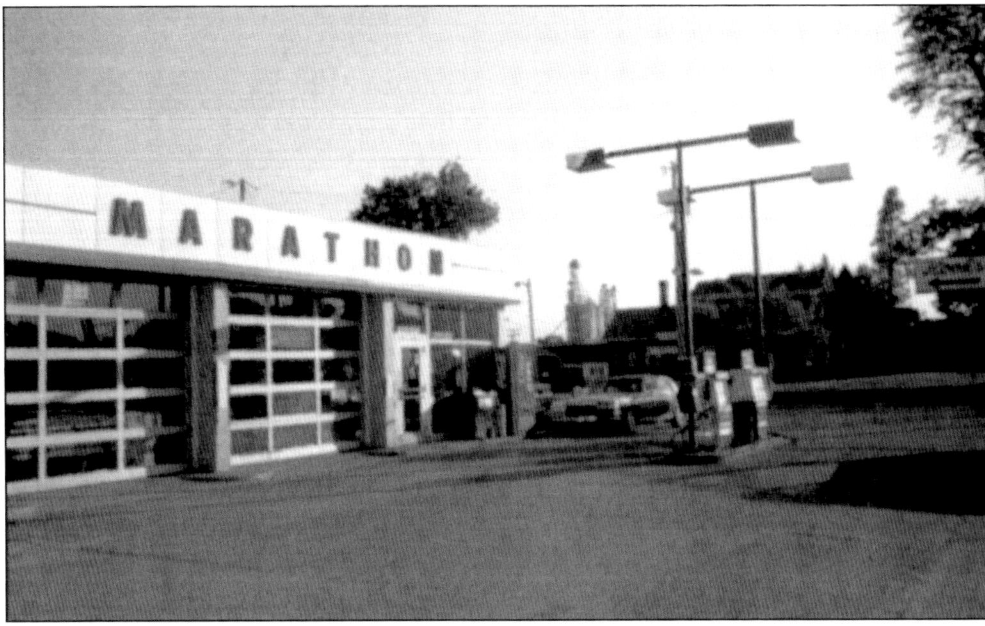

A photograph from about 1990 shows a Marathon gas station on the National Road in Brazil. The flat-roofed, oblong building represents an International-style design popular in the 1950s. White enamel tile panels and steel window and door frames remained popular into the early 1970s, and many of these buildings are still in use along the road today. A Hook's Drugstore sign can be seen at the right of the photograph; the Hook's chain was purchased by Revco in 1994. (Jan Davis.)

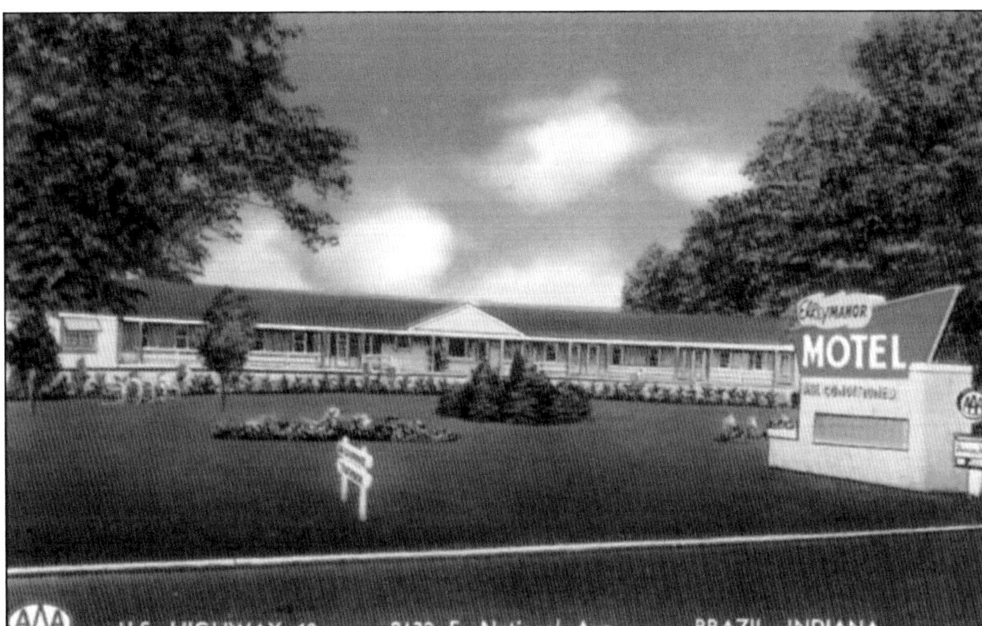

A 1940s-era chrome postcard shows the "Air Conditioned" El Rey Manor Motel on US 40 in Brazil. The card is captioned, "U.S. Highway 40 . . . 2132 E. National Ave. . . . Brazil, Indiana." (Clay County Historical Society.)

A 1940s-era photograph shows the intersection of Main Street and Highway 40 in downtown Brazil. The Sinclair gas station can be seen at right, as well as the Cafe Hotel. Vintage Coca-Cola signs can be seen on both sides of the street. In the distance, the hill on US 40 going west out of town is visible. (Plainfield Library.)

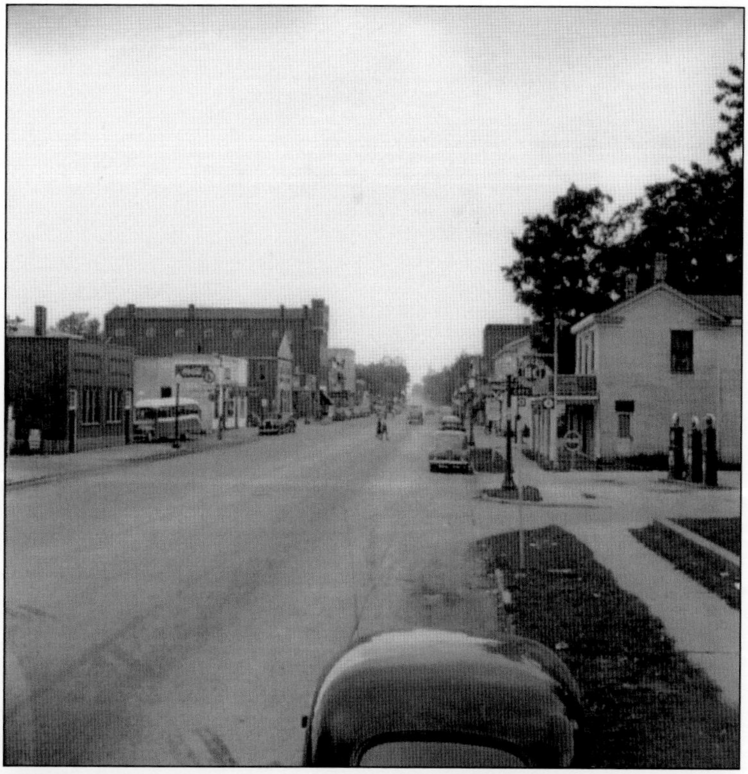

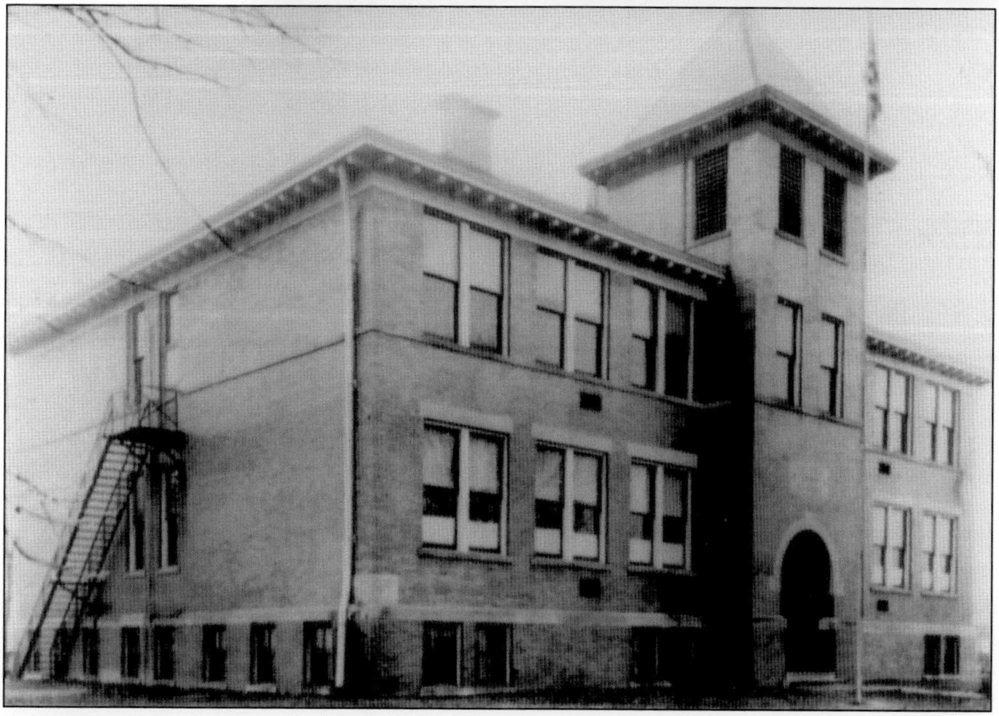

A 1910s–1920s view shows Seelyville's First Glenn High School. Built in 1913, it later became a school for first through seventh grades. (Vigo County Historical Society.)

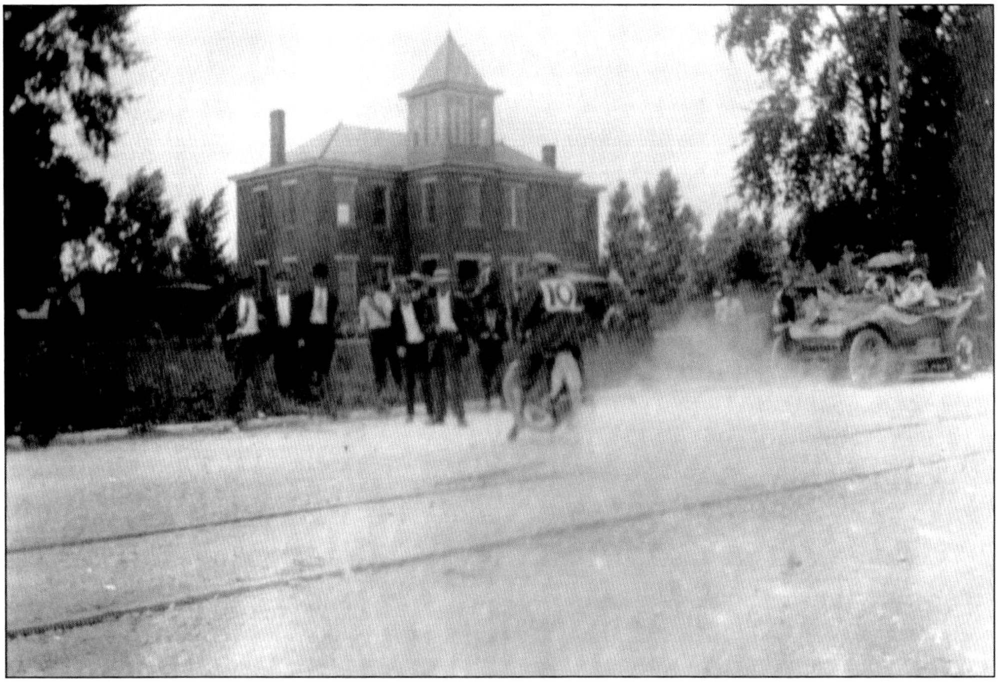

In a photograph of a motorcycle race on the National Road in Seelyville around 1915, the first Glenn High School can be seen in the background. The interurban tracks can be seen on the dirt road in the foreground. (Vigo County Historical Society.)

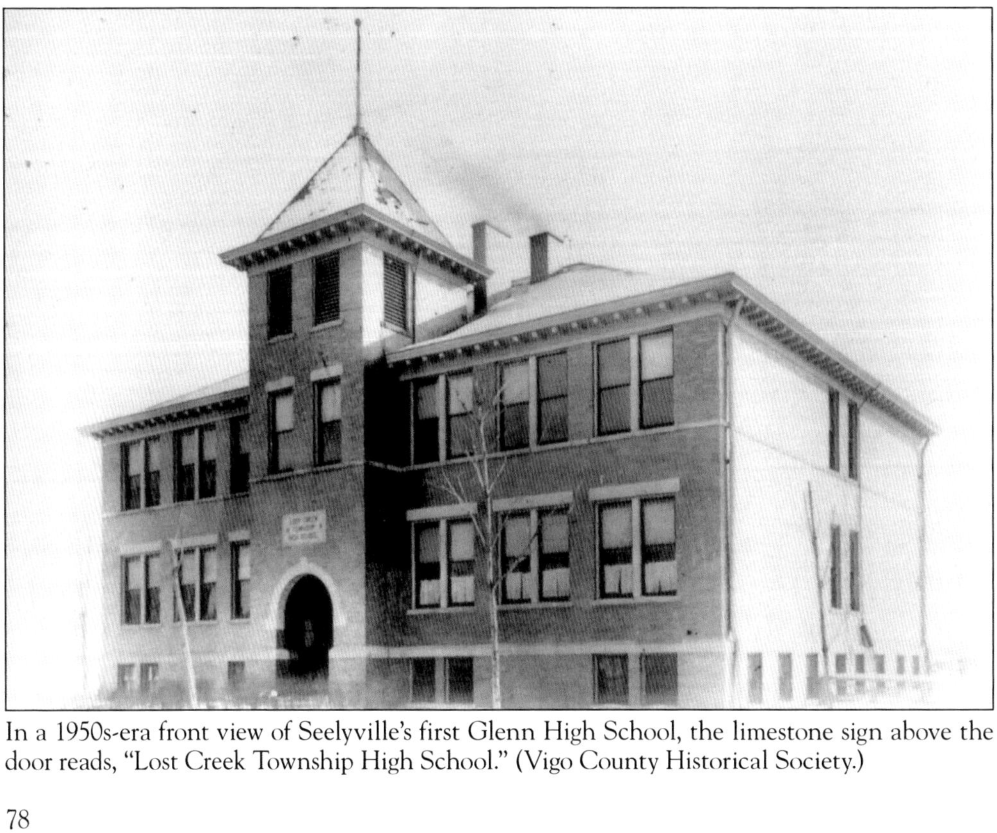

In a 1950s-era front view of Seelyville's first Glenn High School, the limestone sign above the door reads, "Lost Creek Township High School." (Vigo County Historical Society.)

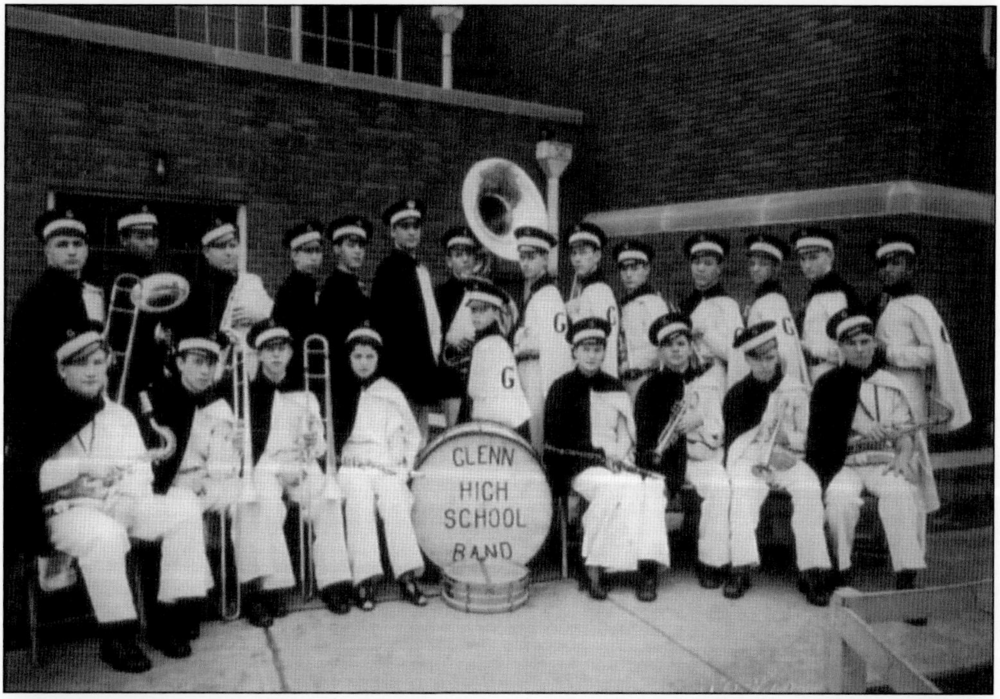

Seelyville's Glenn High School band of 1932 poses outside the school building. The band members are wearing white uniforms with capes and hats. (Jim Webster.)

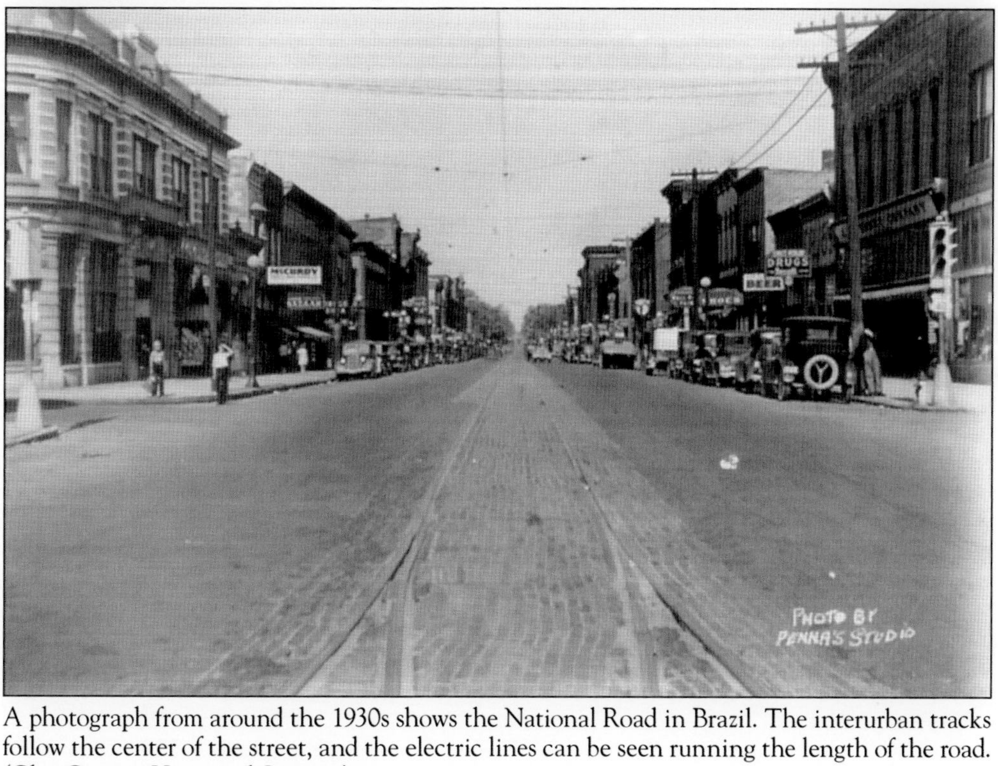

A photograph from around the 1930s shows the National Road in Brazil. The interurban tracks follow the center of the street, and the electric lines can be seen running the length of the road. (Clay County Historical Society.)

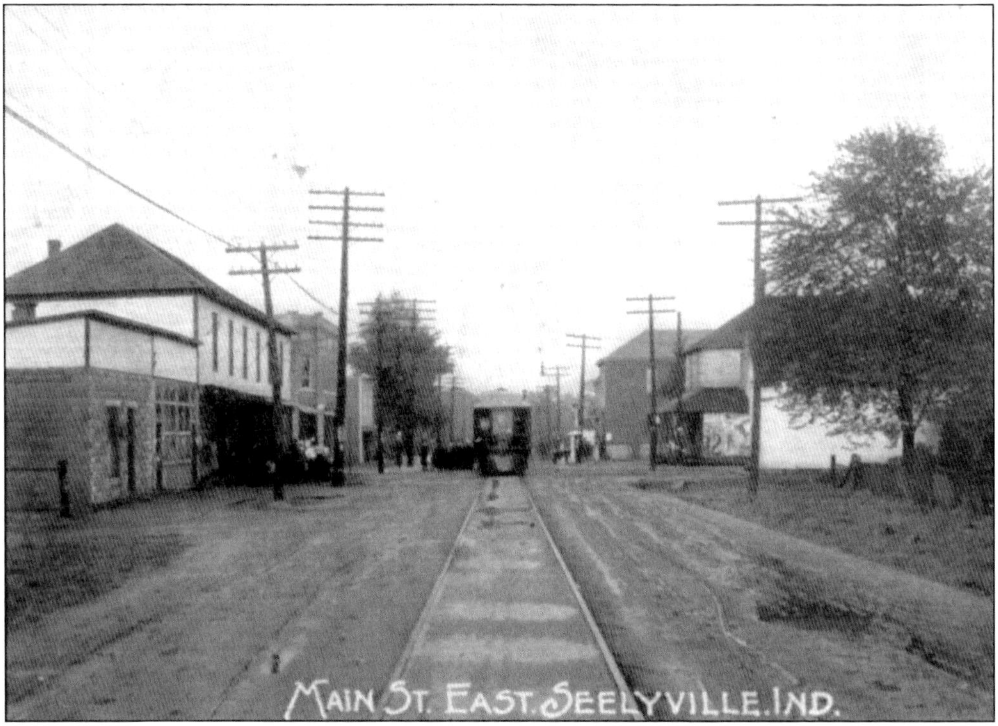

A Seelyville interurban from around 1900 is shown on Main Street in a view looking east. Seelyville was laid out by and named for the town's first postmaster, Jonas Seely, after the opening of the McKeen coal shaft, one of the earliest operated in the county. The mine closed in 1879. East of Terre Haute by nine miles, the early town established a post office in 1878 and operated a station on the Vandalia Railroad. (Vigo County Historical Society.)

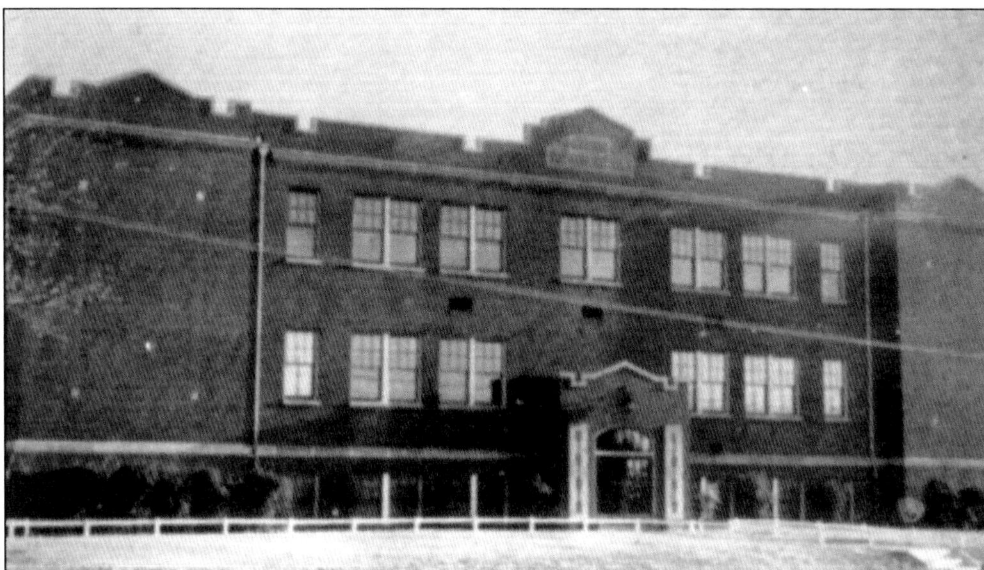

A 1930s-era view shows the exterior of Seelyville's second Glenn High School. The building was demolished in the fall of 2004. (Vigo County Historical Society.)

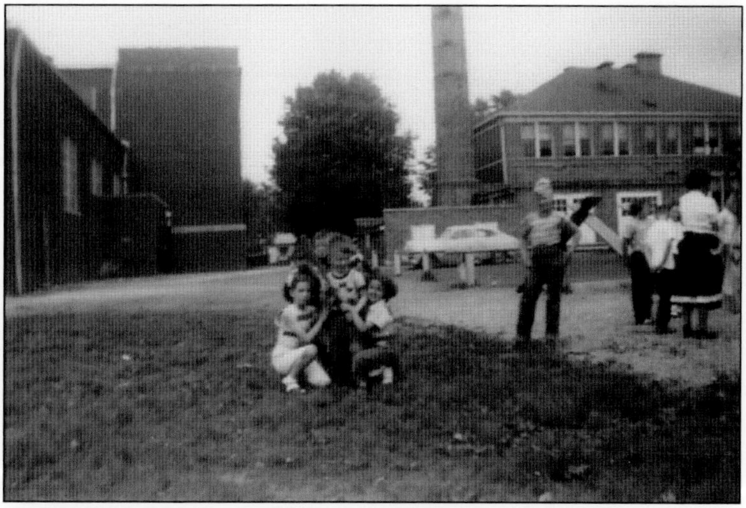

A view from around the 1950s shows the back of Seelyville (left) and Glenn (right) High Schools. The boiler room with its brick smokestack is in the center of the photograph. The children are pictured playing with the old water pump in the foreground, while the teeter-totters remain empty. (Vigo County Historical Society.)

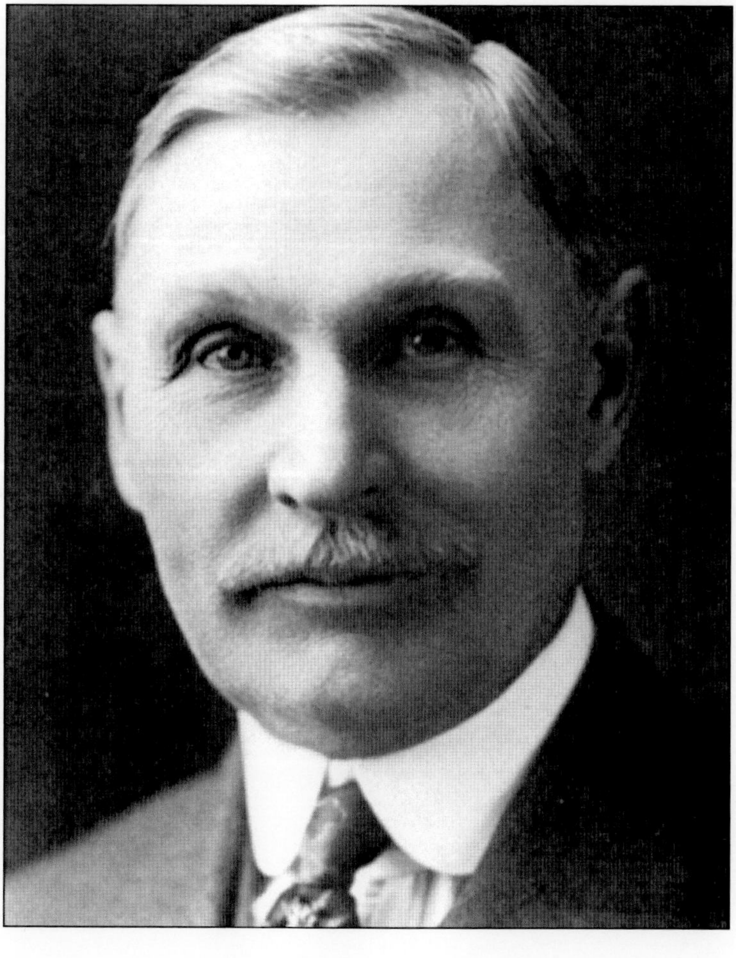

Alexander Samuelson, the Swedish-born plant supervisor at Terre Haute's Root Glass Company, is credited with developing the distinctive shape of the Coca-Cola bottle in 1916. The idea came during a work stoppage at the plant because of the brutal heat of a typical Indiana summer. The Coca-Cola bottle was not the Root Glass Company's only claim to fame; they also invented the Root Mason Jar, which became the famous Ball canning jars. (Root Glass Company.)

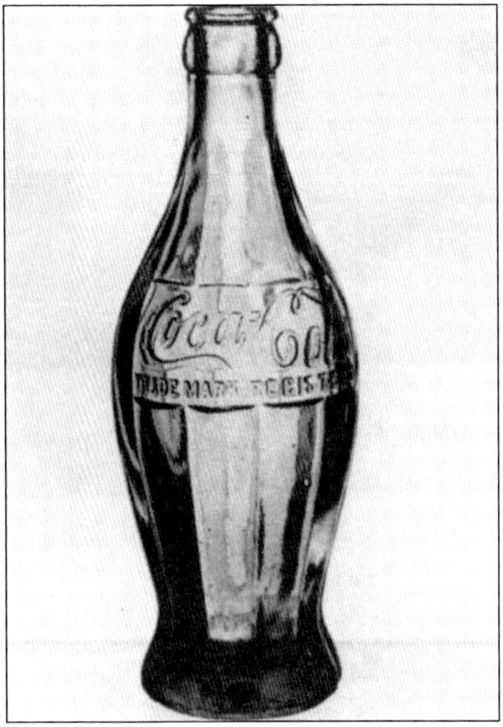

The Coca-Cola bottle is the only Hoosier product that can be identified by blindfolded people in more than 130 countries. Legend has it that the bottle was designed to look like a cacao bean pod; it was one of the first things ever patented because of its shape. (Coca-Cola Company.)

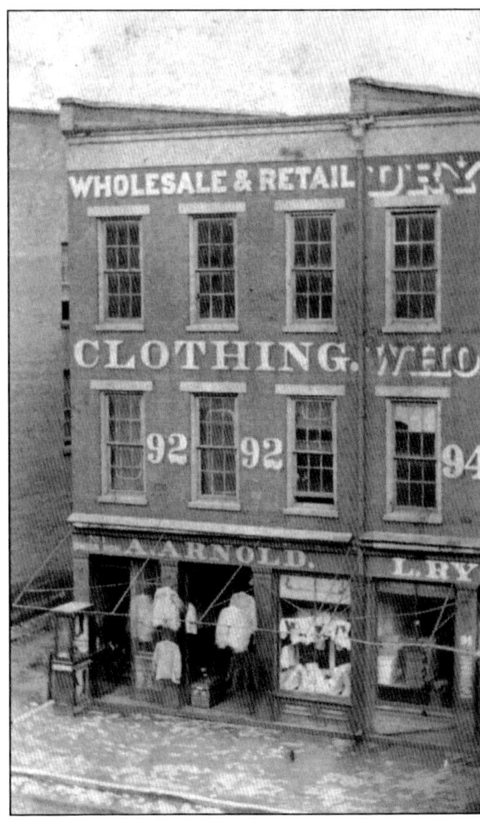

This is one of the earliest *carte de visite* photographs of National Road in Terre Haute taken during the Civil War. Fueled by the war, pork processing became a major industry of the city. The A. Arnold clothing store was located at 92 Main Street. The painted sign reads, "Wholesale & Retail Clothing—A. Arnold." The street address was changed to "No. 1 Union Row" during the Civil War. The back stamp reads, "C. Eppert Photographer No. 87 Main Street, Between Third and Fourth Terre Haute, Ind." (Mick Kissick.)

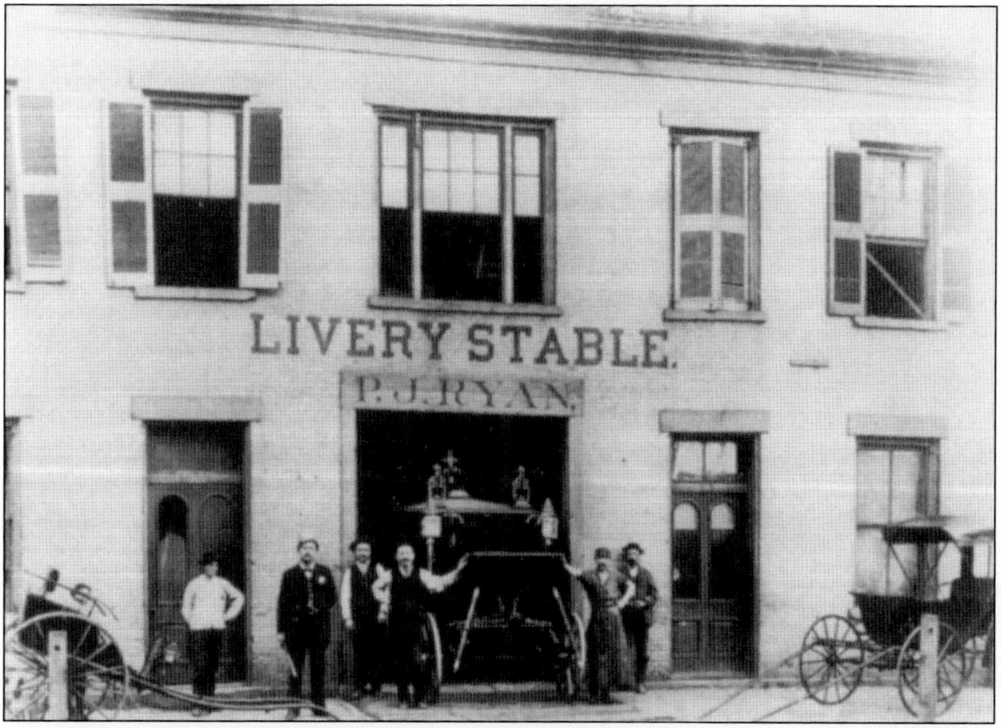

An 1890s-era photograph shows P.J. Ryan Livery Stable in Terre Haute. The image shows a group of men posed proudly with an ornate horse-drawn hearse. (Indianapolis Public Library, Irvington Branch.)

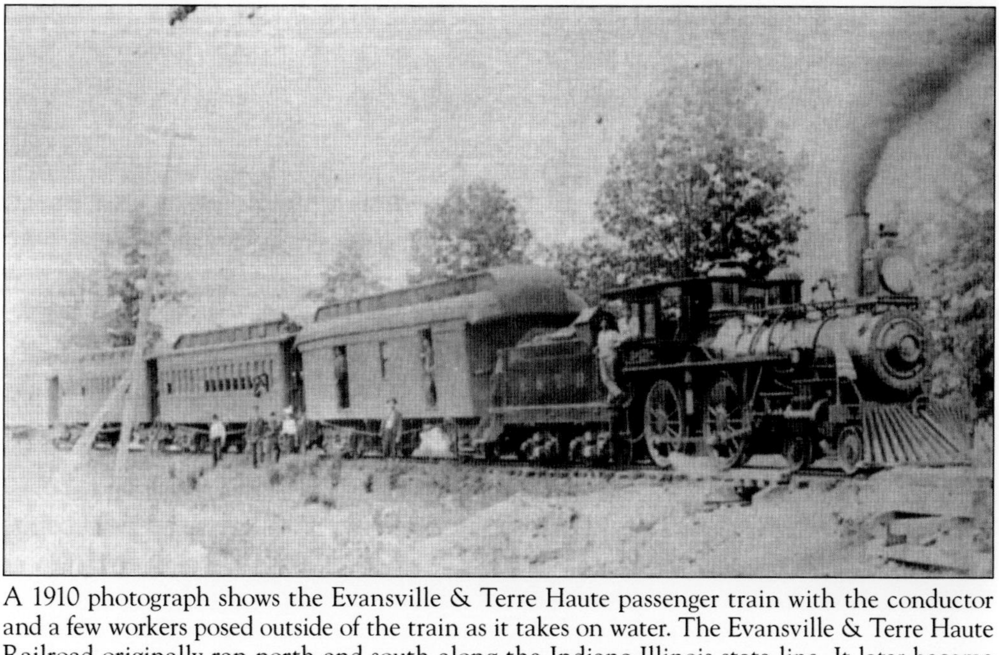

A 1910 photograph shows the Evansville & Terre Haute passenger train with the conductor and a few workers posed outside of the train as it takes on water. The Evansville & Terre Haute Railroad originally ran north and south along the Indiana-Illinois state line. It later became known as the Evansville, Indianapolis & Terre Haute line, with service to the state's capital city soon paralleling the Historic National Road. (Alan E. Hunter.)

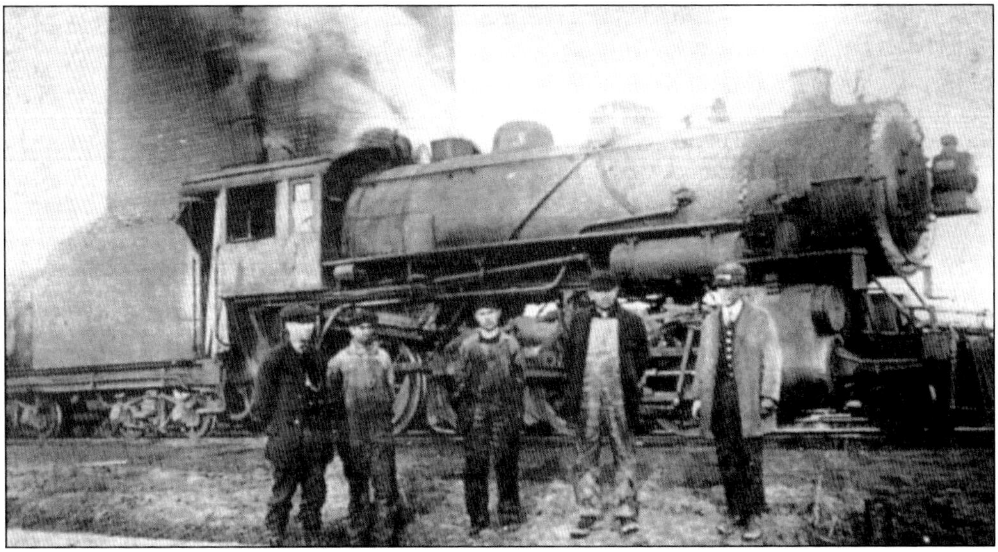

A photograph from around 1910 shows the engine and crew of the Chicago, Terre Haute & Southeastern No. 682. The crew appears to be posed for the photographer during a water stop, as the engine's stack is smoking. (Elmer G. Sulzer.)

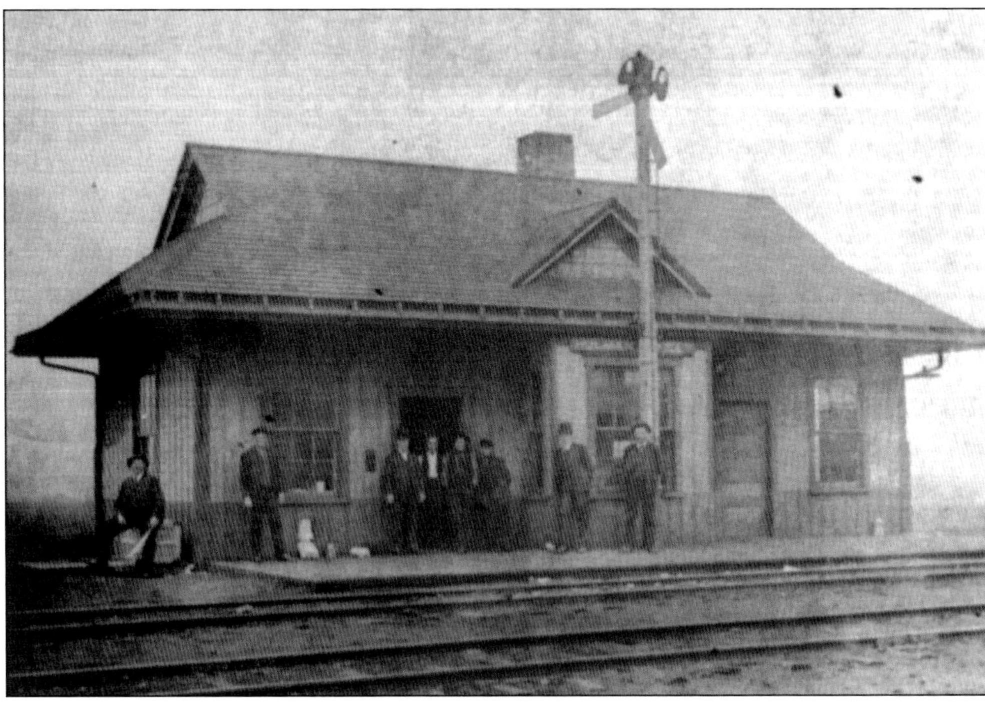

A photograph from around 1910 shows the engine and crew of the Southern Indiana Railway depot at Hulman Street in Terre Haute. Several passengers await the train as a rather menacing looking "railroad bull" sits at the side of the depot with a huge club in his hand, ready to sweep any nonpaying hobos off the train. (C.W. Pearce.)

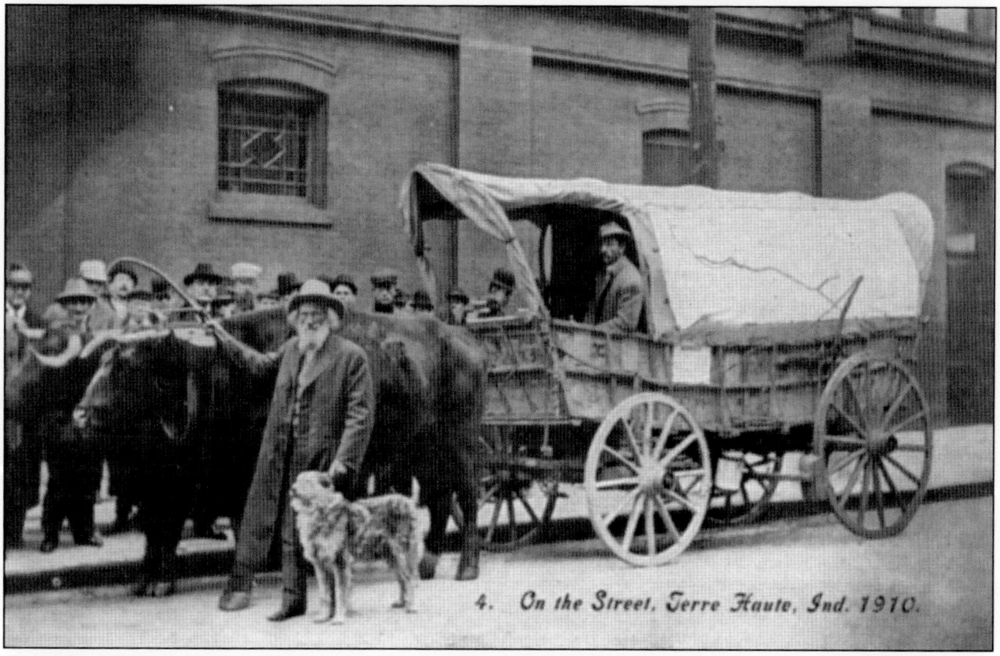

A 1910 postcard view is captioned, "On the Street, Terre Haute, Ind. 1910." The postcard pictures an old man with a bullwhip raised and his dog by his side. He is leading a pioneer wagon pulled by a pair of oxen. A crowd of well-dressed men stands on the sidewalk next to the National Road. (Bill Raney.)

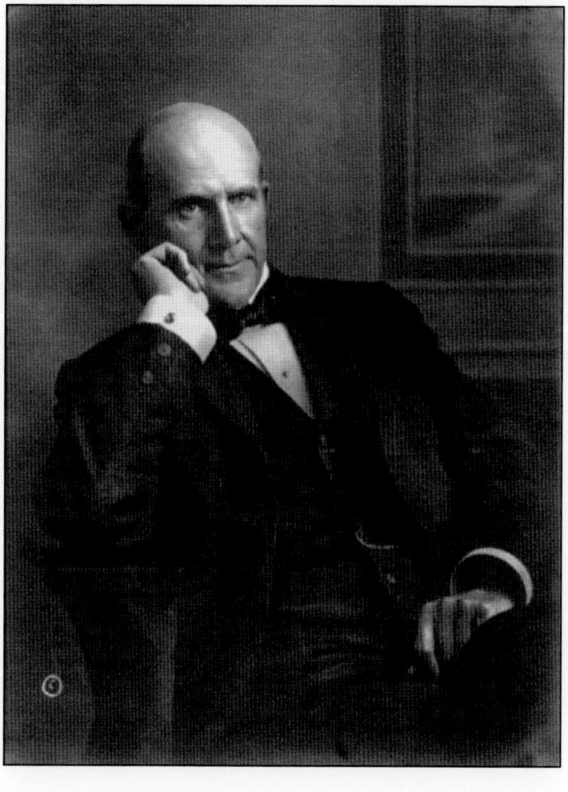

A photograph from about 1920 portrays Eugene V. Debs. Born in Terre Haute on November 5, 1855, Debs was a pioneering labor union leader and five-time candidate for president of the United States. He was one of the founding members of the International Labor Union and the Industrial Workers of the World. Debs's presidential candidacy was as a member of the Social Democratic Party in 1900 and, later, as a member of the Socialist Party of America in 1904, 1908, 1912, and 1920. (Vigo County Historical Society.)

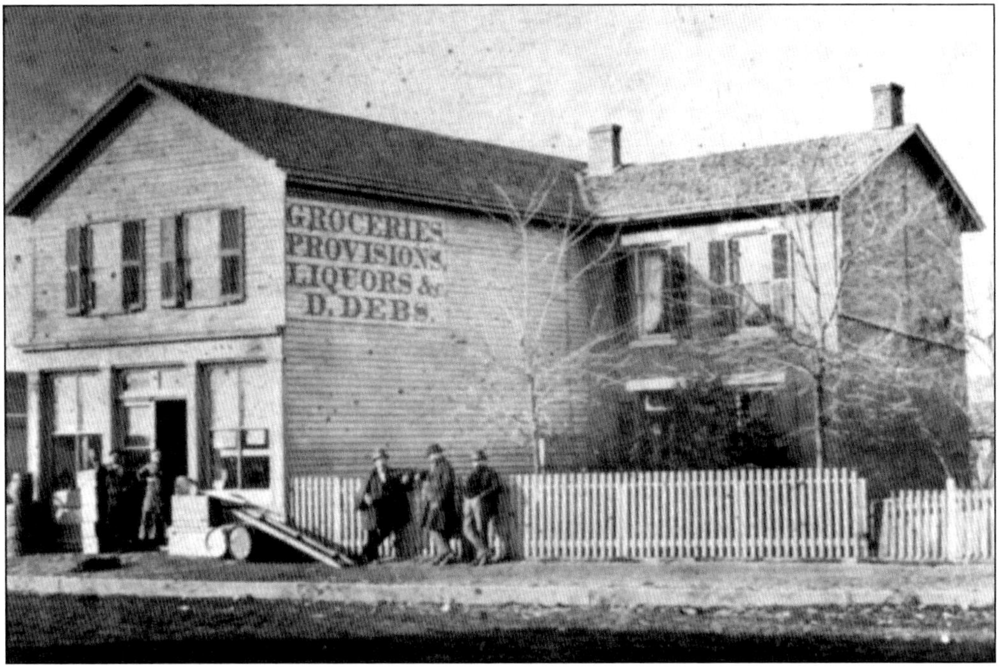

An 1880s-era photograph shows the Debs grocery store in Terre Haute. The store was operated by the family of Eugene V. Debs, whose mother, Marguerite, started the store with the family's last $40, saving them from financial ruin. The Debs family lived on the second floor of the building. Marguerite Debs stands in the doorway. (Indianapolis Public Library, Warren Branch.)

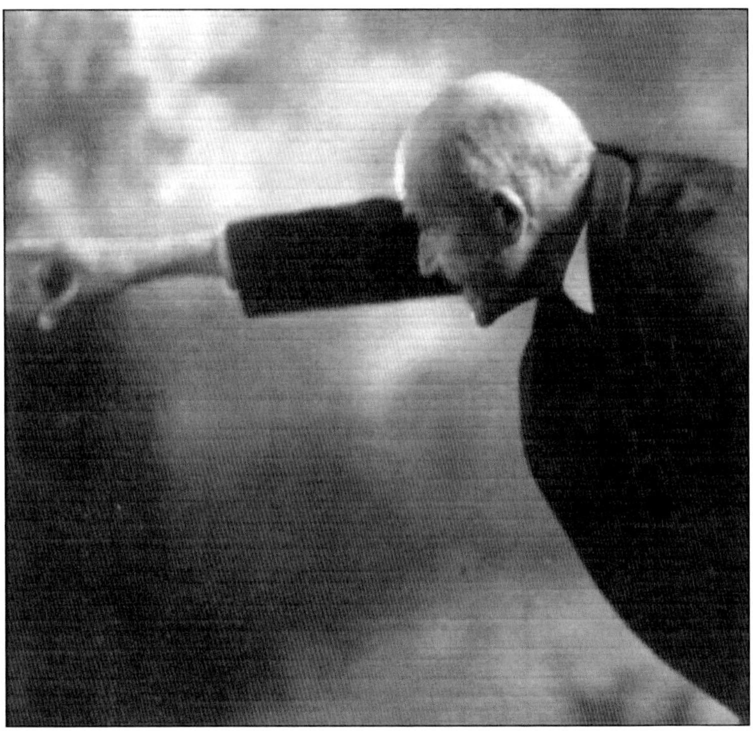
Eugene V. Debs is photographed on the campaign trail while running for president of the United States. Debs was known as a passionate speaker who worked his crowds into frenzies. Debs's speeches against Pres. Woodrow Wilson and the war earned him a trip to the Atlanta Federal Penitentiary in 1919. He ran for president from prison in 1920 and received 913,664 write-in votes, 3.4 percent of the total. (John Pfeiffer.)

A 1994 photograph shows the Eugene V. Debs home at 451 North Eighth Street on the campus of Indiana State University in Terre Haute. Debs and his wife, Kate, built the two-story frame house in 1890 after their fifth wedding anniversary. When Debs died in 1926, a funeral service was given at the house and attended by 5,000 mourners. Used as the Theta Khi fraternity house from 1948 to 1961 and briefly for apartments in 1962, the home was bought by the Eugene V. Debs Foundation. Declared a National Historic Landmark in 1966, today the house is a museum. (Jan Davis.)

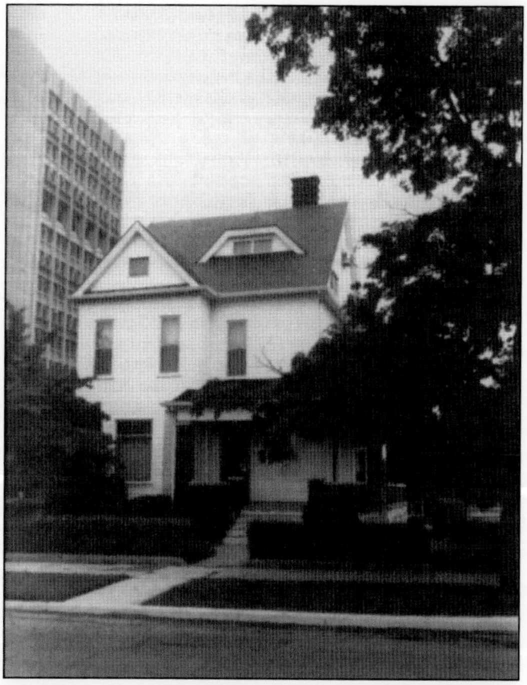

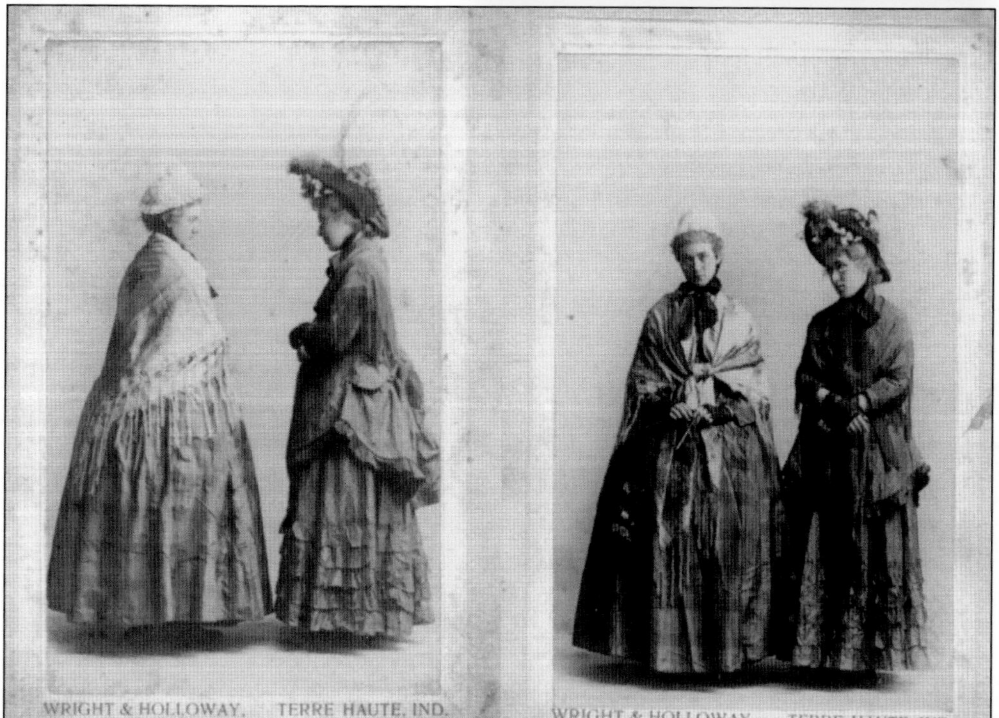

These two 1894 cabinet photographs show a pair of women in dresses. Each photograph features women posed in hoop skirts and bonnets, and both read, "Wright & Holloway, Terre Haute, Ind." The photographs have been captioned on the back: "Two maids of ye olden times Feb. 24, 1894." (Alan E. Hunter.)

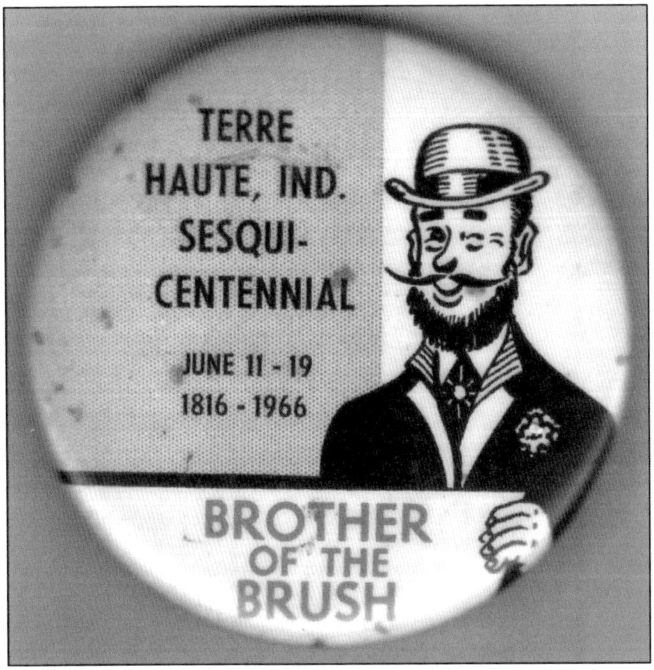

Terre Haute is known as the Crossroads of the Nation for the downtown intersection of US 40 and US 41. The intersection lost an important piece of its history when the famed Terre Haute House was demolished after a long struggle to preserve it. Since the loss of the Terre Haute House, advocates have made significant strides in the preservation and promotion of National Road heritage in the city. This pin celebrates Terre Haute's sesquicentennial in 1966. (Alan E. Hunter.)

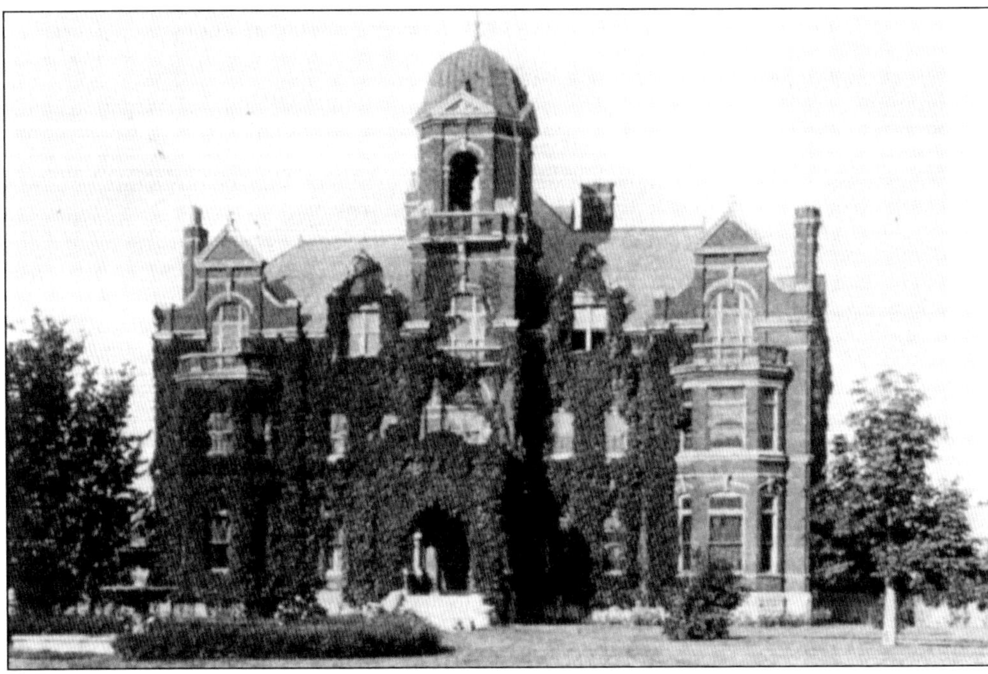

A 1907 photograph shows Terre Haute's Rose Orphan's Home at the corner of Old National Road and Twenty-fifth Street. The home served as a refuge for parentless, half-orphan, and destitute children from 1884 until 1949. The cornerstone of the building was laid in 1883, and the first children were enrolled on September 4, 1884. The main building was flanked by a chapel on the west and handsome cottages and dormitories on the east. It could house as many as 150 children. A study in 1929 concluded that the home was the "nations finest" children's institution. (Indianapolis Public Library, Warren Branch.)

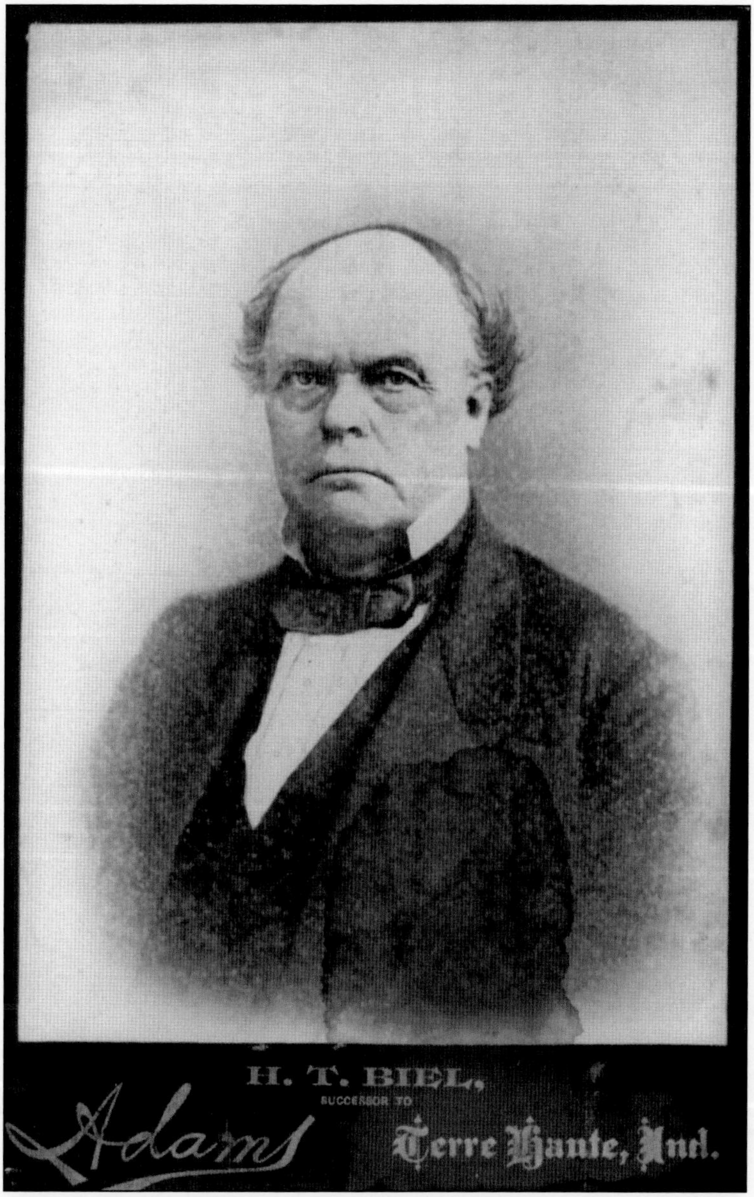

An 1870s-era cabinet photograph portrays the "Father of Terre Haute." The caption reads, "H. T. Biel, successor to Adams Terre Haute, Ind," denoting the photographer and studio, respectively. Chauncey Rose was the principal founder of the Terre Haute & Richmond Railroad, which was renamed the Terre Haute & Indianapolis Railroad in 1865. He was instrumental in getting the US Army Corps of Engineers (supervisors of the construction of the Cumberland Road—the National Road—under Maj. Cornelius A. Ogden) to relocate their headquarters from Indianapolis to Terre Haute. Rose was generous with his money in Terre Haute, where his philanthropic activities were reported in an 1875 *New York Times* article to have exceeded two million dollars in the currency of that day. Among his numerous benefactors were the Providence Hospital, the Free Dispensary, and the Rose Orphan's Home, to which he endowed enough money to ensure it would remain permanent. Rose also contributed enough money to build and endow the Rose Polytechnic Institute, now the Rose-Hulman Institute of Technology. (Vigo County Historical Society.)

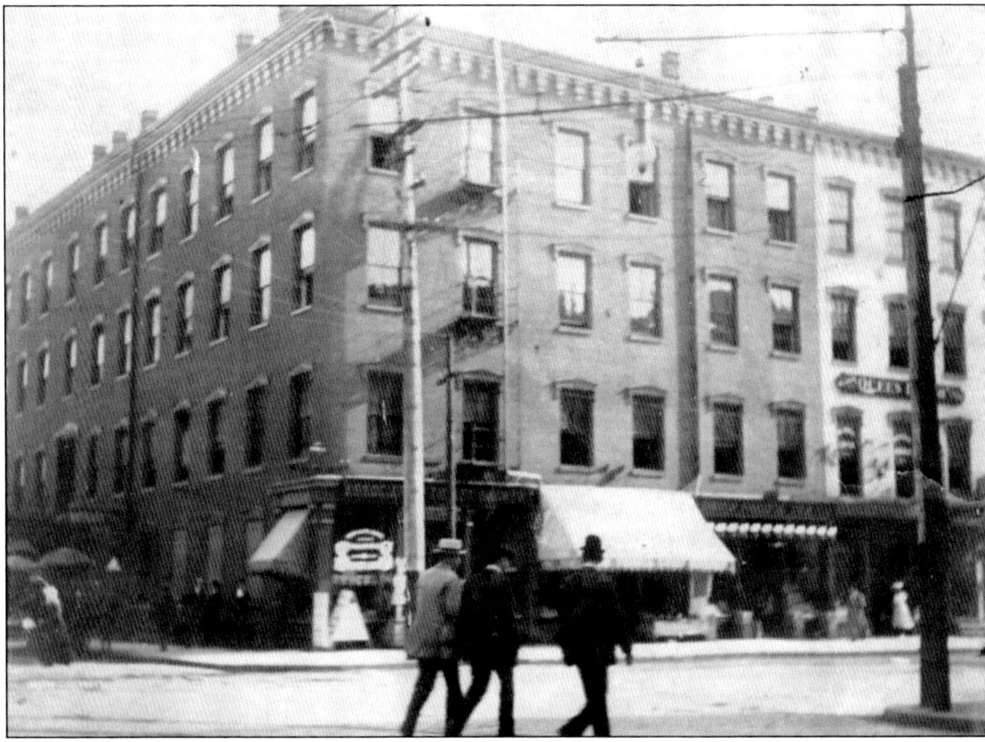

The National House hotel was located at the corner of Sixth Street and Wabash Avenue, shown here in 1897. The Associated Ticket Broker travel agency can be seen on the ground-floor corner. (Vigo County Historical Society.)

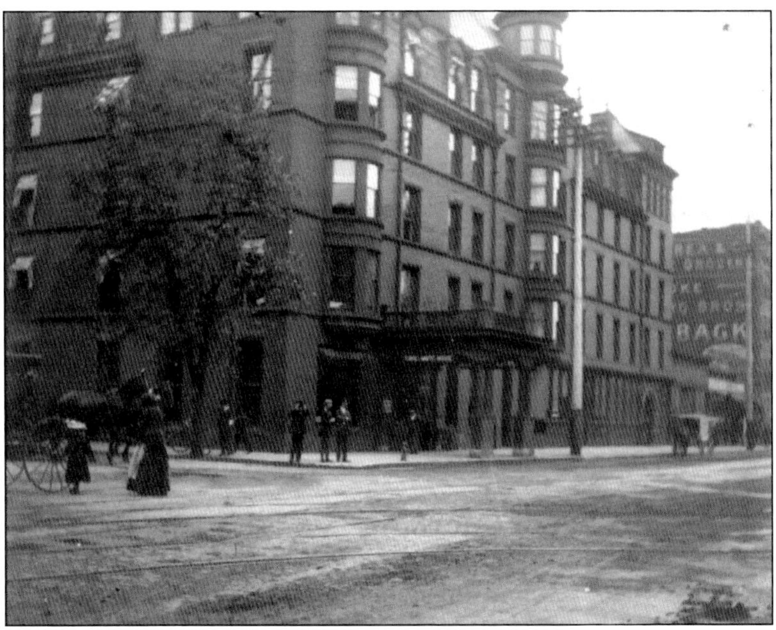

The Terre Haute House hotel is shown in May 1897; people stand on the street corner, and a doorman is posed outside the front door. Chairs can be seen on the balcony above, although there is no doorway, meaning that a person would have to climb through the window to sit there. (Vigo County Historical Society.)

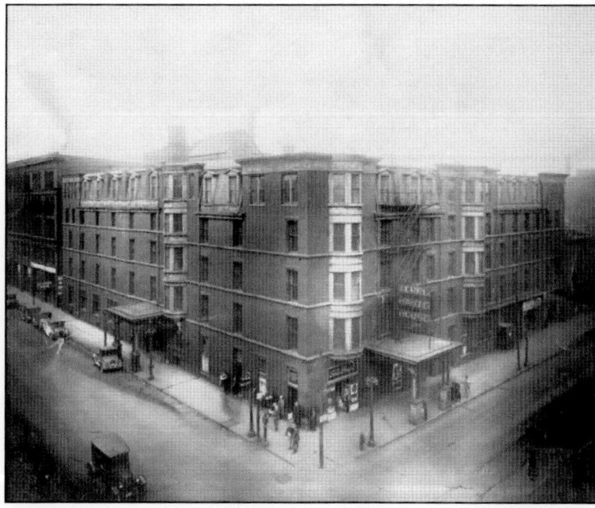

This R.B. Hare photograph shows the Terre Haute House hotel between 1923 and 1927. Legend claims that both Al Capone and John Dillinger stayed at this hotel. Advertising for the hotel from around 1880 boasts, "Steam Heat and Electric Lights in All Rooms. Private Ice Plant. Artesian Water. Bar. Barber Shop. Billiard Rooms. Large Convention Hall. Western Union Telegraph. Long Distance Telephone. Railroad Ticket Offices. Service Throughout the House Perfect. . . . $2.50 $3.00 $3.50 $4.00 Per day." (Vigo County Historical Society.)

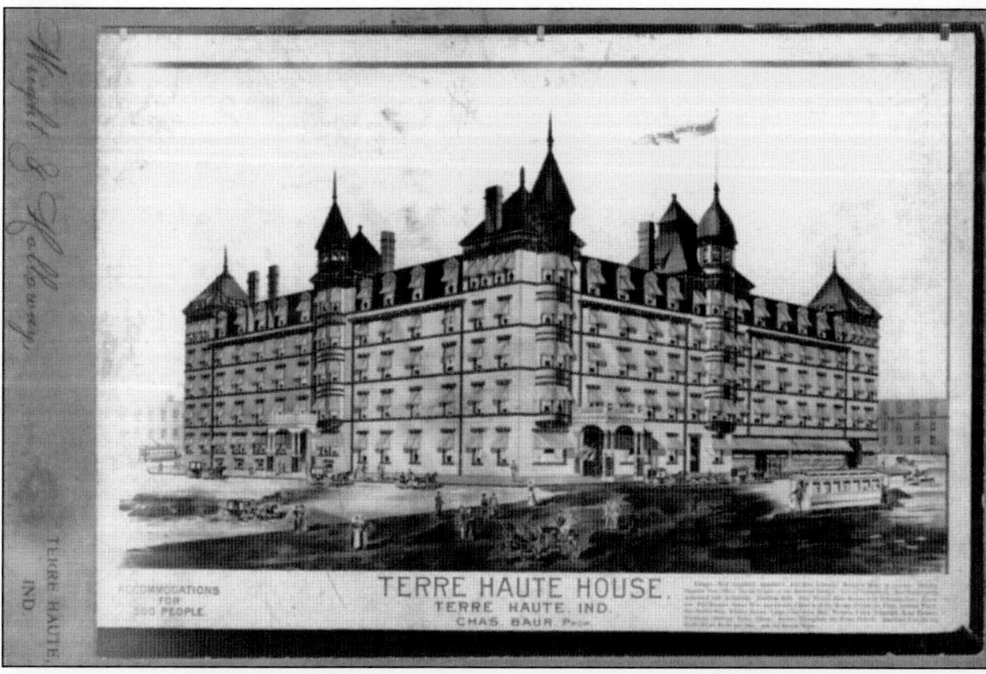

The caption for an 1880s-era Wright & Holloway cabinet photograph by Gast Art Litho St. Louis advertises, "Terre Haute House—Terre Haute, Ind.—Chas. Bauer Prop.—Accommodations for 500 People." The text to the right reads, "Largest, Most Elegantly Appointed, and Most Liberally Managed Hotel in Indiana. Directly Opposite Post Office. In the Center of the Business District. . . . Most Sumptuously Appointed Cafe in Indiana. Faultless Beds. Sixty Private Bath Rooms with Porcelain Tubs. Elevators. Fire Escapes." (Vigo County Historical Society.)

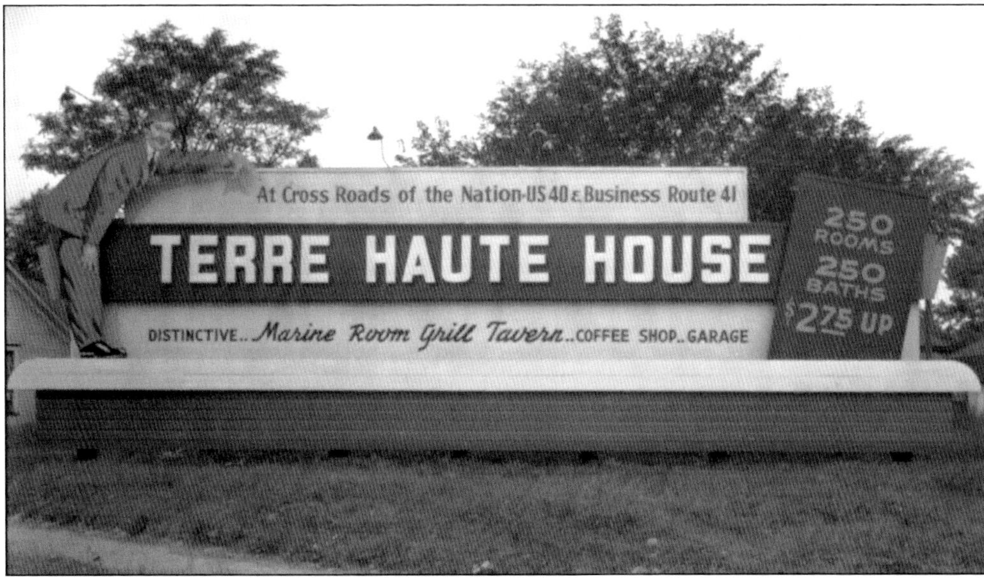

A large billboard located on the National Road during the early 1940s features a man pointing to the sign that reads, "At Cross Roads of the Nation-US 40 & Business Route 41—Terre Haute House—Distinctive . . Marine Room Grill Tavern . . Coffee Shop . . Garage—250 Rooms 250 Baths $2.75 Up." (Vigo County Historical Society.)

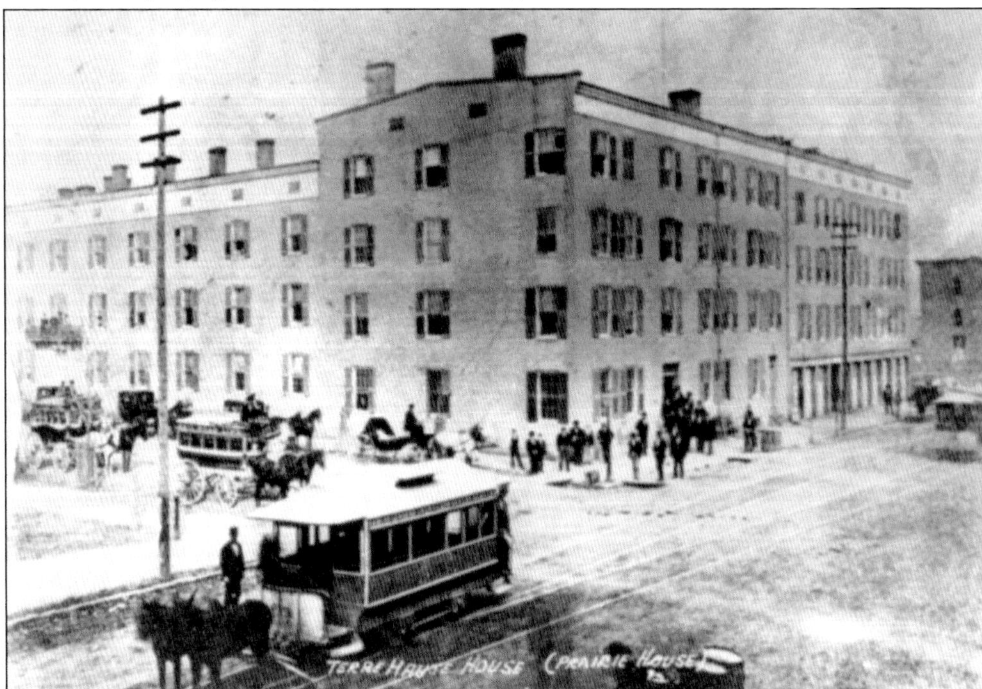

The Prairie House hotel is shown as it appeared in 1869. The building would be remodeled and renamed the Terre Haute House hotel. This photograph shows horse-drawn vehicles (trolleys and coaches) and people at the corner and on the balcony of the building. (Vigo County Historical Society.)

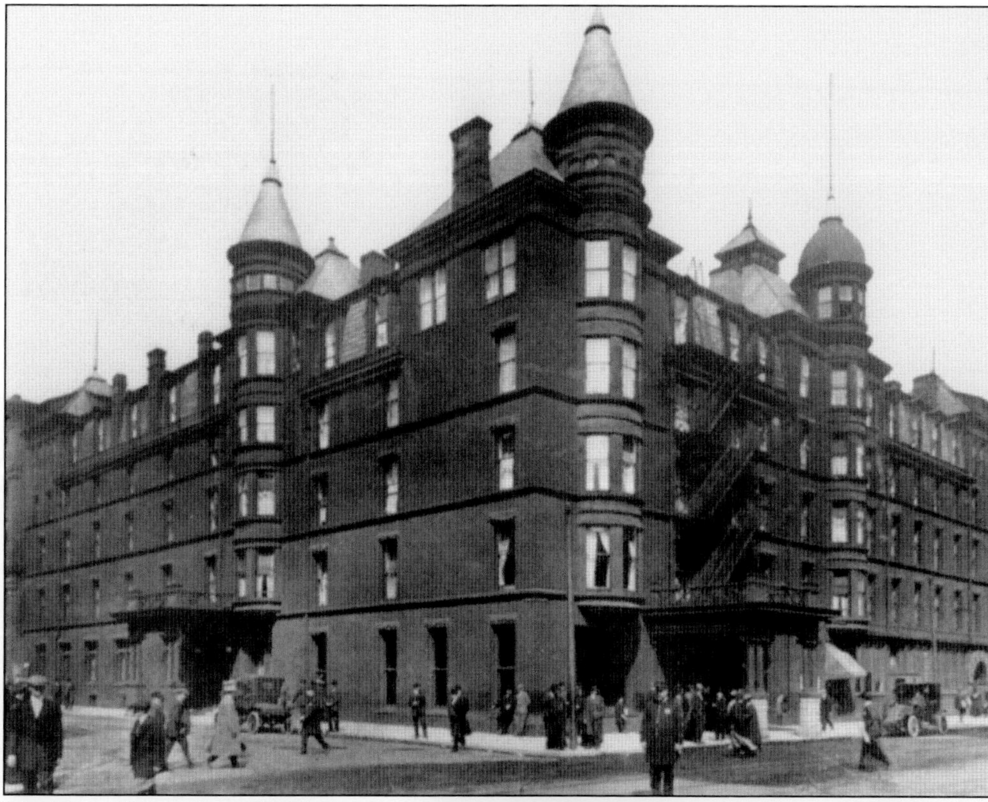

The Terre Haute House hotel is shown around 1900 with three turrets and a fire escape facing Wabash Avenue. A policeman directs traffic in the middle of the street before the advent of traffic lights, and people are scurrying about. This photograph first appeared on page 102 of the *Terre Haute Pictorial* book printed in 1900. (Vigo County Historical Society.)

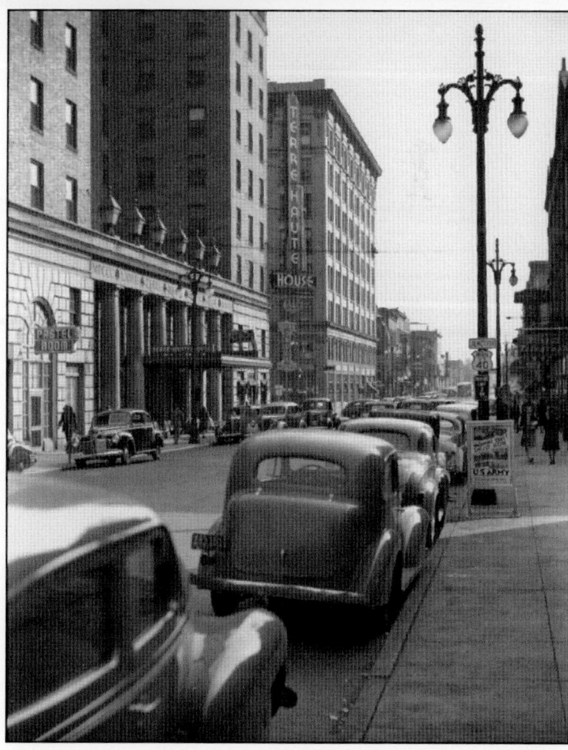

A photograph taken at Seventh Street, looking south on US 41 from a point just north of the junction of US 41 and US 40, shows the Terre Haute House hotel and its neon sign on the left. A neon sign for the Pastel Room can be seen, and a US 40 sign is visible on the right of this Sebree Studio photograph. (Vigo County Historical Society.)

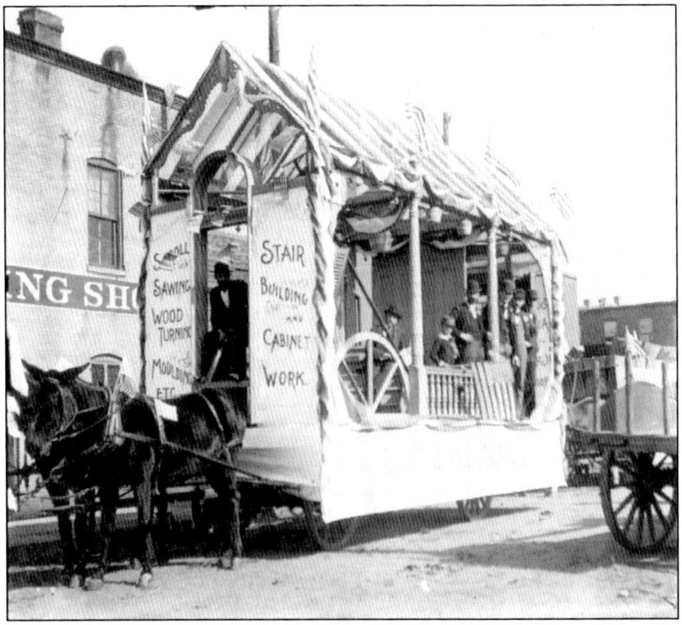

A Clift and Williams Co. float for the first Terre Haute street fair on Wabash Avenue is marked, "Scroll—Sawing—Wood Turning—Moulding—Etc." and "Stair Building and Cabinet Work." The fair took place in 1899. (Vigo County Historical Society.)

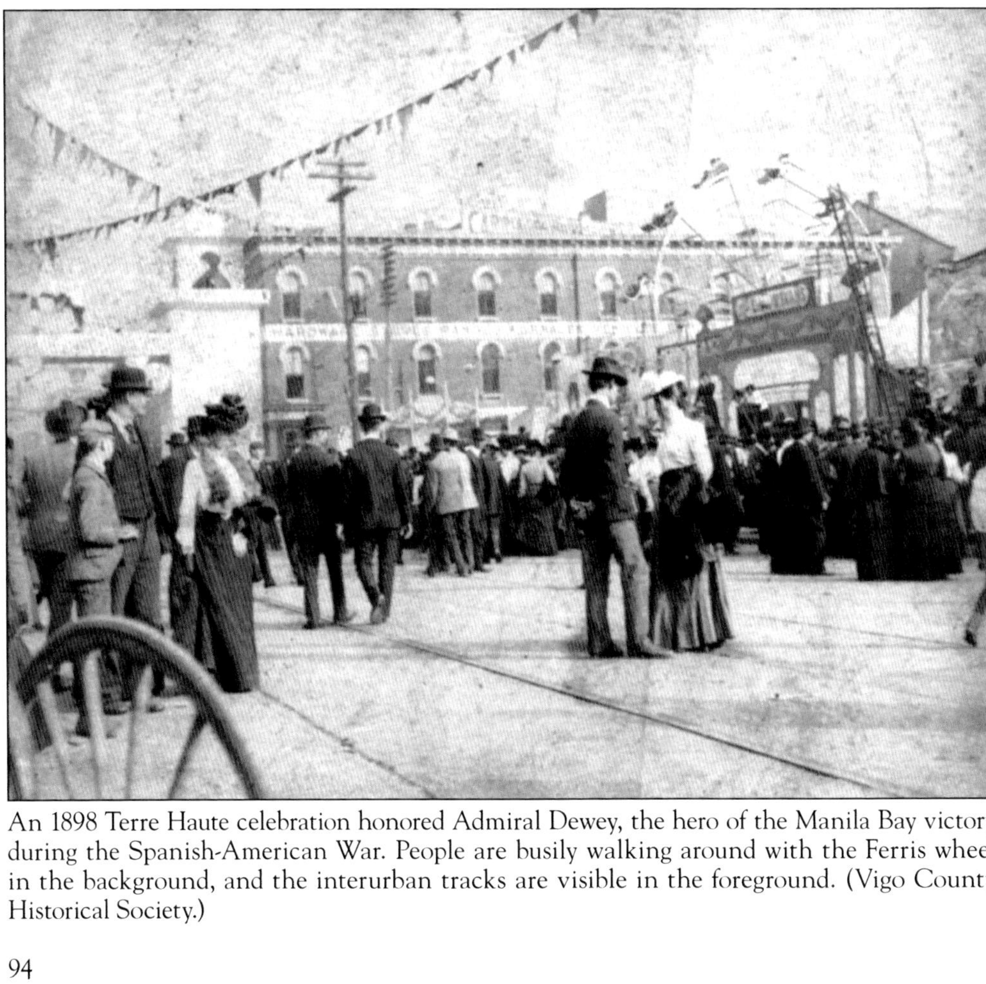

An 1898 Terre Haute celebration honored Admiral Dewey, the hero of the Manila Bay victory during the Spanish-American War. People are busily walking around with the Ferris wheel in the background, and the interurban tracks are visible in the foreground. (Vigo County Historical Society.)

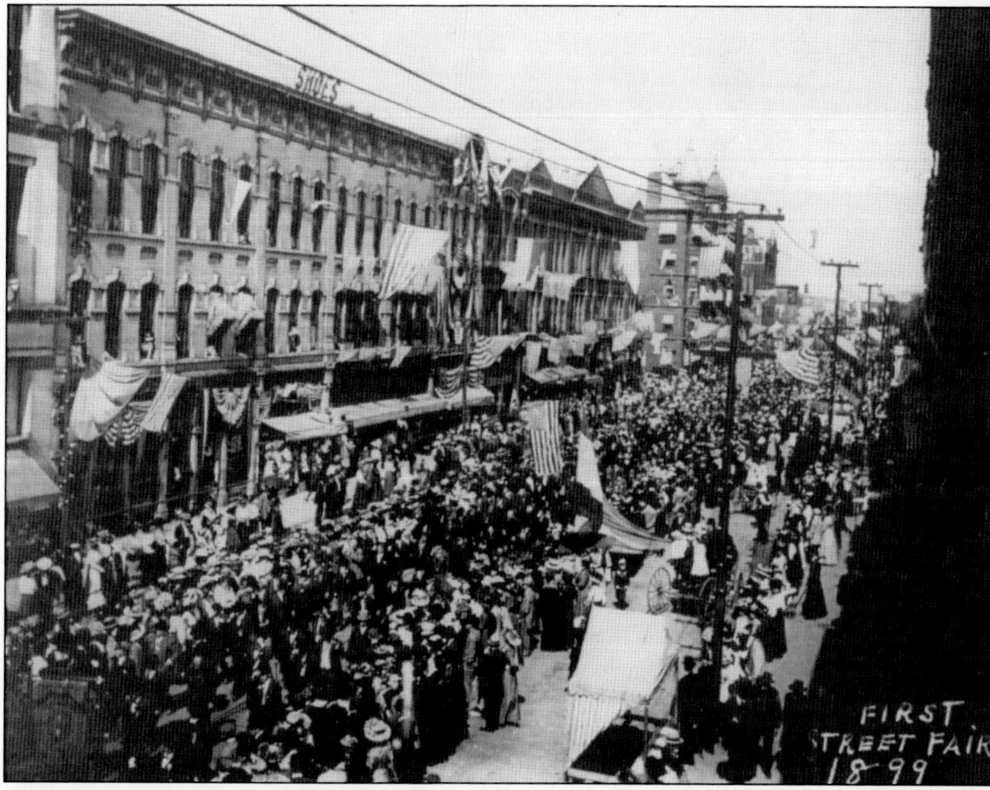

This photograph taken at Eighth Street and Wabash Avenue looking east is captioned, "First Street Fair 1899." The streets and sidewalks are choked with people as Civil War veterans march past. (Vigo County Historical Society.)

An 1876 view looking west shows the United States centennial celebration arch built at Sixth Street and Wabash Avenue. The buildings on both sides of the road are decked with flags and portraits of the presidents. The National Road is still a dirt road with streetcar tracks in the middle. (Vigo County Historical Society.)

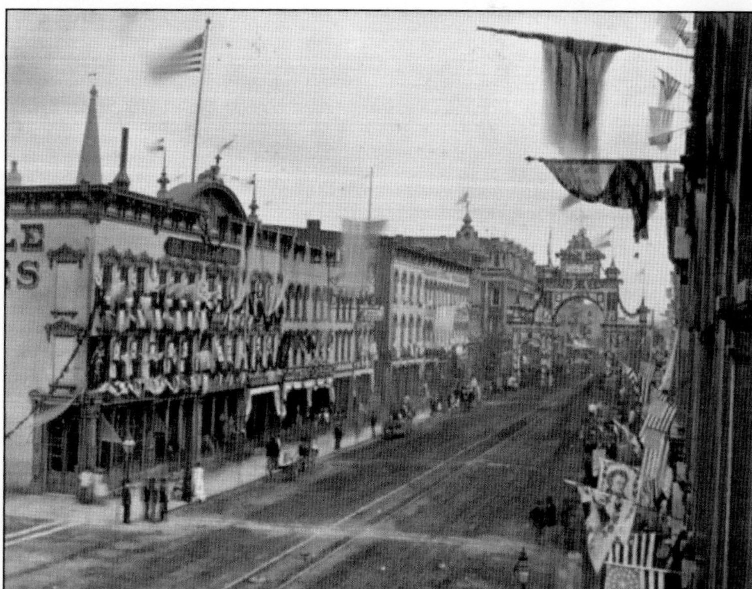

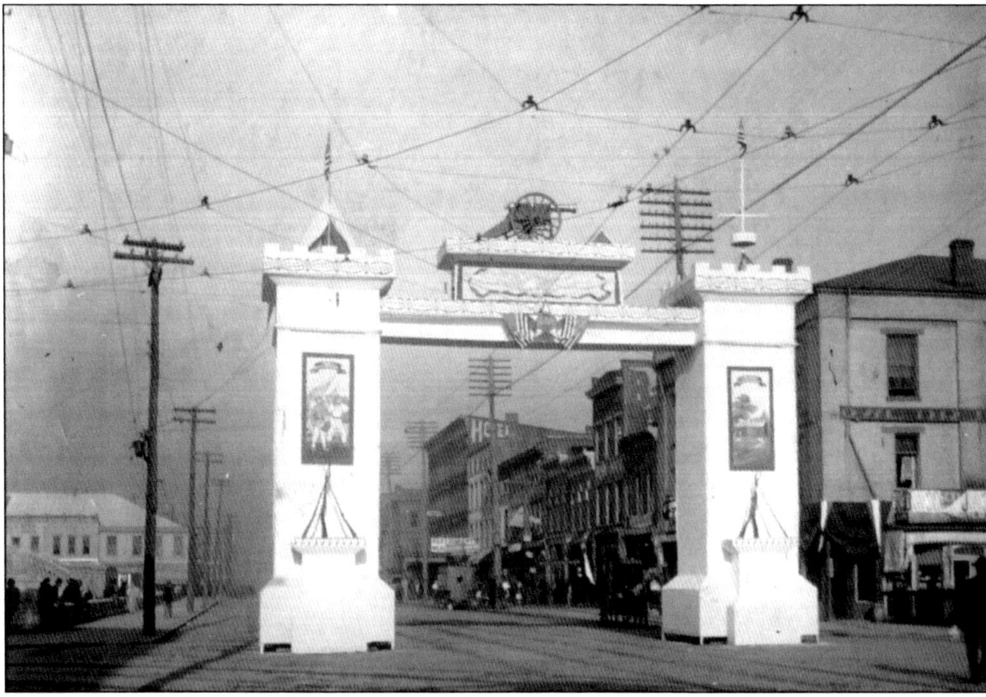

At the Terre Haute celebration in honor of Admiral Dewey in 1898, people walk around Third and Ohio Streets. This view looks north. (Vigo County Historical Society.)

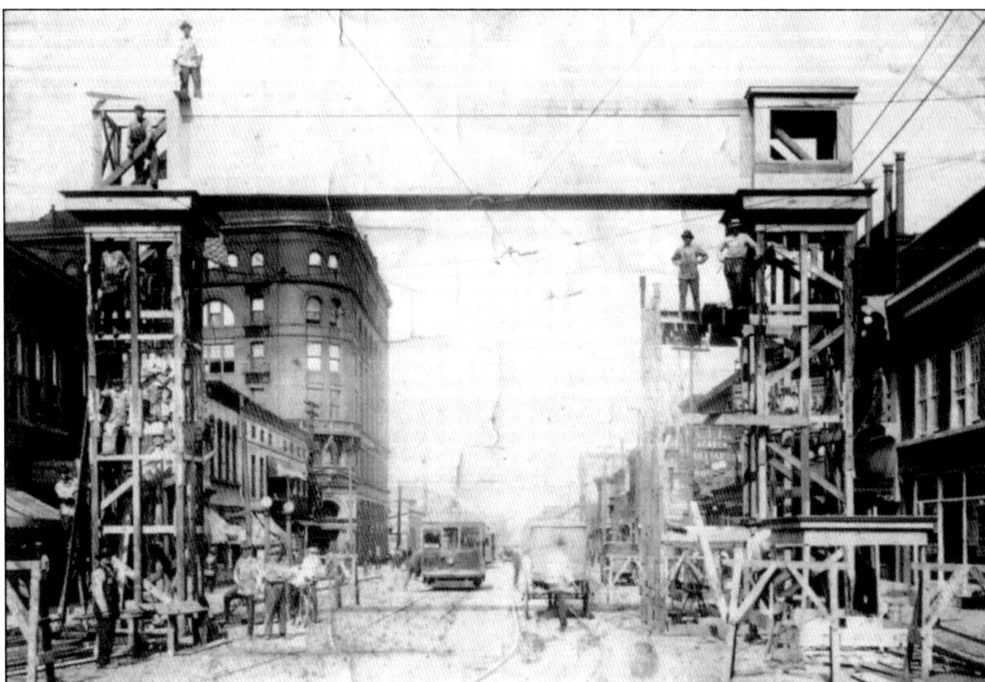

This view taken during Terre Haute's 1898 celebration in honor of Adm. George Dewey looks east, showing men building arches at Ninth Street and Wabash Avenue. (Vigo County Historical Society.)

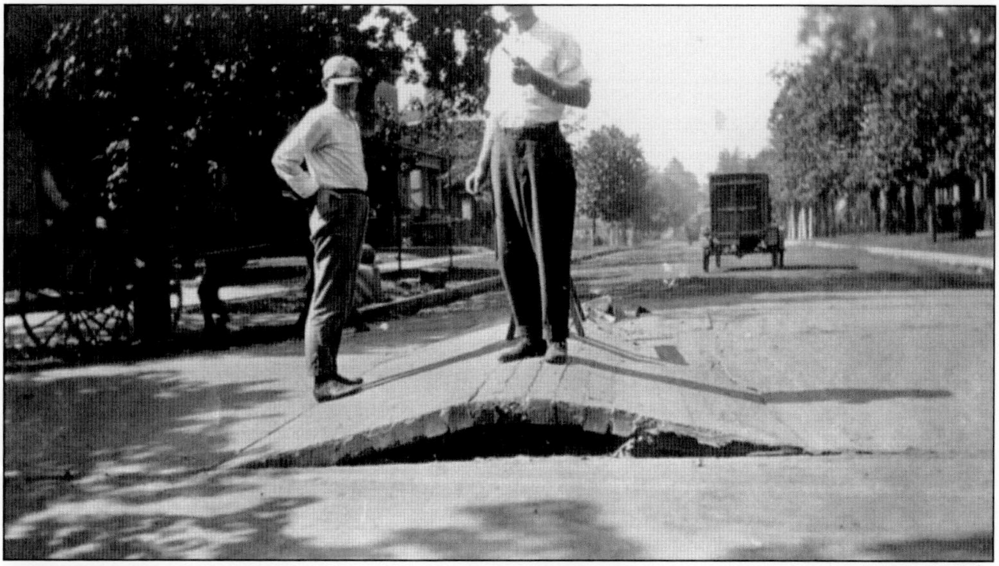

An August 1916 view shows how the National Road buckled because of high temperatures. The image is captioned, "Effect of intense heat on Wabash street temperature at 100 degrees in shade for one week. Terre Haute, Ind. Aug. 1916." A man standing atop the domed section calmly smokes a pipe. (Vigo County Historical Society.)

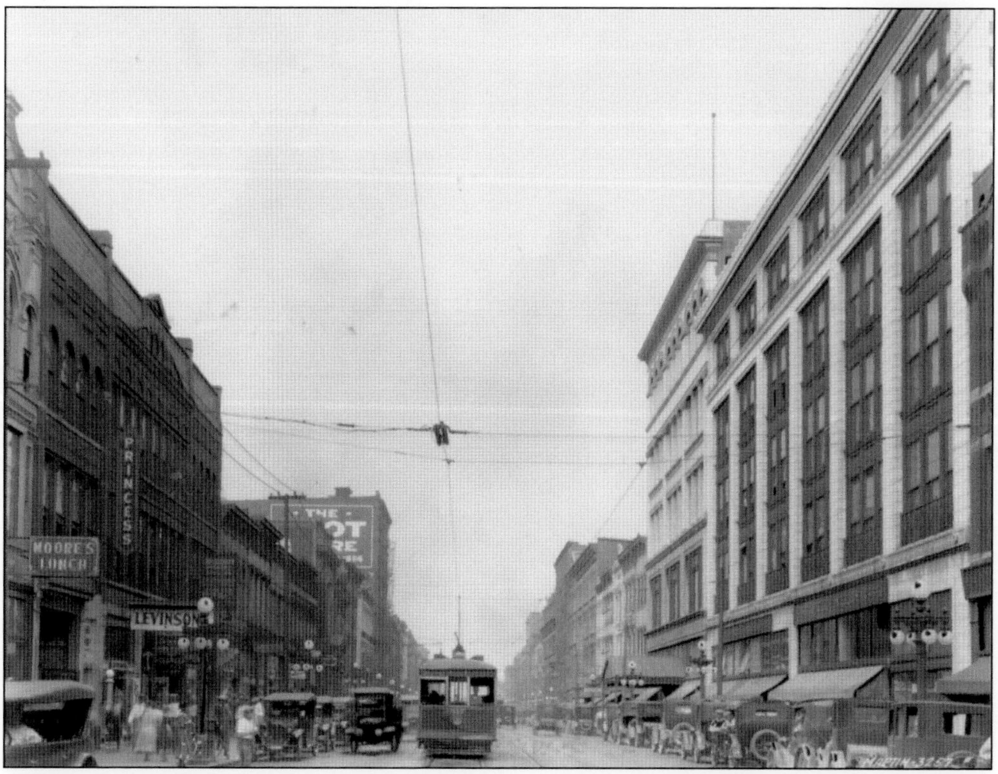

A street view of Terre Haute from about 1900 looks west at Seventh Street and Wabash Avenue. The Princess Theater can be seen above the Levinson's store at left, and the Piggly Wiggly is in the right foreground. (Vigo County Historical Society.)

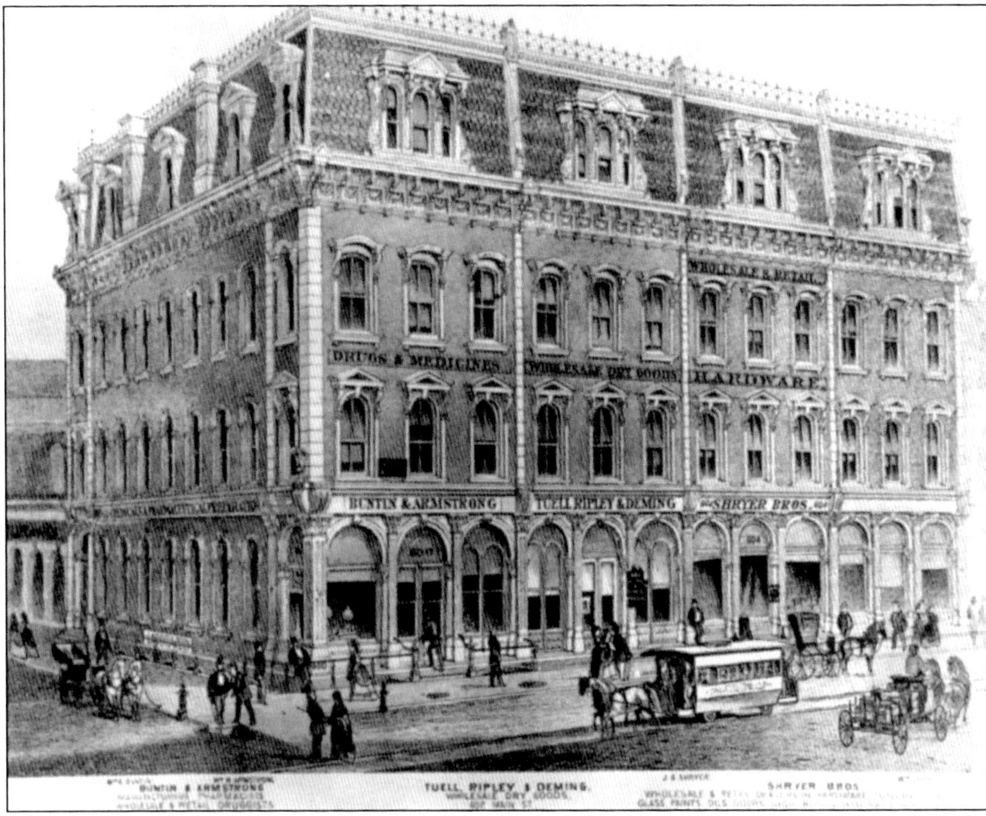

A woodcut from around 1880 portrays Hotel Deming at the northeast corner of Sixth Street and Wabash Avenue. The caption reads, "Buntin & Armstrong—Manufacturing Pharmacists —Wholesale & Retail Druggists—No. 600 Main St. Cor. Sixth—Tuell, Ripley & Deming—Wholesale Dry Goods—602 Main St.—Terre Haute, Ind.—Shryer Bros.—Wholesale and Retail Dealers in Hardware, Cutlery, Guns &c.—Glass, Paints, Oils, Doors, Sash, Blinds, Iron Nails, Horse-Shoes—Cordage, Rope, Packing, Leather Belting, Lead Pipes, Fire Brick." (Vigo County Historical Society.)

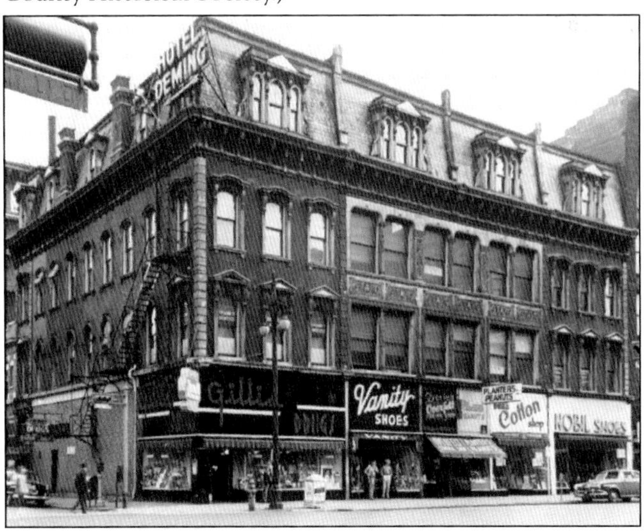

A May 1950 photograph looking northeast from the corner at Sixth Street and Wabash Avenue shows Terre Haute's Hotel Deming building. The familiar Coca-Cola sign has not yet appeared. (Vigo County Historical Society.)

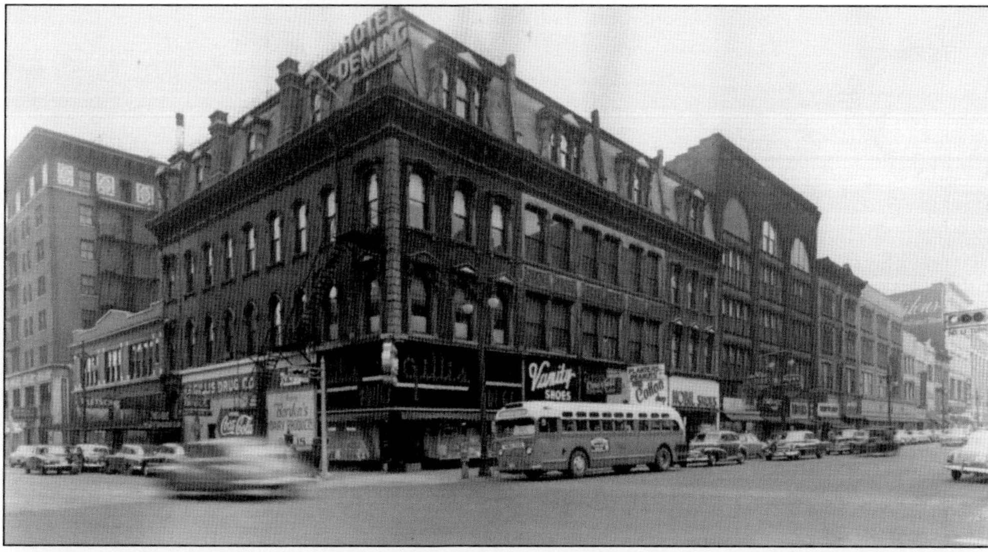

A 1951 photograph looking northeast from the corner of Sixth Street and Wabash Avenue shows Terre Haute's Hotel Deming. The Coca-Cola sign has been painted on the brick sidewall of the Gillis Drugstore. (Vigo County Historical Society.)

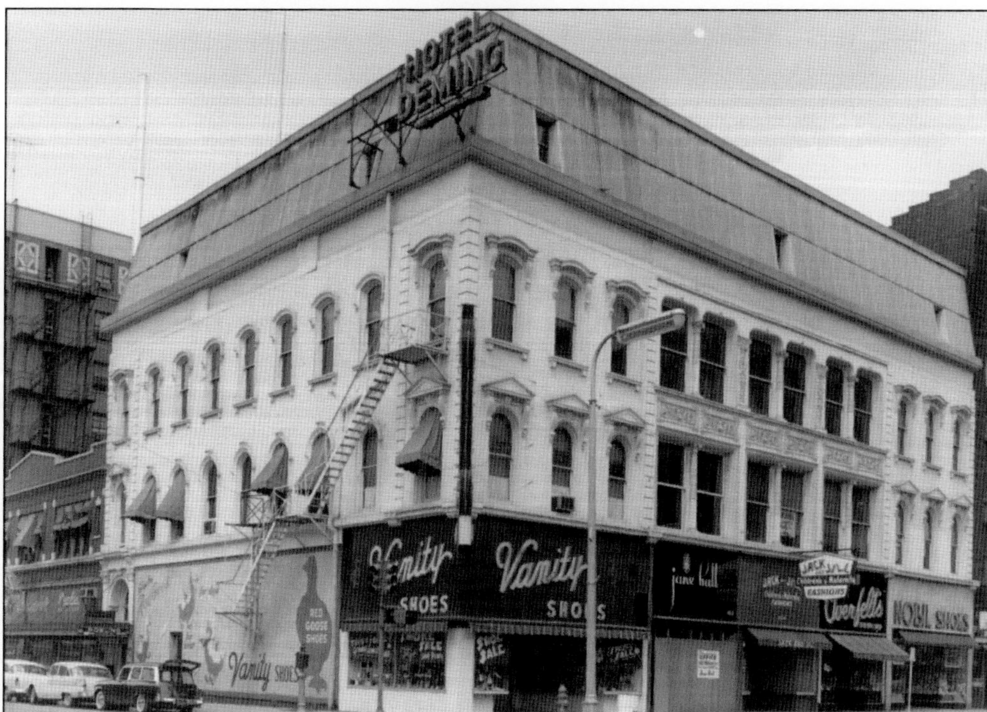

A late-1950s view facing west from the south side of Sixth Street and Wabash Avenue shows the Hotel Deming. A Red Goose shoes sign is painted on the side of the Vanity shoe store building. Other stores include Jane Hall, Jack and Jill's clothing, Overfelt's Camera shop, and Nobil Shoes. (Vigo County Historical Society.)

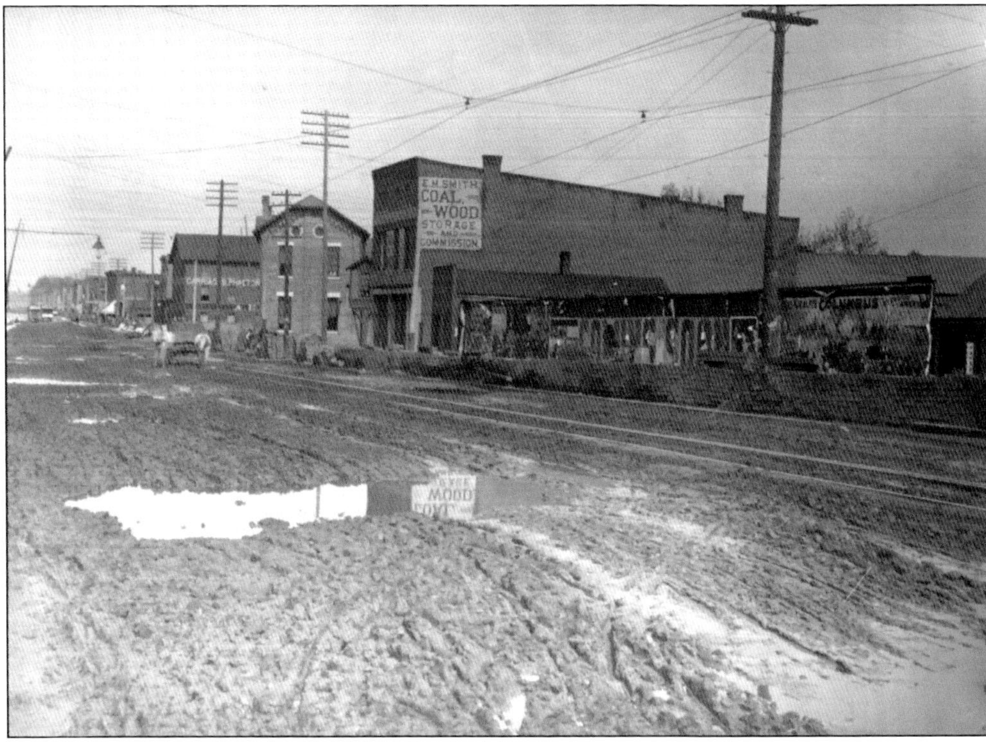

An 1882 view looks east, capturing a muddy road with tracks in the middle at Ninth Street and Wabash Avenue. This image was taken just before the street was made into a brick thoroughfare. Curbs and stacks of bricks are piled high at the side of the street. The long, wooden sign next to the E.M. Smith Coal, Wood, Storage and Commission has been plastered with a sign for the Kiralfy Brothers show *Columbus and the Discovery of America*, "Coming Soon to Terre Haute May 30." (Vigo County Historical Society.)

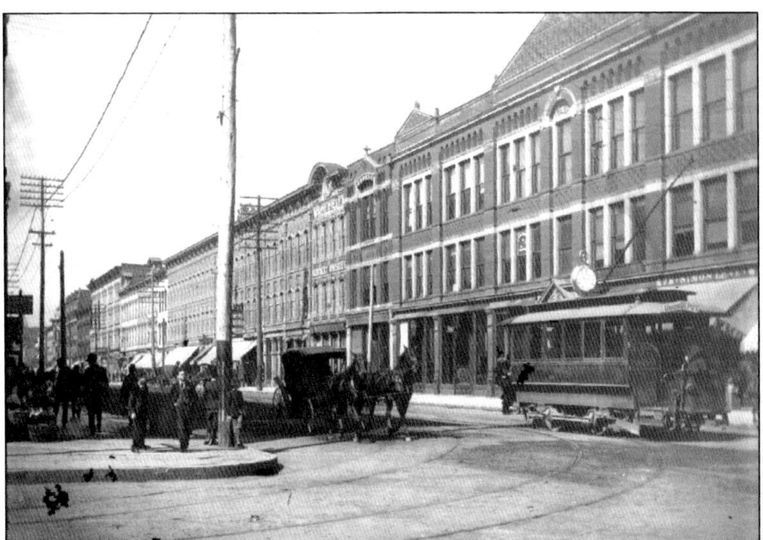

This image was taken about 1892 at Seventh Street and Wabash Avenue, looking northwest. The Union Depot electric streetcar can be seen pulling away at right. (Vigo County Historical Society.)

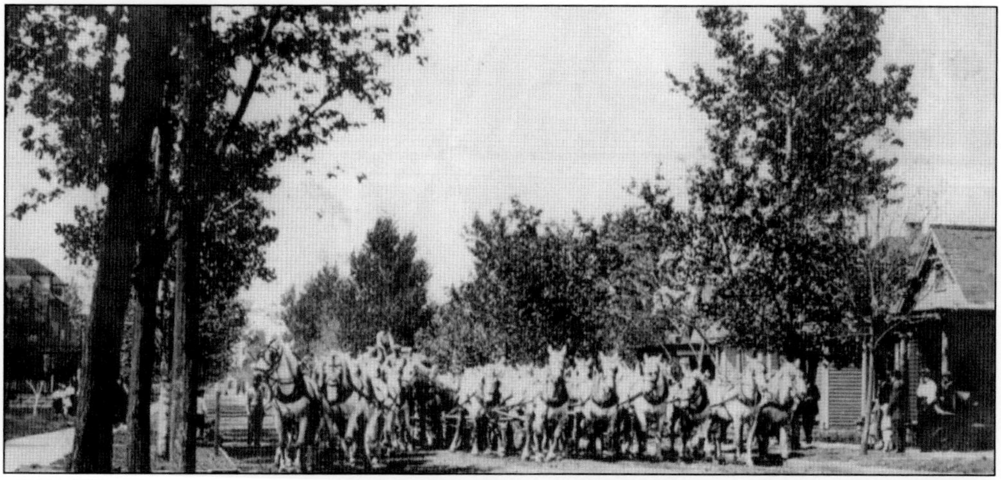

A 1916 photograph shows a Terre Haute horse-drawn tow truck. The image is captioned, "30 Horse team pulling wagon from Mud hole 1916 at Wabash." (Vigo County Historical Society.)

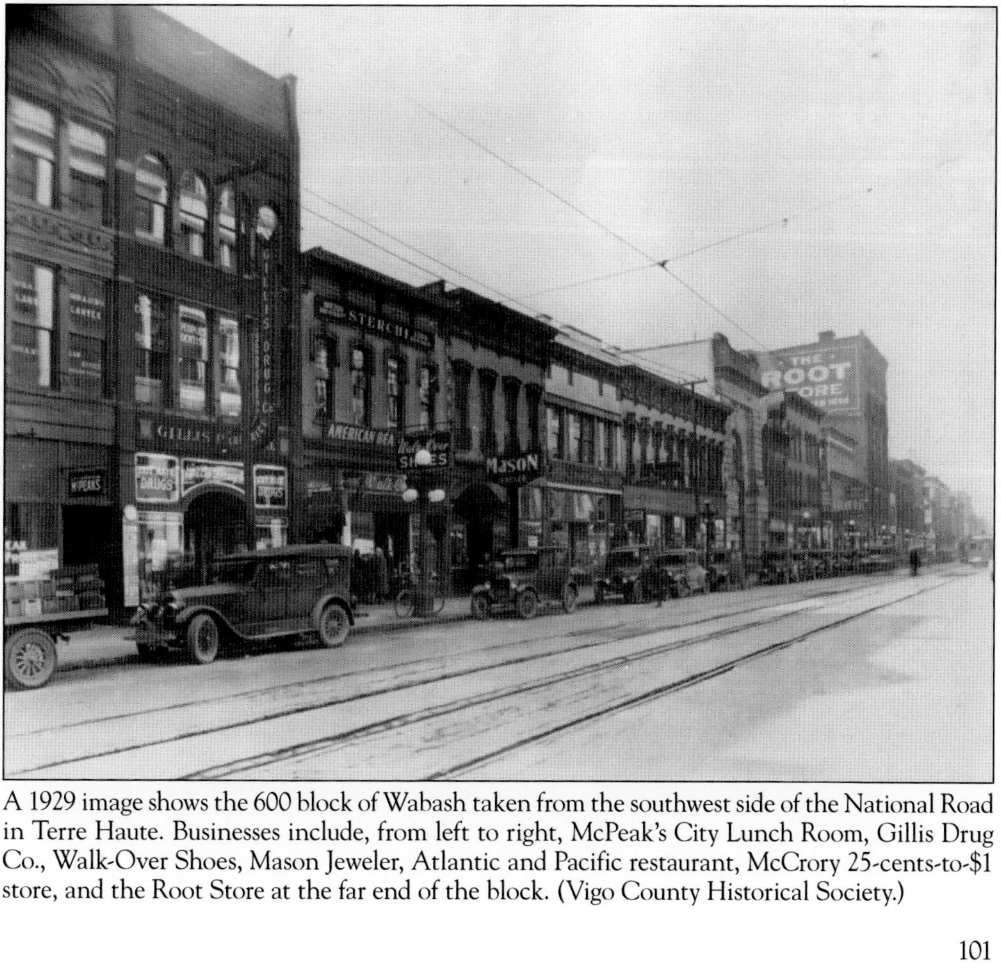

A 1929 image shows the 600 block of Wabash taken from the southwest side of the National Road in Terre Haute. Businesses include, from left to right, McPeak's City Lunch Room, Gillis Drug Co., Walk-Over Shoes, Mason Jeweler, Atlantic and Pacific restaurant, McCrory 25-cents-to-$1 store, and the Root Store at the far end of the block. (Vigo County Historical Society.)

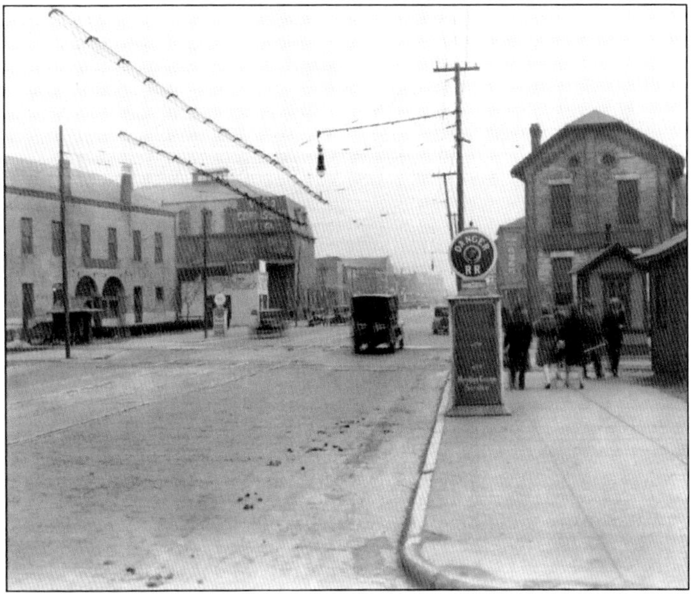

This c. 1920 view faces west at the railroad crossing at Tenth Street and Wabash Avenue and shows advertising for Hotel Severin Indianapolis and Meridian Garage Service on the flashing railroad signal at right and the Chicago & Eastern Illinois Railroad depot and the Nickel Inn (with Coca-Cola and Purol Gasoline pump signs) on the left. First-generation streetlights hang over the centers of the roads. (Vigo County Historical Society.)

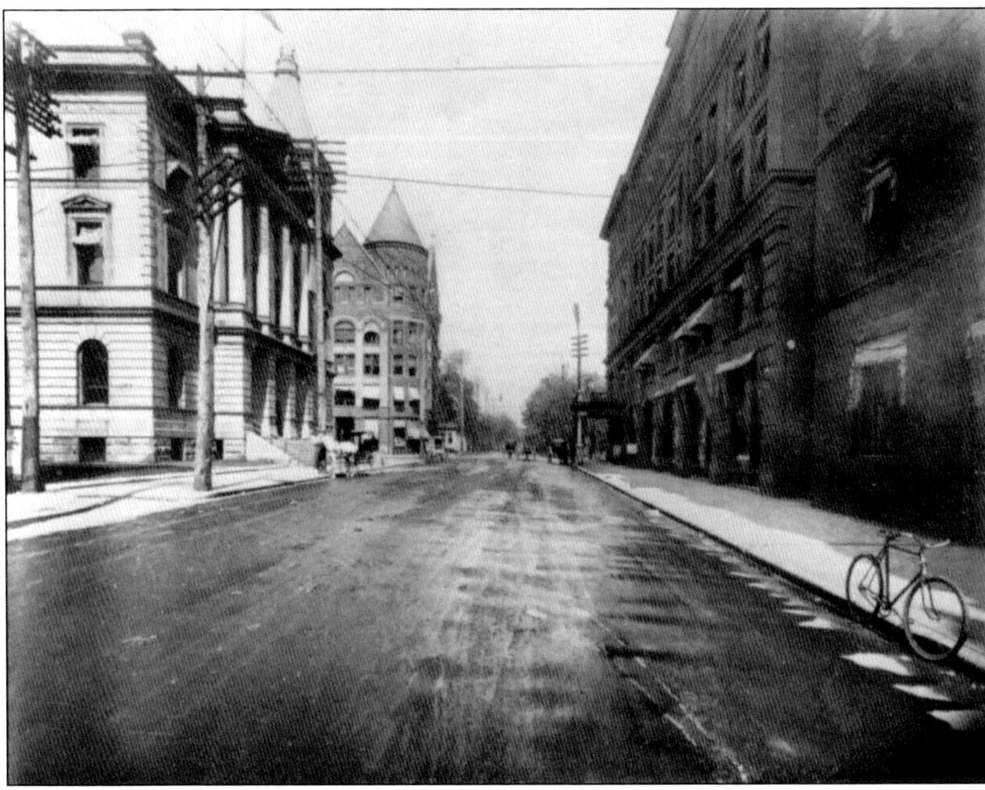

A 1903 scene looks north on Seventh Street from Main Street (now Wabash Avenue), showing the Government Building in Terre Haute. The Grand Opera House and the Block and Rose Dispensary building can be seen in the background. (Vigo County Historical Society.)

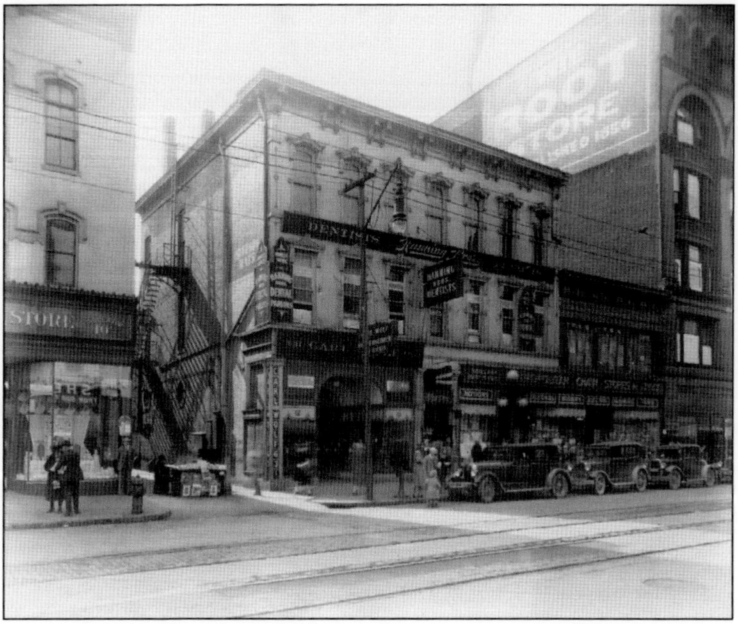

The 600 block of Wabash is shown in a westward view from the alley at 6½ Wabash Avenue. The S.S. Kresge five-and-dime store is at far left. The Carl Wolf hat company advertises Stetson hats next door to the Hanning Bros. dentists, who advertise via a set of teeth hanging above the door. The Root Store building is at far right. This is likely a 1930s-era photograph. (Vigo County Historical Society.)

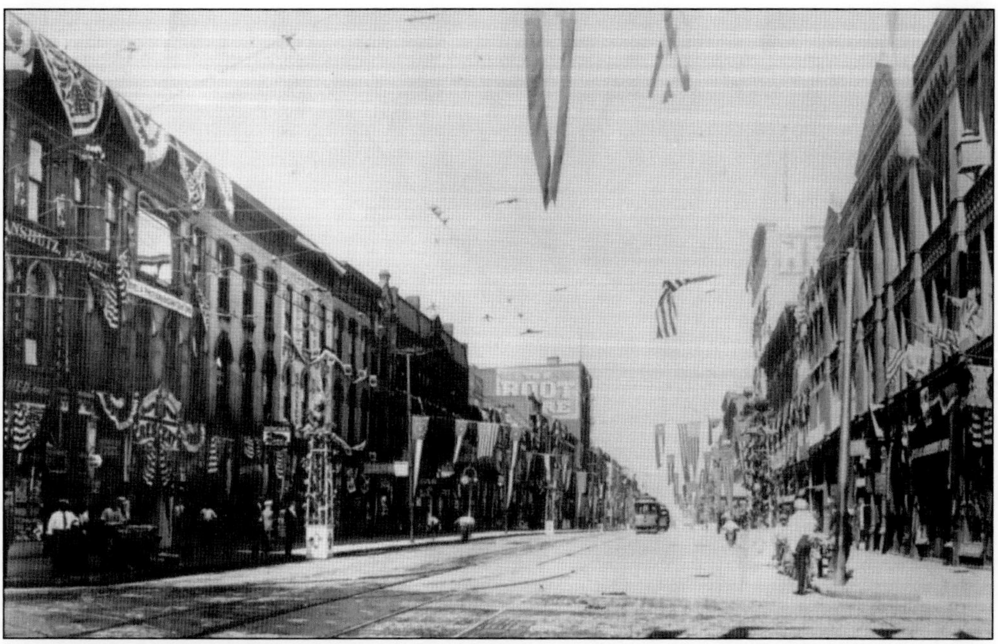

In a 1907–1910 Terre Haute scene, an electrified streetcar is coming up the road toward the intersection of Seventh Street and Wabash Avenue. The street is decorated with flags for a parade. Buildings in the photograph include Silverstein Brothers Furniture, Carpet and Rugs, the Crescent, and the Root Store on the left and the Freemason's Lodge on the right. (Vigo County Historical Society.)

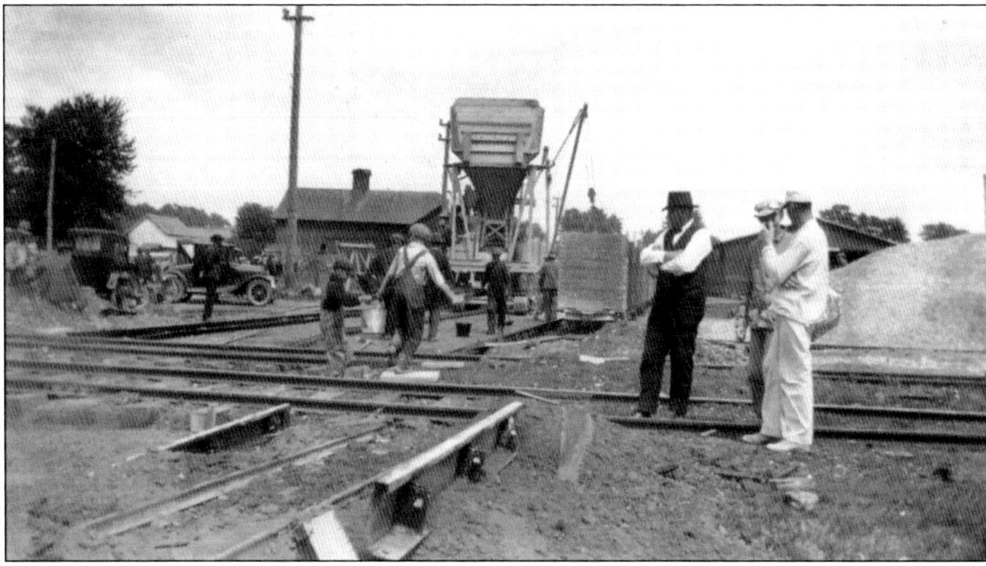

A photograph from about 1931 shows the paving of Wabash Avenue in Terre Haute. While the boys seen carrying the bucket in the center of the photograph might be thought of as child laborers, what they are most likely doing is collecting chunks of coal (uncovered by workmen) that had fallen from passing trains to sell door-to-door for extra money. (Vigo County Historical Society.)

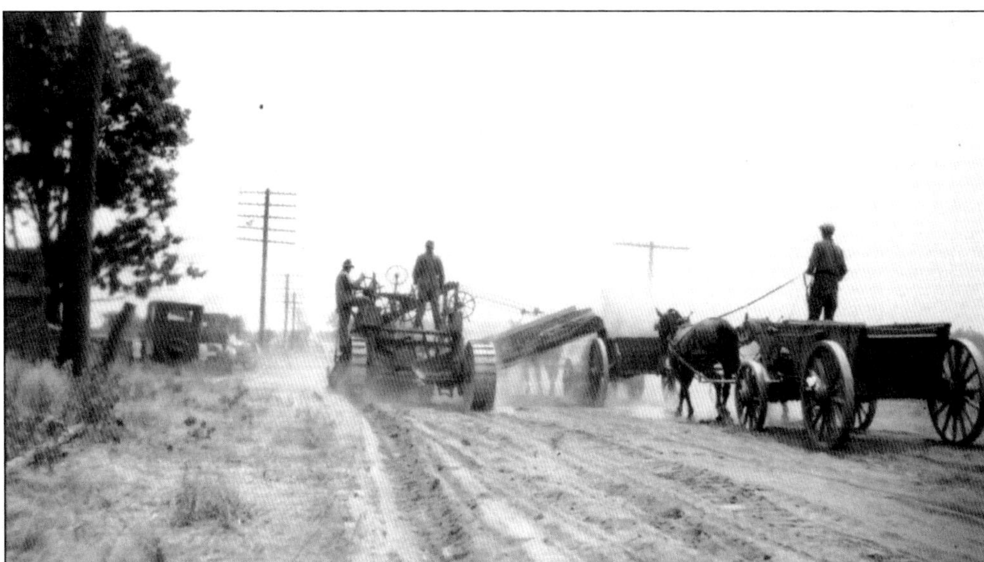

Another c. 1931 photograph shows the paving of Wabash Avenue with horse-drawn construction equipment and vintage, 1920s-era runabout cars parked at the side. (Vigo County Historical Society.)

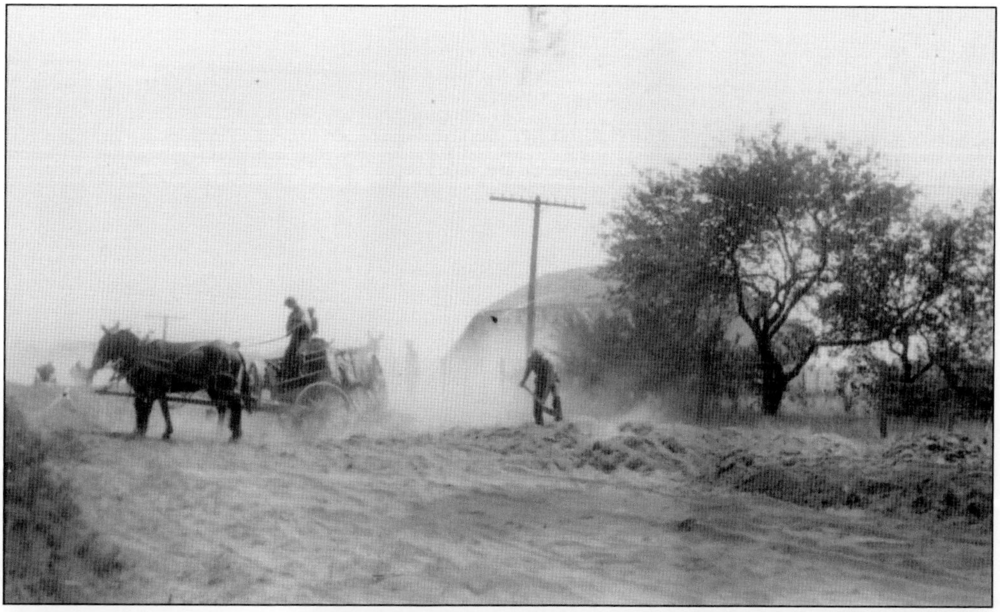

Another photograph from about 1931 shows horse-drawn construction equipment and shovel-wielding workmen paving Wabash Avenue. (Vigo County Historical Society.)

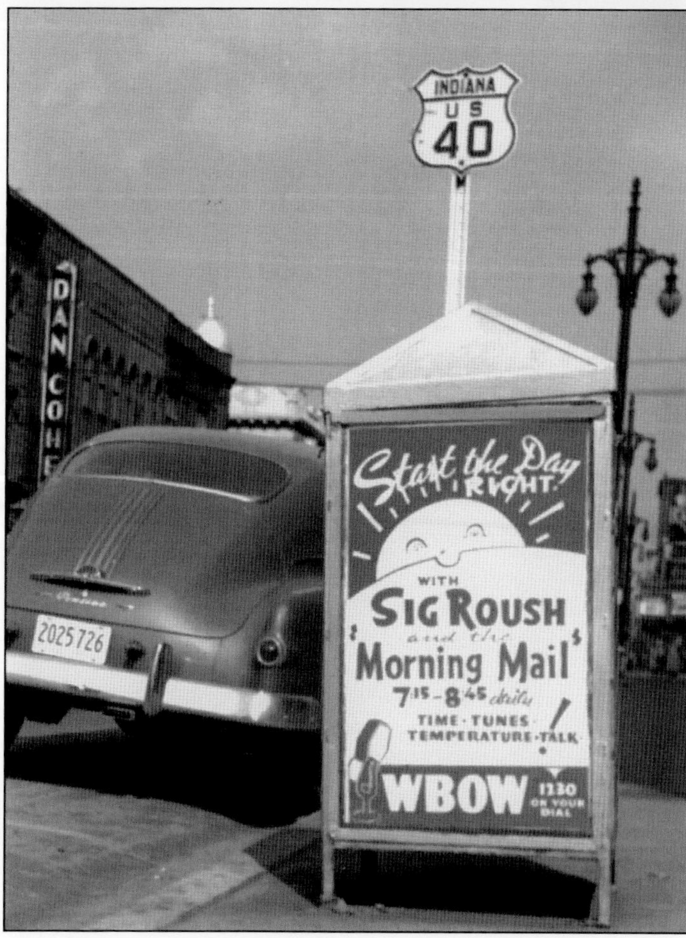

In a 1950 photograph, an Indiana US 40 Highway marker rises above a Pontiac automobile parked across from Dan Cohen's store on Wabash Avenue. The WBOW radio poster on the trash container reads: "Start the day right with Sig Roush and the 'Morning Mail' 7:15 - 8:45 daily—Time Tunes Temperature Talk—WBOW 1230 on your dial." (Vigo County Historical Society.)

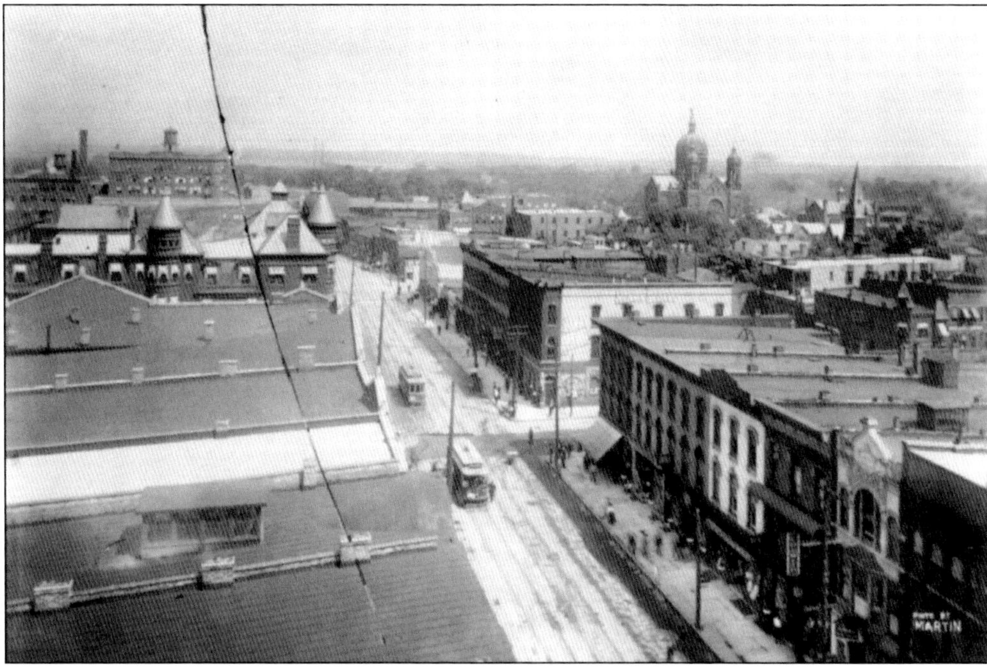

A one-of-a-kind glass plate negative photograph from the Martin Photograph shop looks east on Terre Haute's Wabash Avenue. Dated 1909, the image shows electric streetcars and St. Benedicts Church before the fire. The Terre Haute House hotel is easily identifiable by its turrets, and the Hulman and Co. building is in the background. The glass negative has been broken and repaired. (Vigo County Historical Society.)

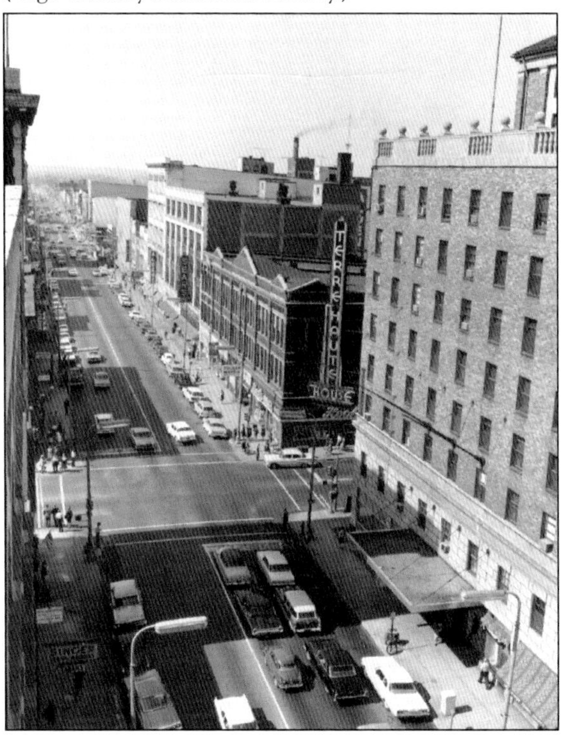

A 1960s westward view of Terre Haute's Wabash Avenue shows the Terre Haute House hotel, Hook's, Sears, and Aldens. A "Tucker for Mayor Headquarters" sign can be seen hanging from the light pole. Ralph Tucker was the longest serving mayor in Terre Haute history, holding office from 1948 to 1968. (Vigo County Historical Society.)

In a view looking east from Eighth to Ninth Streets on Wabash Avenue in the early 1950s, the State Theater can be seen with a marquee featuring *Prisoner of War*, starring future president Ronald Reagan, whose name has been misspelled as "Regan." The Inn Hotel is at right, and the Sunbeam electric company is on the left. (Vigo County Historical Society.)

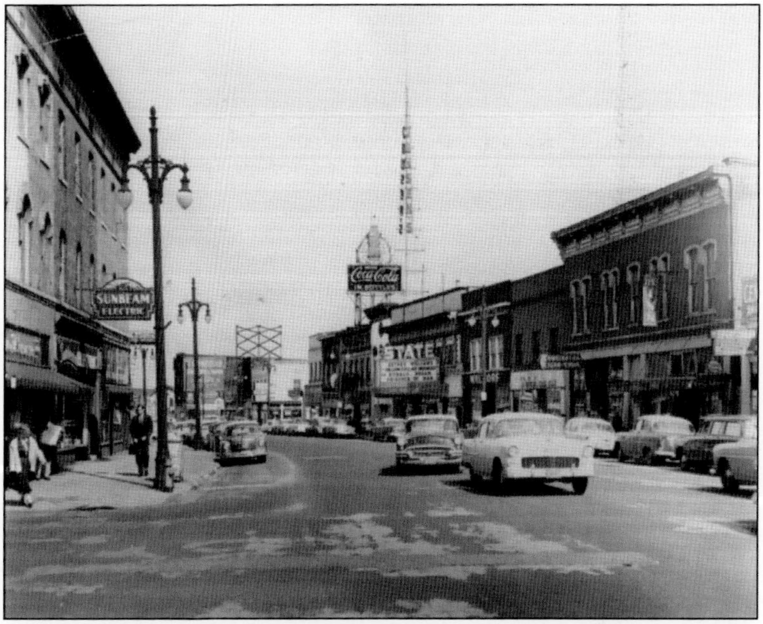

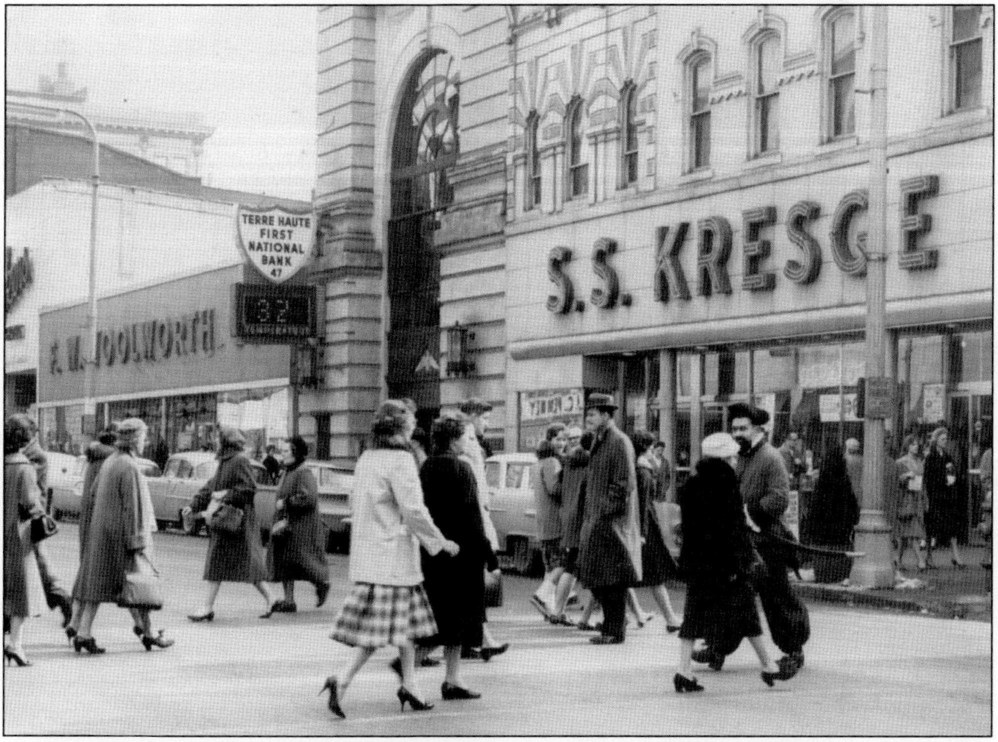

A 1960–1970s Terre Haute Street scene looks west from Seventh Street and Wabash Avenue. The S.S. Kresge and F.W. Woolworth Department stores rest on either side of the Terre Haute First National Bank. A pirate in a tricornered hat walks through the crosswalk among unconcerned passersby—no doubt a character from one of the two department stores' in-house promotions. (Vigo County Historical Society.)

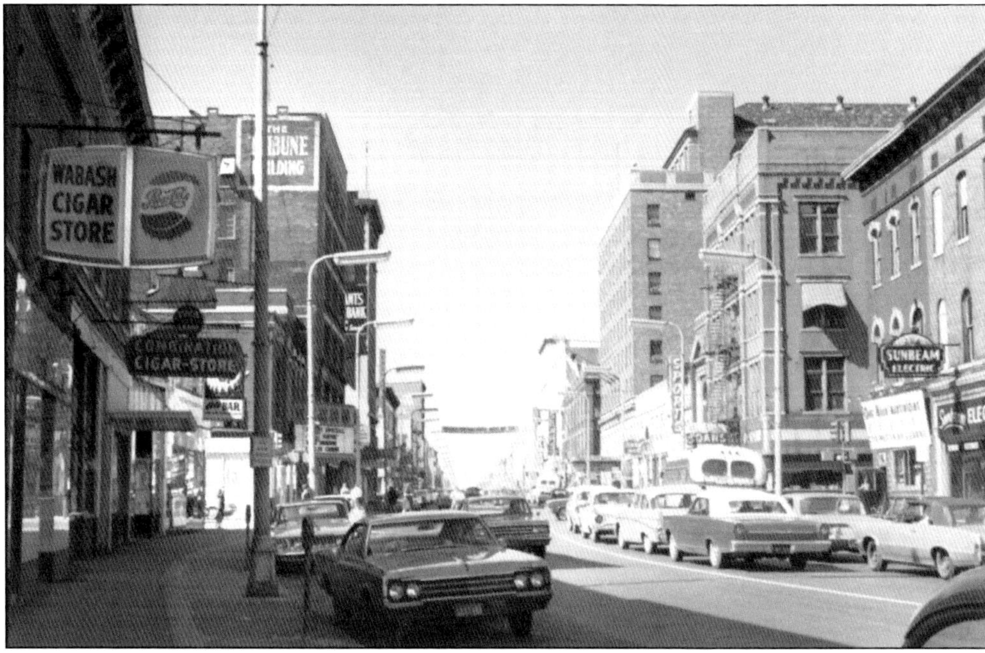

Terre Haute is seen from Eighth Street and Wabash Avenue, looking west. The Tribune Building, Wabash Cigar store (with Pepsi-Cola sign), and the Grand Theater, advertising the Rock Hudson movie *A Very Special Favor*, can be seen in the image. The 1965 photograph shows a "College Football" banner strung above the road. (Vigo County Historical Society.)

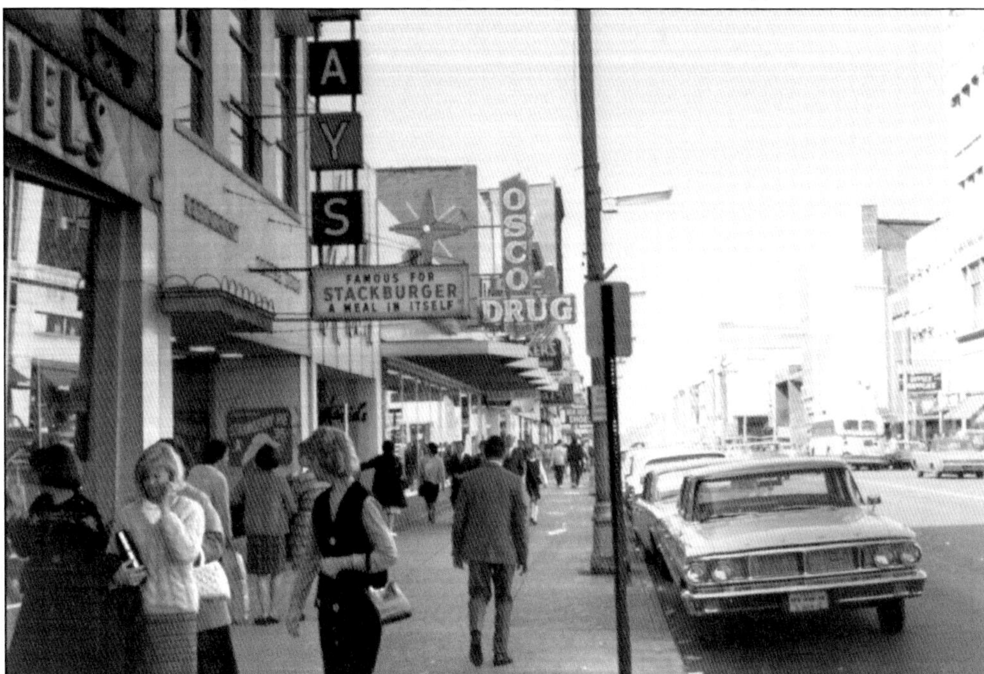

A 1960s-era photograph at Seventh Street and Wabash Avenue looks west, showing O'Days Restaurant, "Famous for Stackburger," and Osco Drug. (Vigo County Historical Society.)

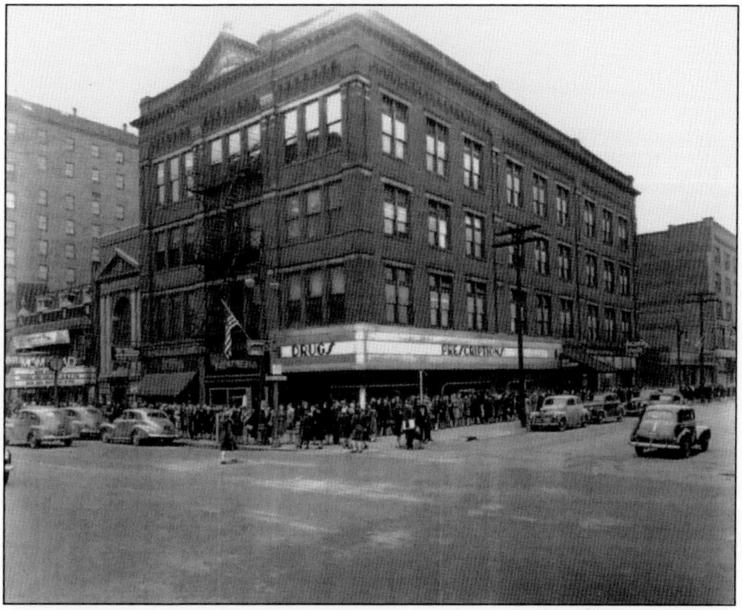

In a c. 1943 photograph of the Grand Theater at Eighth Street and Wabash Avenue, the theater has been taken over by an event called "Mom and Dad." This was likely a World War II war-rationing event of some sort. The sidewalk is full of women waiting in line. The Bement-Rea Building and Carl Riggs Drugstore are visible at right. (Vigo County Historical Society.)

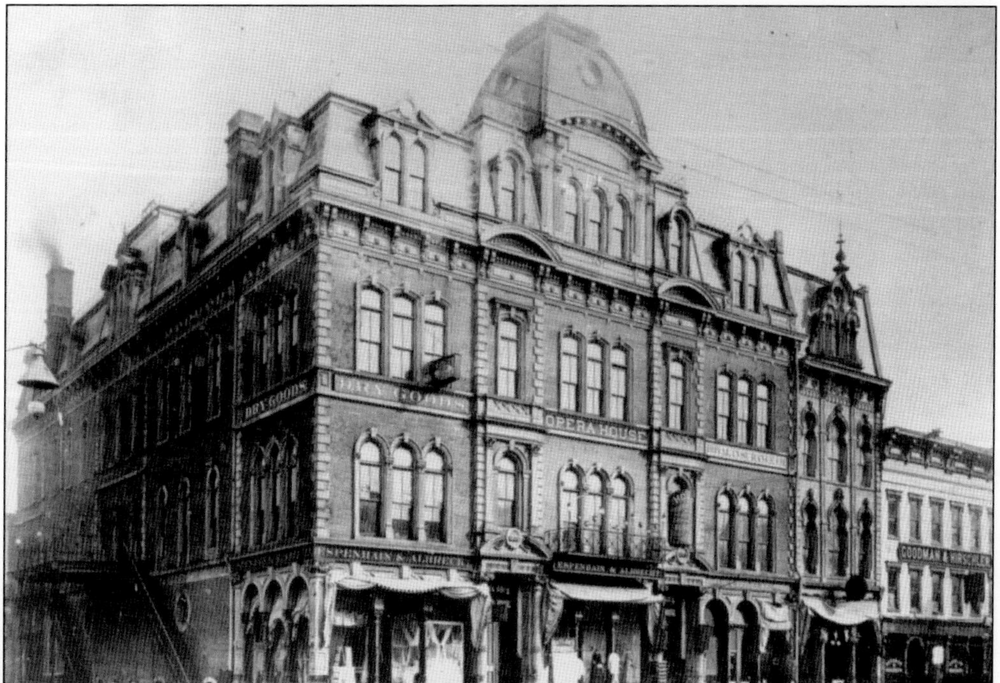

Terre Haute's Naylor Opera House is shown as it appeared in the 1890s from the northeast corner of Fourth and Main Streets. The businesses housed in the grand building when this photograph was taken included Espenhain and Albrecht Dry Goods store, Stationer E.L. Godecke, and Goodman and Hirschler clothiers. The sign for Masonic Lodge No. 86 can be seen at the top. (Vigo County Historical Society.)

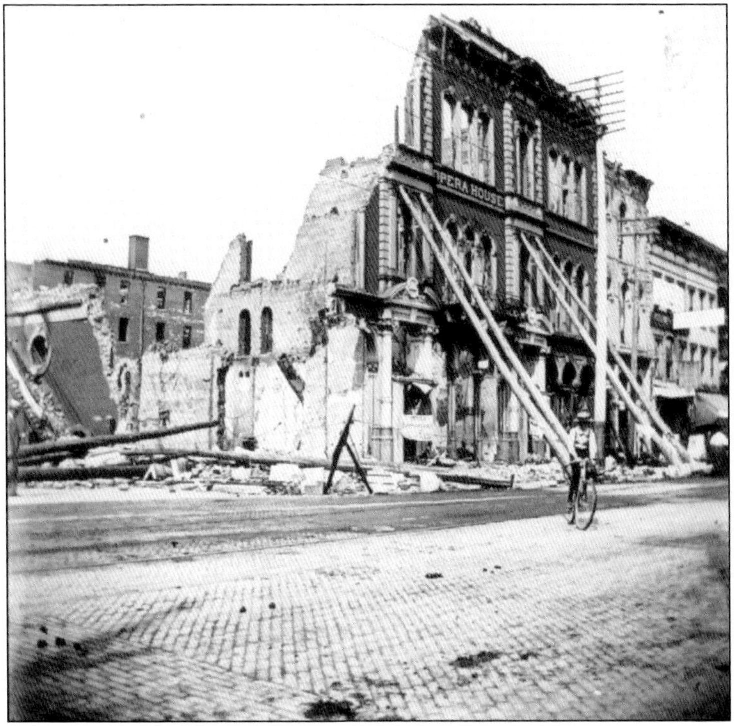

An 1896 view shows fire damage at the Naylor Opera House in Terre Haute as a man casually rides his bike on the empty street. Buffalo Bill and Wild Bill Hickok performed at the opera house on October 9, 10, and 11, 1873. (Vigo County Historical Society.)

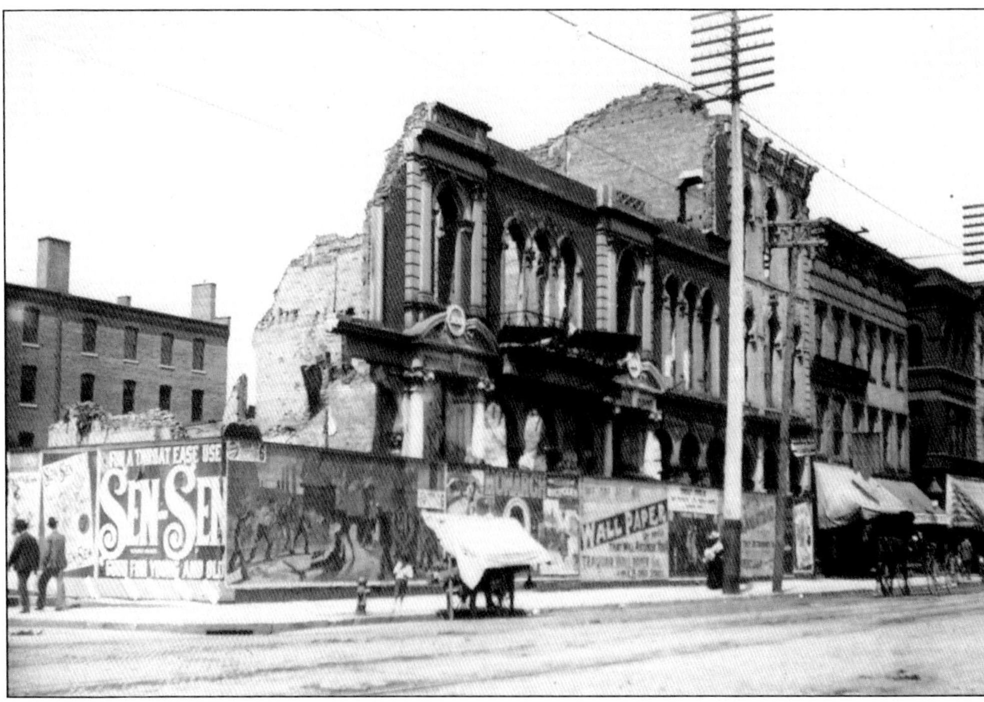

Another 1896 view portrays fire damage at the Naylor Opera House. Signs for Sen-Sen gum, Monarch Bicycles, and the play *Master and Man* can be seen in front. Ironically, there is a young boy standing on the corner staring at the fire hydrant in front of the burned building. (Vigo County Historical Society.)

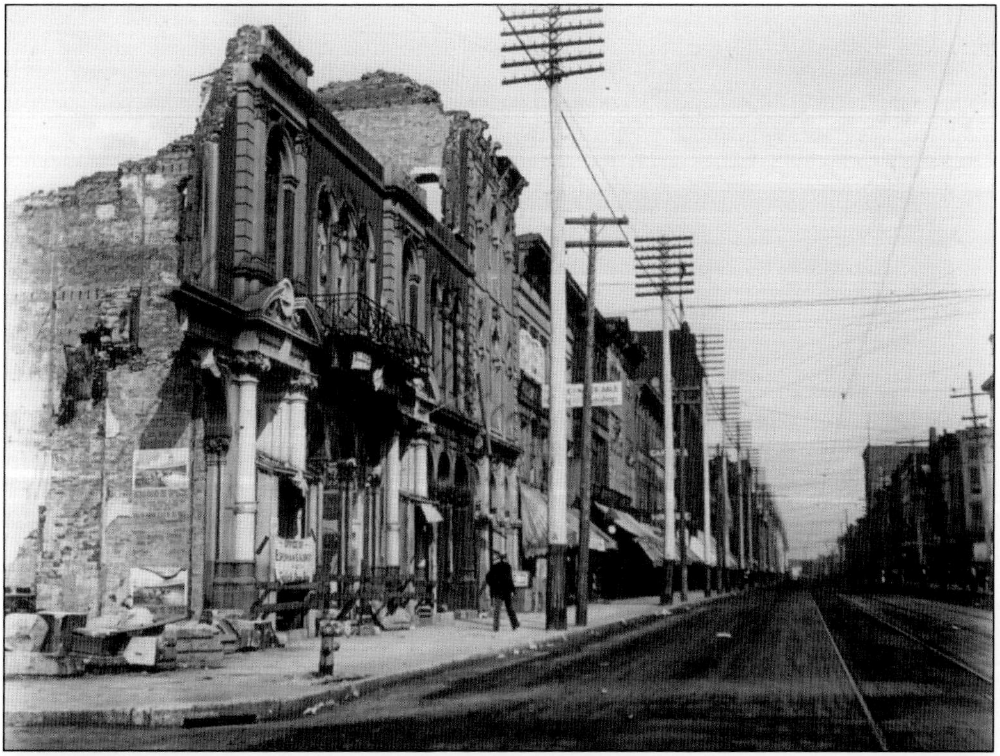

In another 1896 image of fire damage at the Naylor Opera House, it is apparent that no time was wasted before plastering the crumbling walls with posters for upcoming events. (Vigo County Historical Society.)

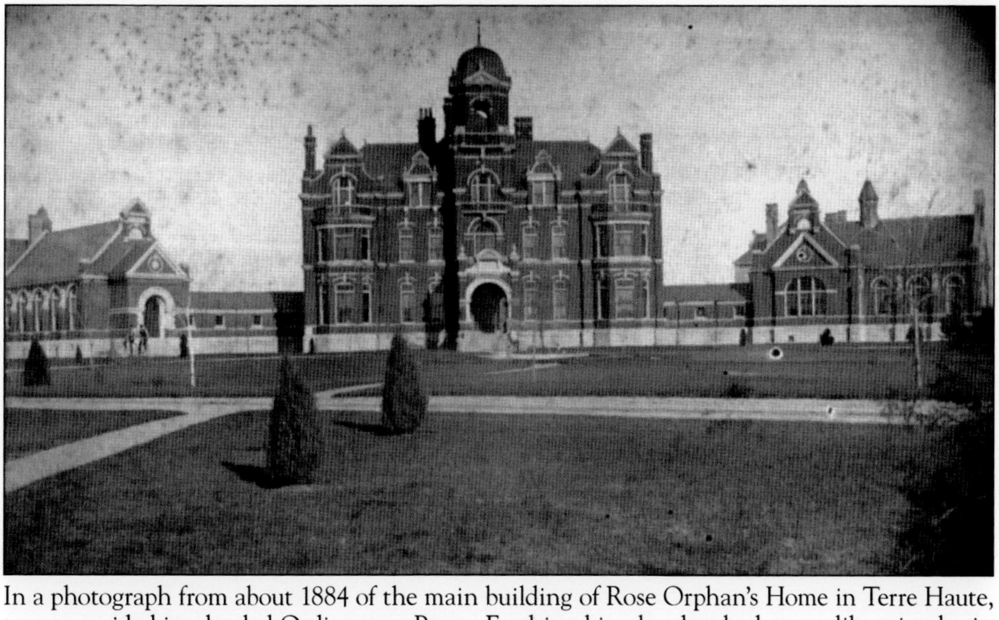

In a photograph from about 1884 of the main building of Rose Orphan's Home in Terre Haute, two men ride big-wheeled Ordinary or Penny Farthing bicycles that look more like tricycles in front of the building on the left. By 1885, these clumsy bikes had fallen out of favor. (Vigo County Historical Society.)

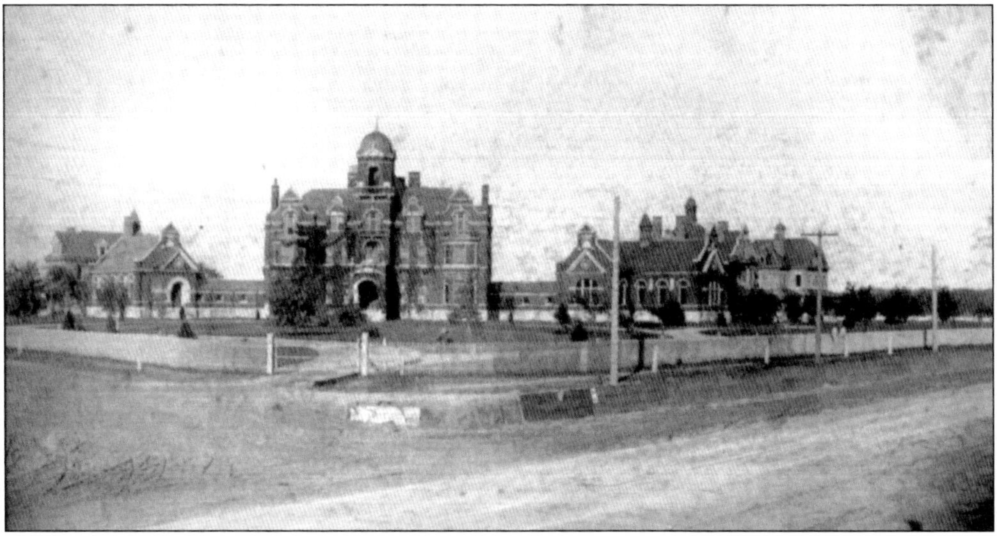

This photograph of Terre Haute's Rose Orphan's Home campus was taken around 1890. Standing approximately at the corner of the National Road and Twenty-fifth Street, the home served children from 1884 until 1949. (Vigo County Historical Society.)

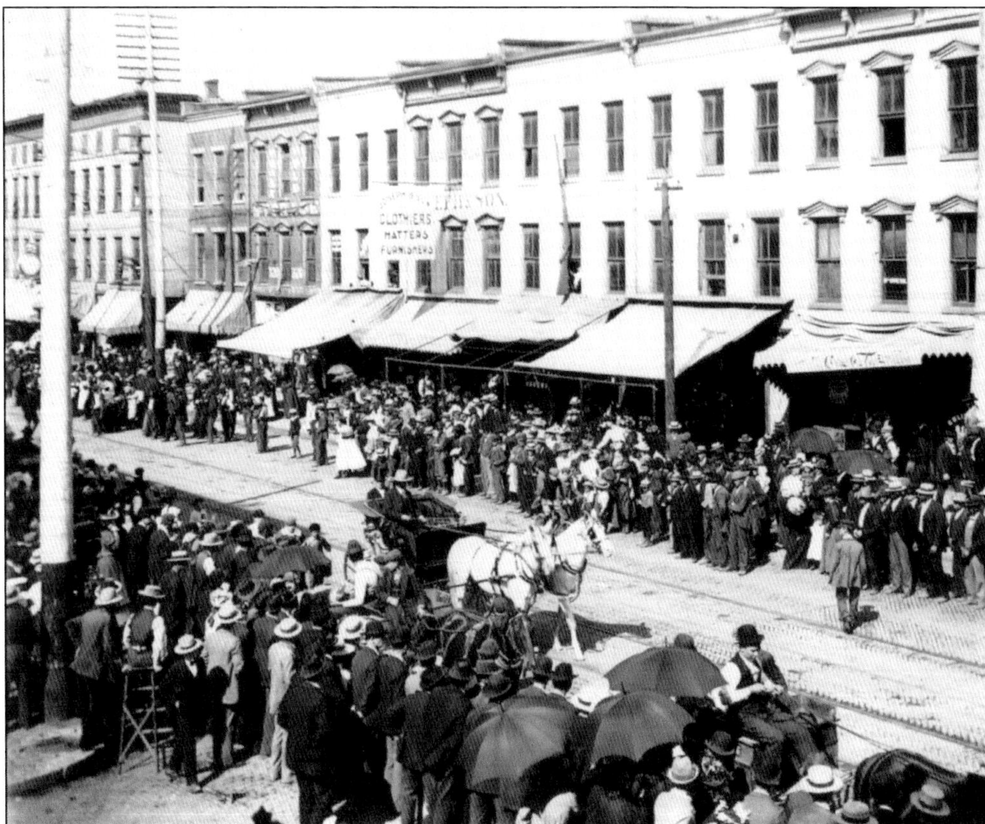

Buffalo Bill Cody, star of the Wild West show parade on Wabash Avenue, rides in the carriage on June 25, 1896. (Vigo County Historical Society.)

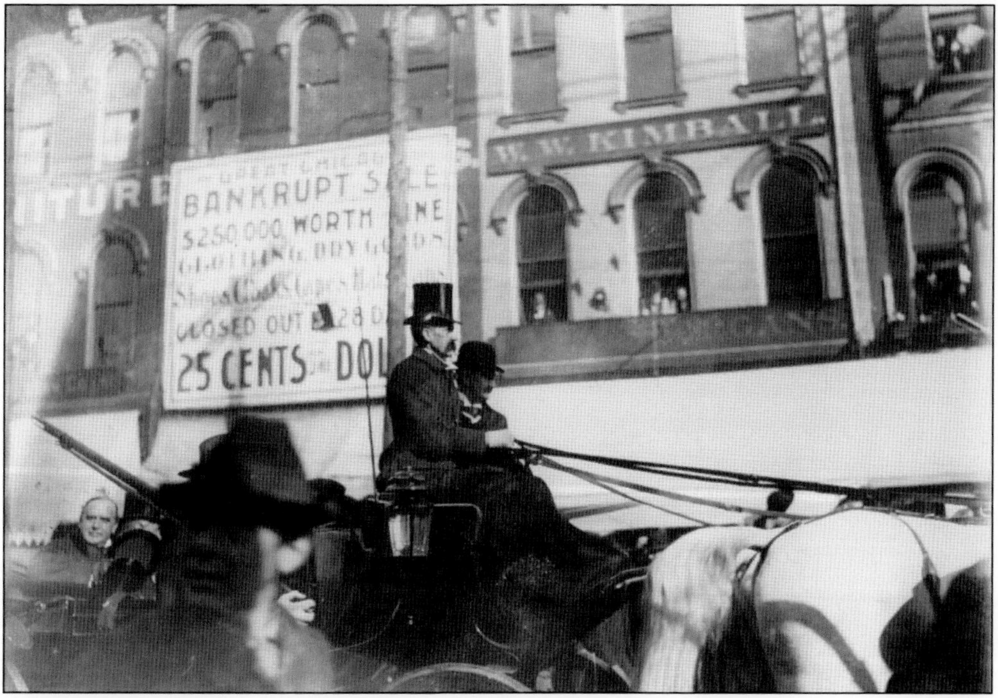

In a campaign parade on Wabash Avenue in Terre Haute, President McKinley is riding in a horse-drawn carriage as he passes the Kimball Organ factory, and, ironically, a furniture factory with a huge bankruptcy sale sign. (Vigo County Historical Society.)

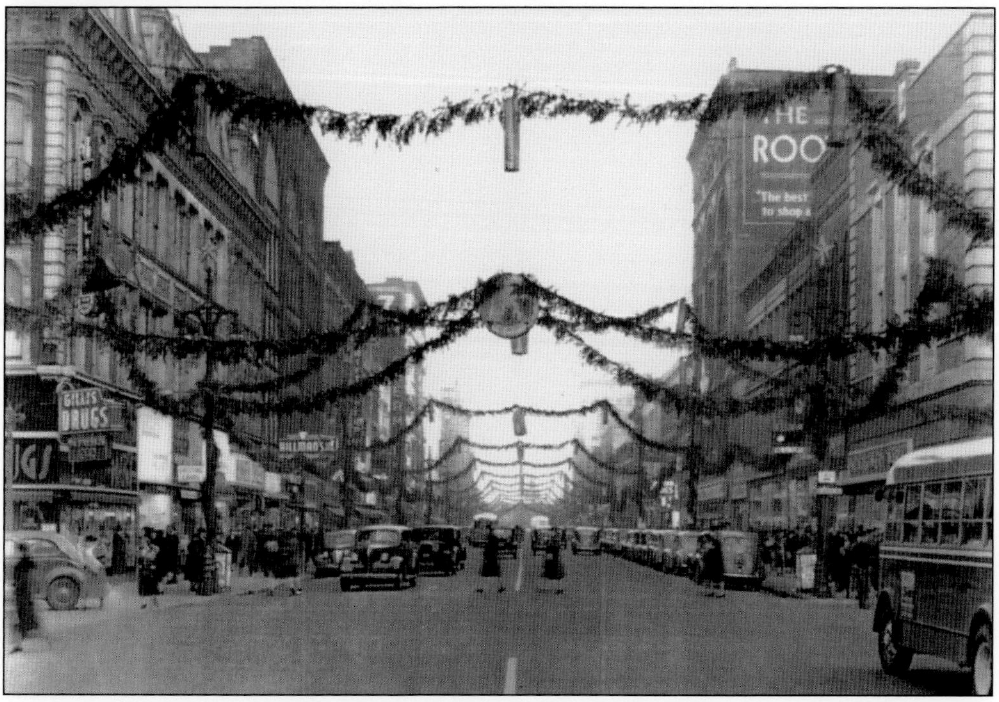

A westward 1940s view of Sixth Street and Wabash Avenue shows decorations for the Christmas holiday. (Vigo County Historical Society.)

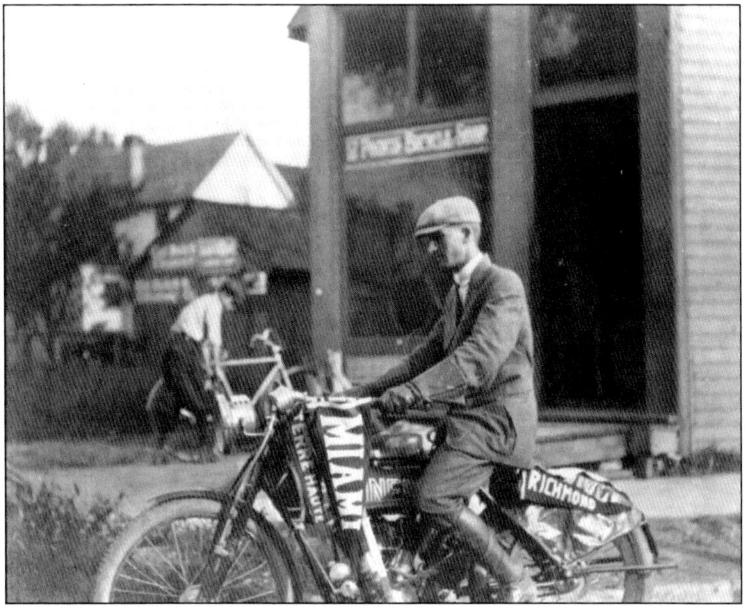

This photograph portrays Herman A. Reinhard after completing his National Road, Terre Haute-to-Richmond motorcycle trip. Reinhard had a bicycle repair shop in Twelve Points in North Terre Haute. The Miami of Ohio University graduate festooned his bike with pennants from his alma mater, Richmond, and Terre Haute. (Vigo County Historical Society.)

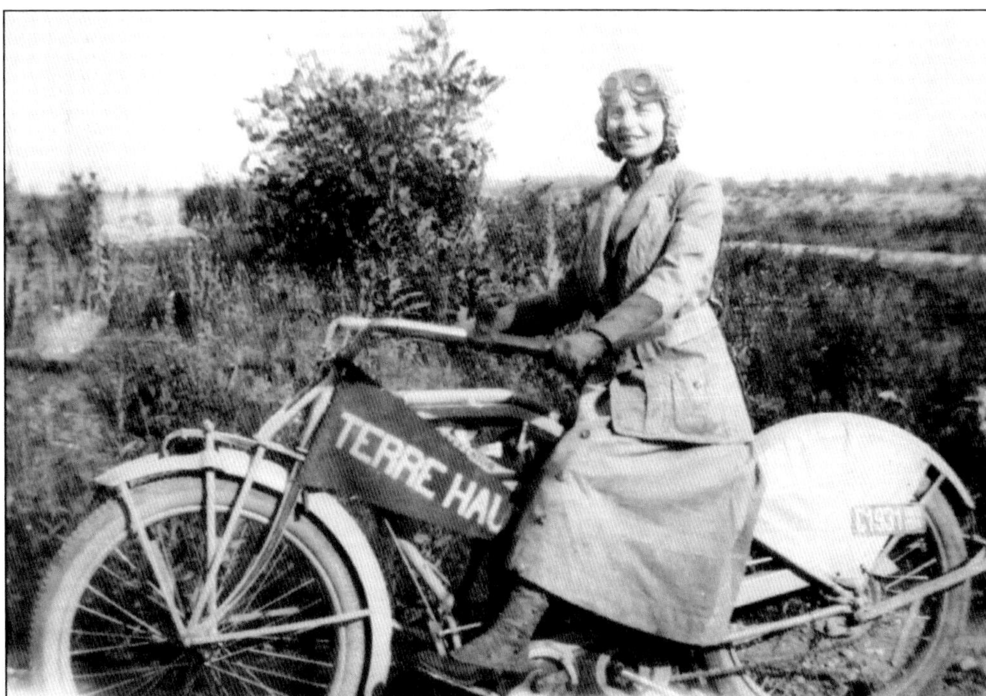

A real-photo postcard shows an unidentified woman on an Excelsior motorcycle in front of the bridge over the Wabash River in Terre Haute. She has attached a Terre Haute pennant to the side of her bike. The motorcycle has a 1914 Indiana license plate attached to the side. (Vigo County Historical Society.)

A photograph from about 1915 shows an unidentified woman on an Excelsior motorcycle in front of the bridge over the Wabash River in Terre Haute. It is captioned "Mrs. A.C.F." (Vigo County Historical Society.)

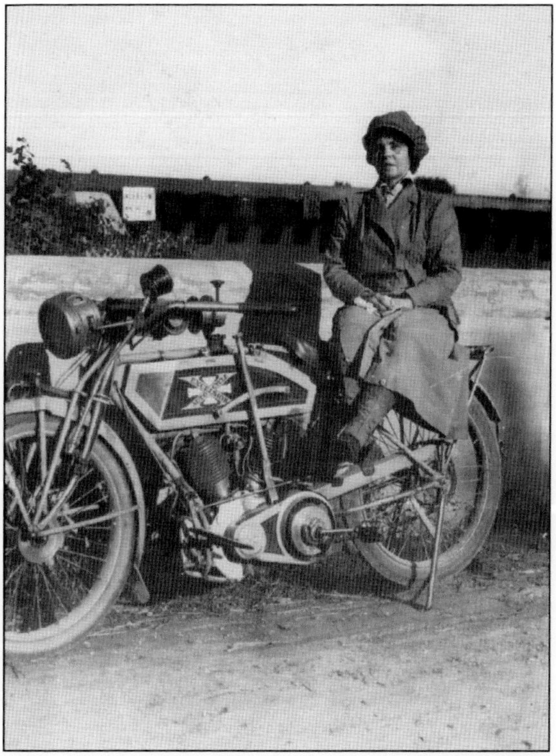

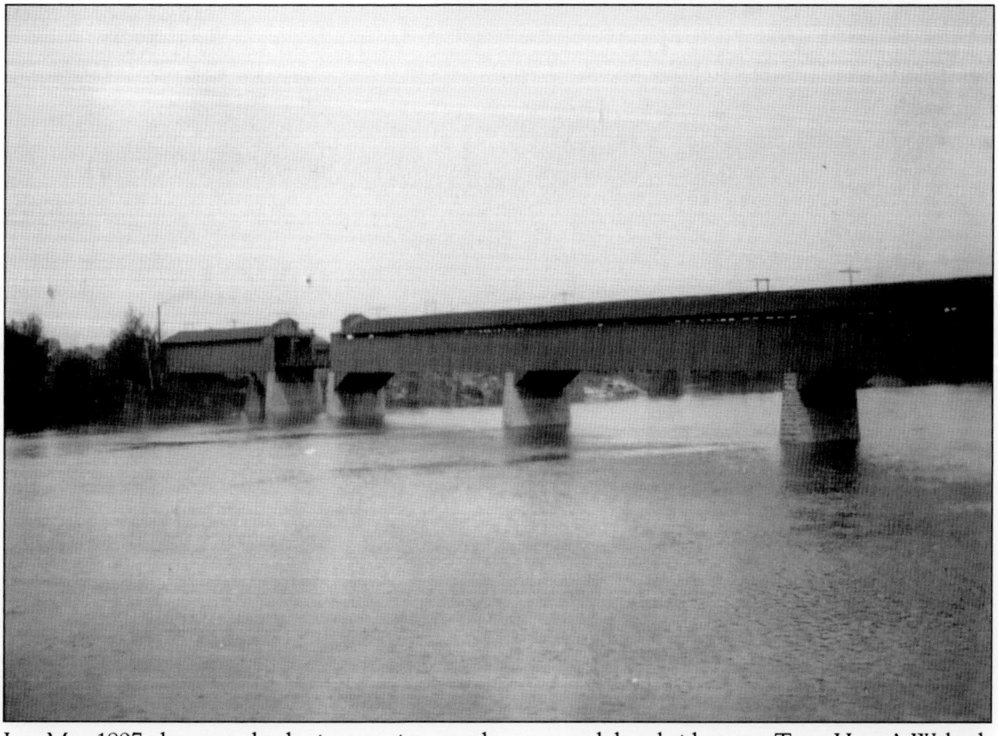

In a May 1897 photograph, the innovative wooden, covered drawbridge over Terre Haute's Wabash River is pictured, with the draw section visible at left. (Vigo County Historical Society.)

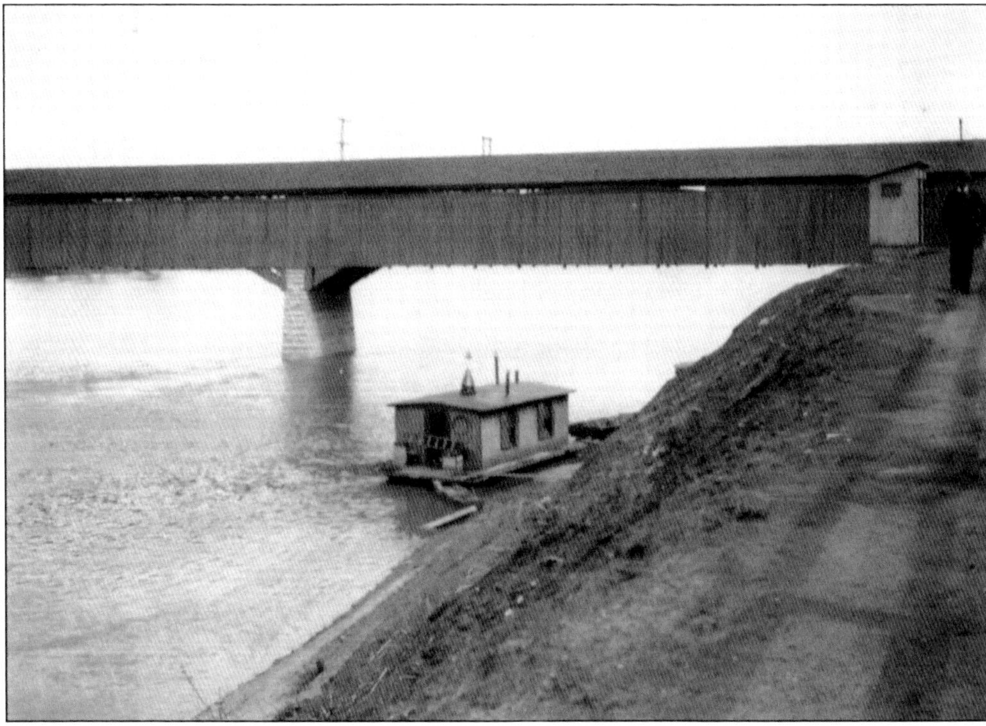

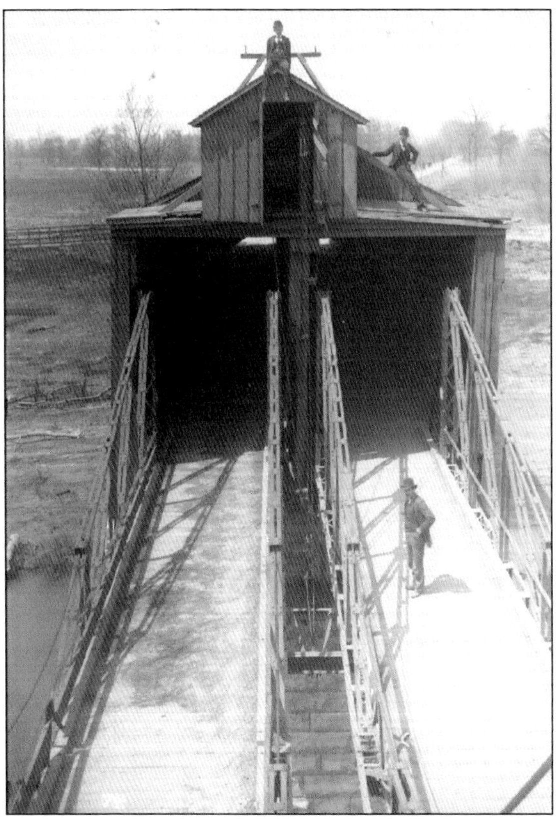

A photograph taken in May 1897 shows the wooden bridge over the Wabash River, with a repair boat docked nearby and pedestrians walking on the trail above. The tollhouse can be seen on the right side. (Vigo County Historical Society.)

Men stand on the roof near the drawbridge section of the covered bridge over Terre Haute's Wabash River sometime in 1892. (Vigo County Historical Society.)

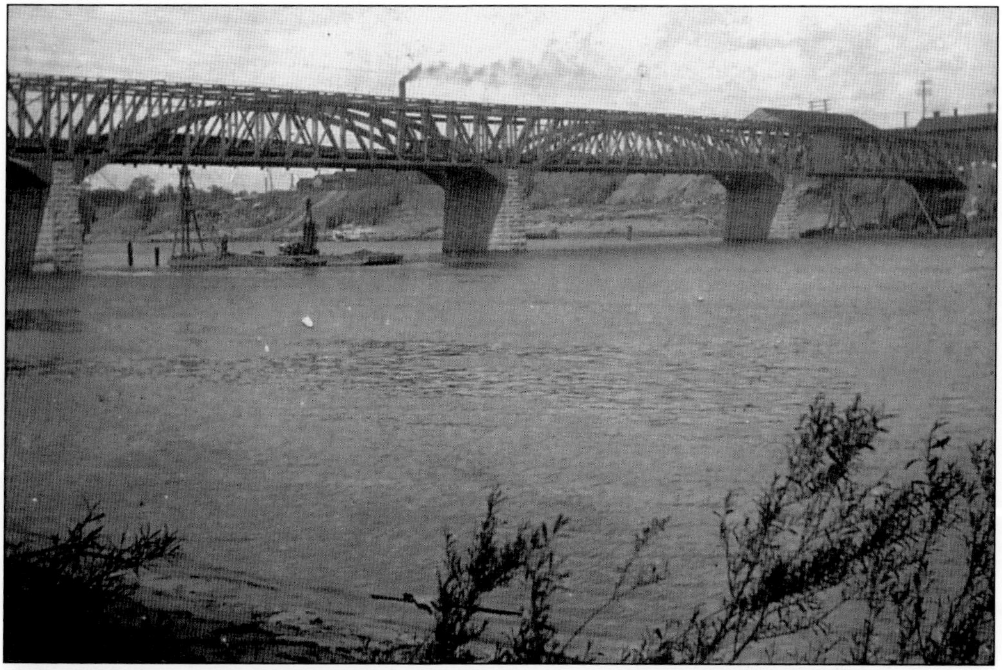

During the 1904 removal of the old wooden bridge over the Wabash River, men ascend a wooden ladder from the barge floating in the river to the bridge. (Vigo County Historical Society.)

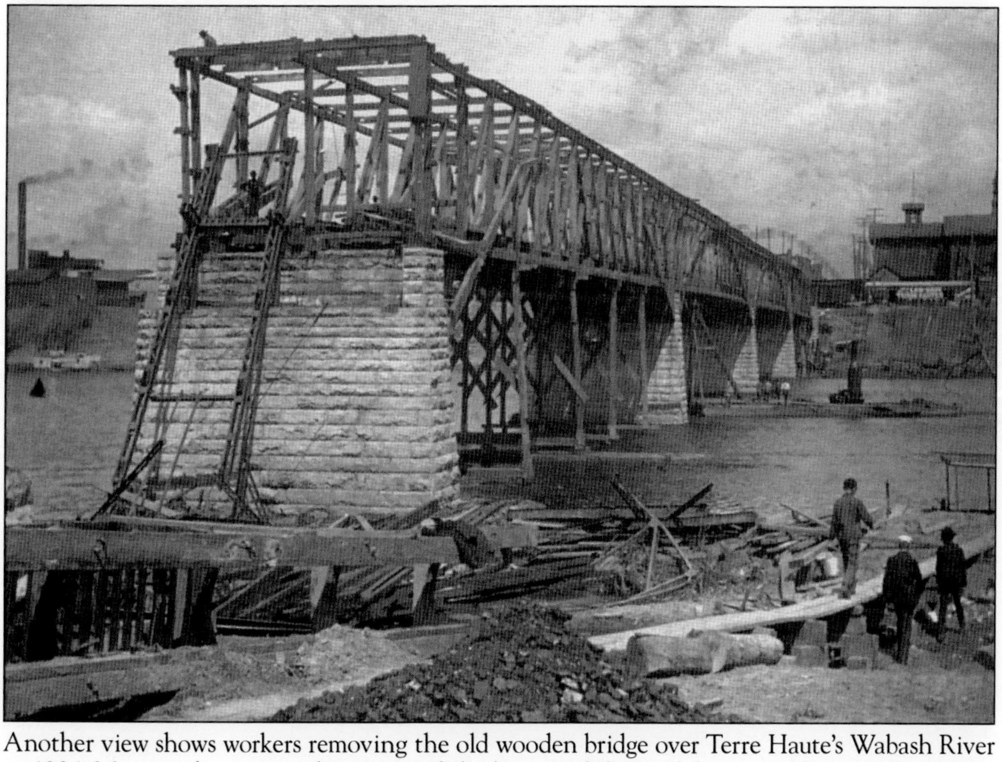

Another view shows workers removing the old wooden bridge over Terre Haute's Wabash River in 1904. Men can be seen working around the base, and the work barge can be seen floating in the river. (Vigo County Historical Society.)

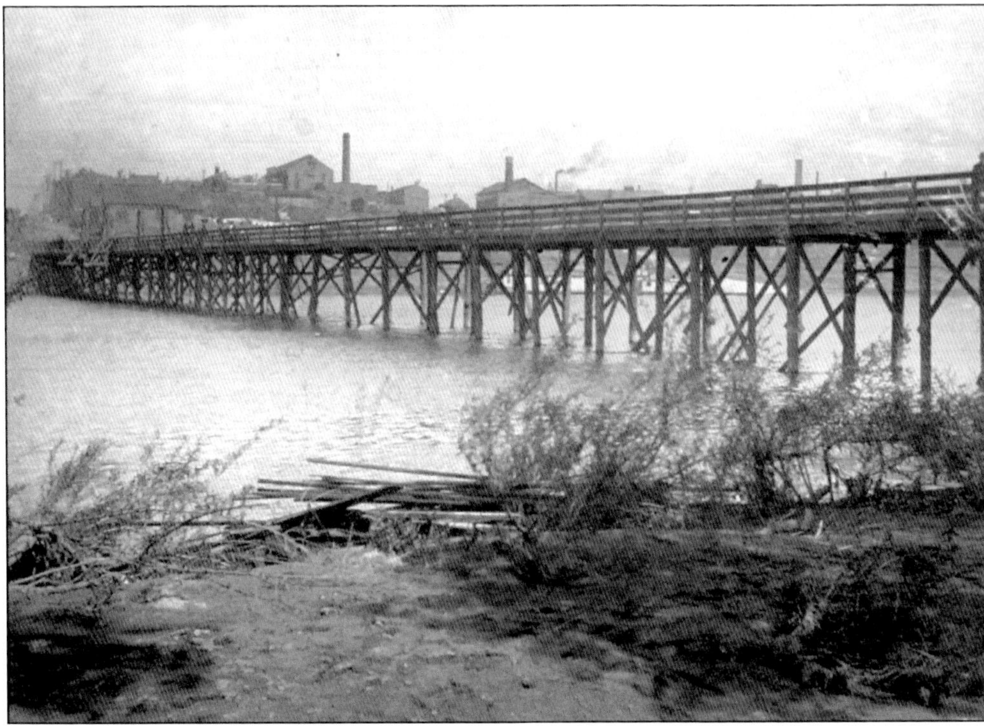

The temporary bridge over Terre Haute's covered drawbridge spanning the Wabash River is shown as it looked in 1904. The tollhouse keeper can be seen at far right, and men drive horse-drawn wagons across the bridge. (Vigo County Historical Society.)

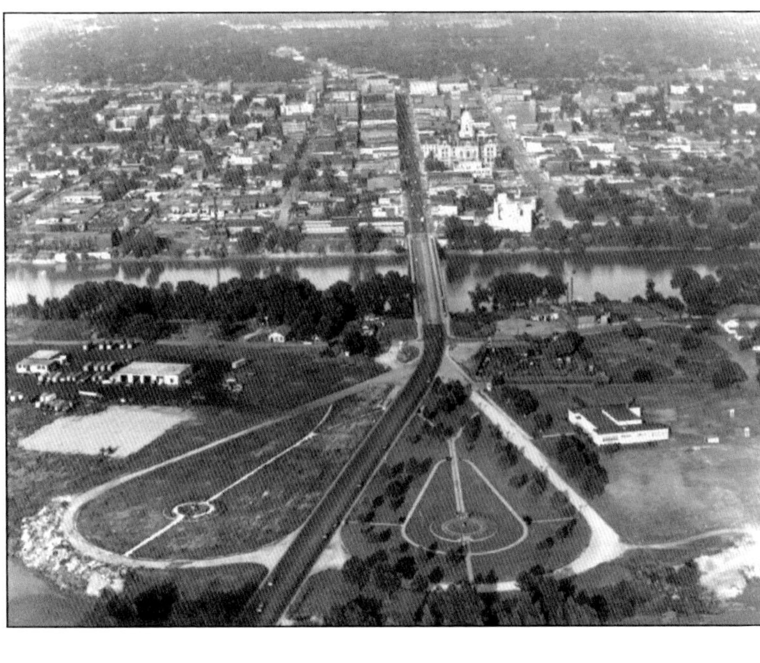

An early-1950s–era view looking east into downtown Terre Haute shows the modern US 40 bridge over the Wabash River. (Vigo County Historical Society.)

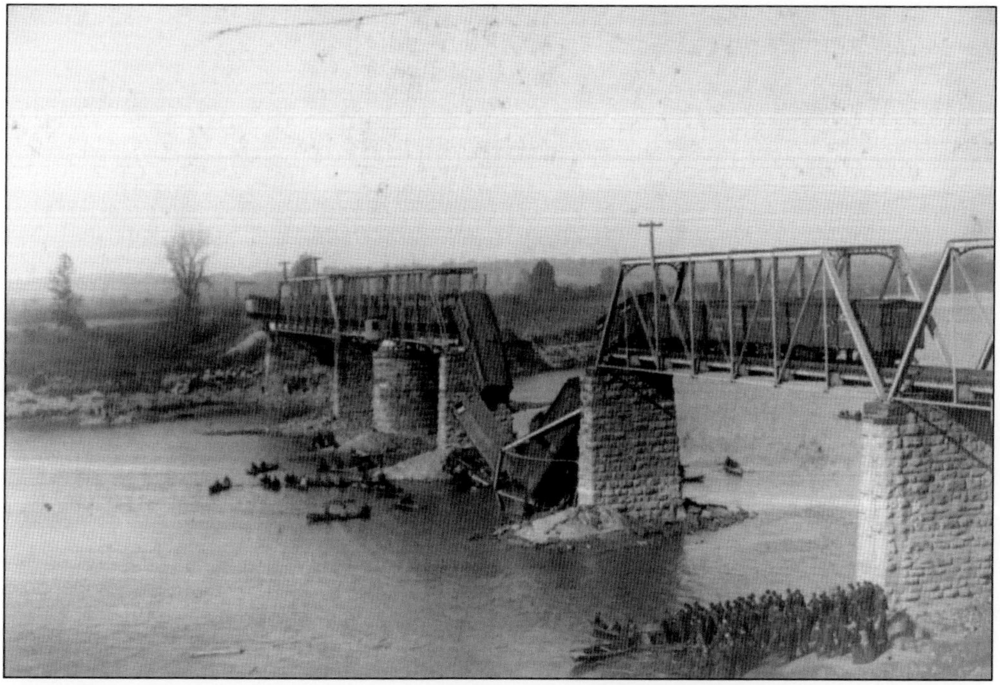

After a Terre Haute Railroad accident on the Wabash River Bridge on October 28, 1892, the engine is still buried in mud, visible in an "extra finish" cabinet photograph by Wright and Holloway (located at 510½ Wabash Avenue). (Both, Vigo County Historical Society.)

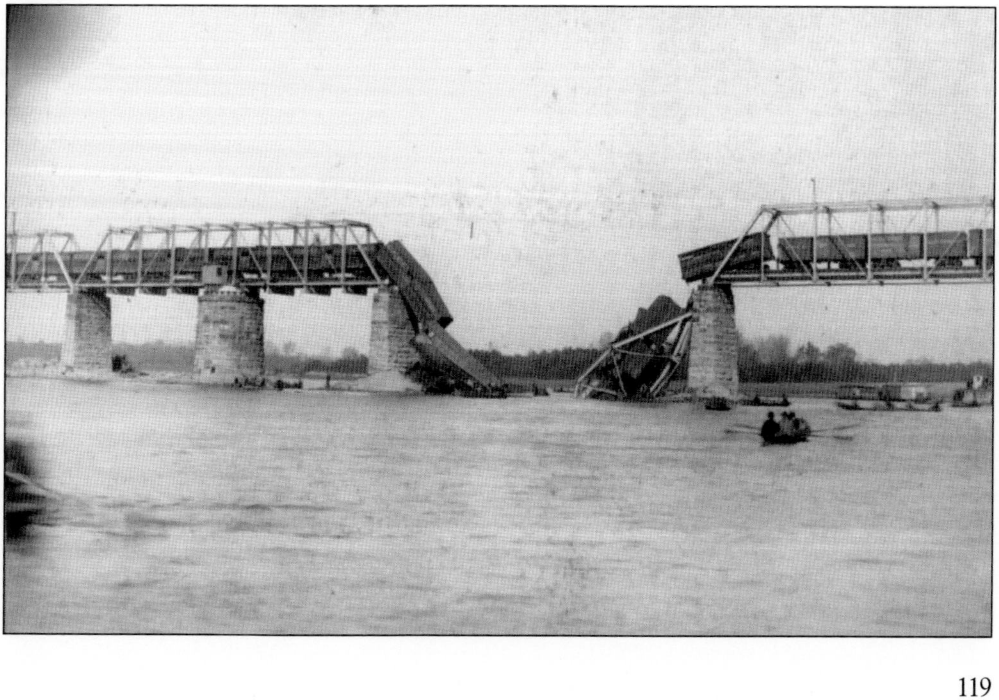

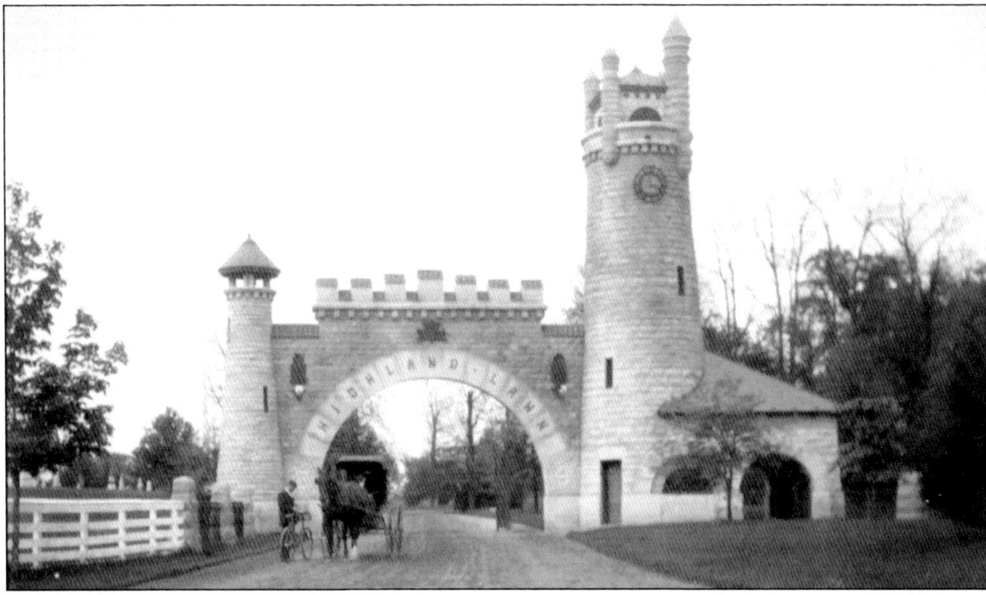

Terre Haute's Highland Lawn Cemetery entrance is pictured in May 1897. Comprising 139 acres and located at 4420 East Wabash Avenue on the National Road, Highland Lawn Cemetery opened in 1884. The first interment, Samantha McPherson, who died of typhoid fever at age 30, was buried on October 29, 1884. Designed in 1884 by Joseph Earnshaw, Highland Lawn Cemetery exhibits typical Romantic landscapes: graceful, meandering paths among plantings of trees and shrubs, lakes, vistas, and open spaces. (Vigo County Historical Society.)

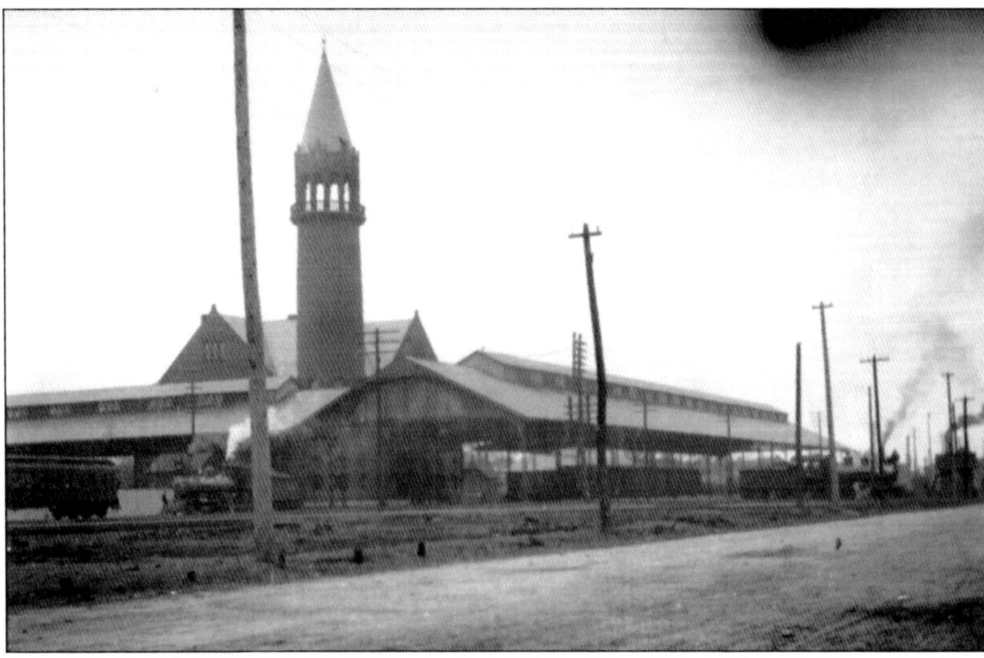

The E.I. Railroad Shed is shown in a May 1897 view from behind the tracks at the Union Railroad Depot in Terre Haute. The city's Union Station was built in the late 19th century and demolished in 1960. Terre Haute, the seat of Vigo County, earned the nickname "Crossroads of America" because of its extensive rail and road network. (Vigo County Historical Society.)

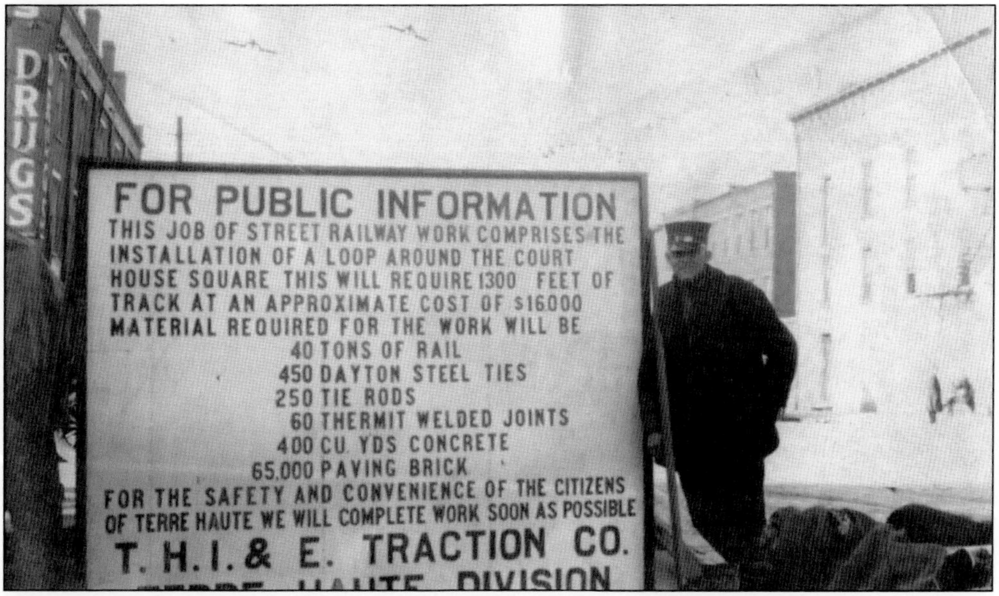

This 1920s-era photograph shows an interurban conductor for the Terre Haute, Indianapolis & Eastern Traction Co. posed beside a sign explaining the construction loop around the courthouse at Third Street and Wabash Avenue between 1921 and 1925. (Vigo County Historical Society.)

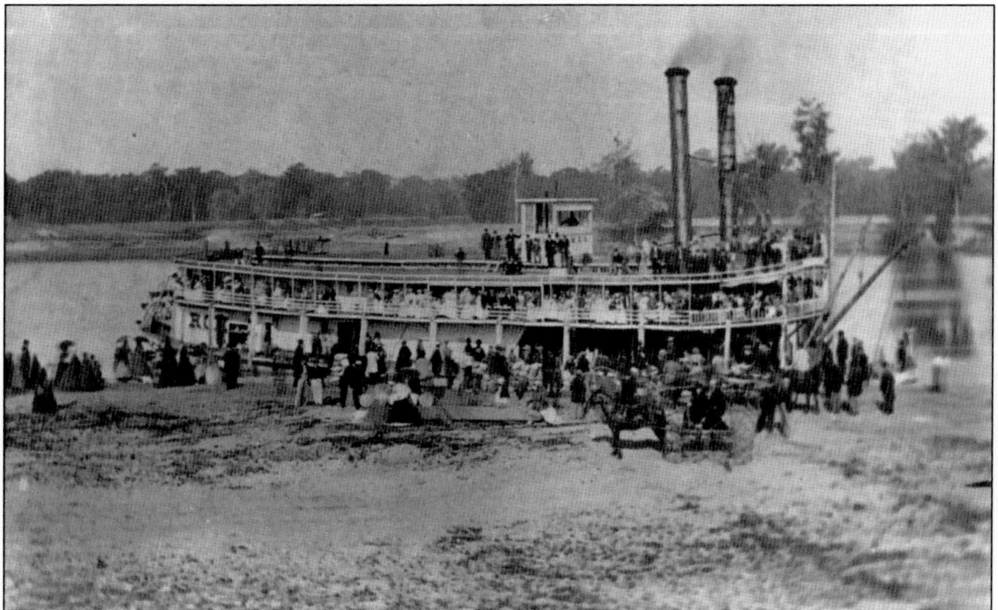

To the generations born before and immediately after the Civil War, traveling the National Road might well have involved transport by boat from Indiana to Illinois across the Wabash River. Here is an image of the Terre Haute Steamboat *Romeo* leaving at the foot of Walnut Street in 1858. (Vigo County Historical Society.)

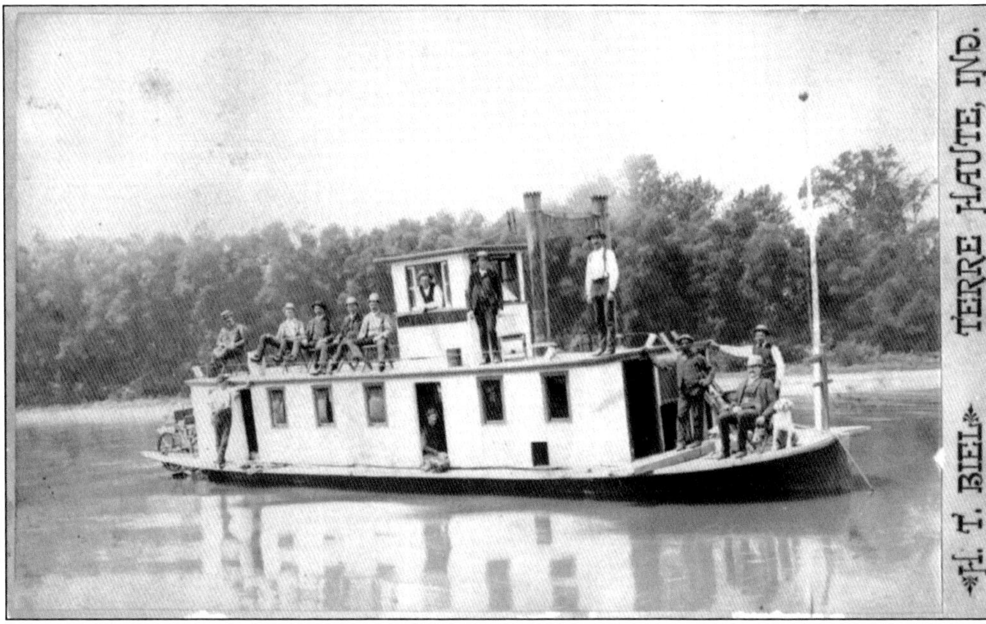

This is an 1880s cabinet photograph of the Terre Haute steamboat *Juantata* leaving from the site of Fort Harrison on the Wabash River. Several well-dressed men are posed atop the hull of the ship, and the skipper can be seen leaning out of the pilot house. A dog and his master are posed proudly on the bow of the ship. This and the next two images were donated by Charles King, secretary of Eugene V. Deb's foundation, after they were found among Margueritte Debs Cooper's possessions. (Vigo County Historical Society.)

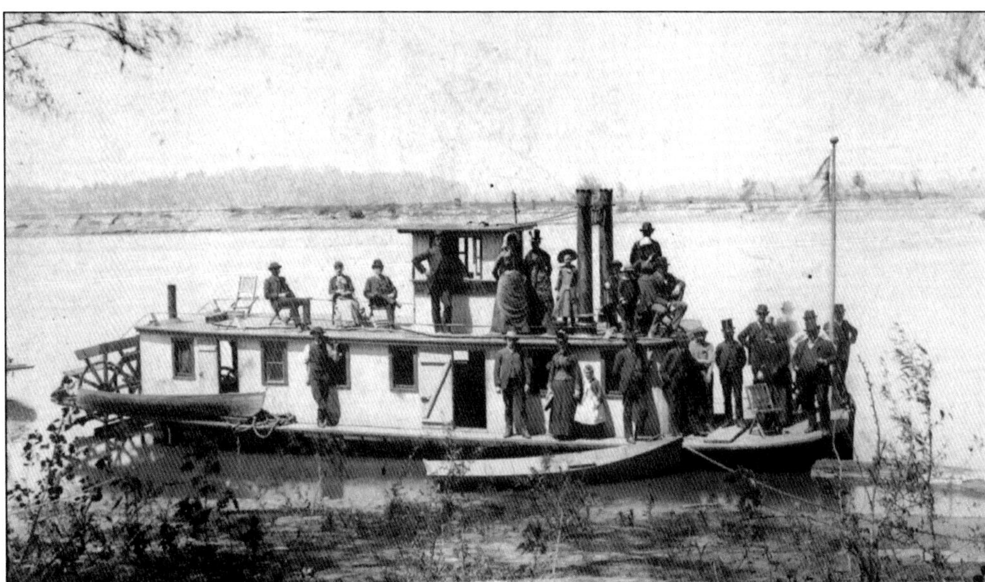

Several well-dressed men and women pose on the decks of the *Juantata* on what looks to be a family outing for a day spent on the river in the 1880s. The ship's flag has been run up the flag pole, and it looks like they are ready to depart Fort Harrison. (Vigo County Historical Society.)

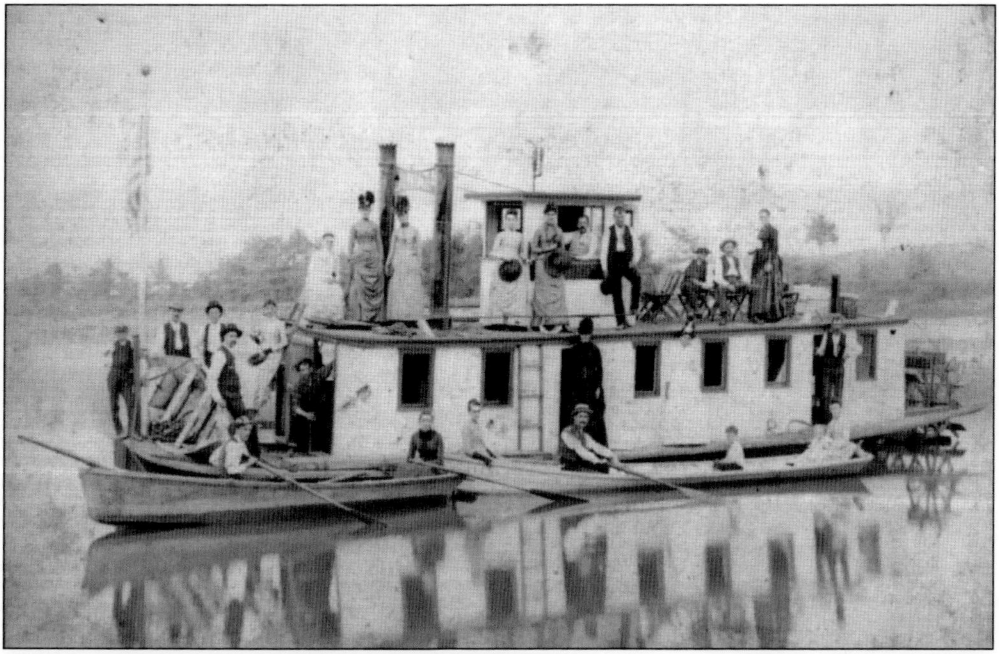

Employees prepare to ferry passengers from ship to shore via canoes. (Vigo County Historical Society.)

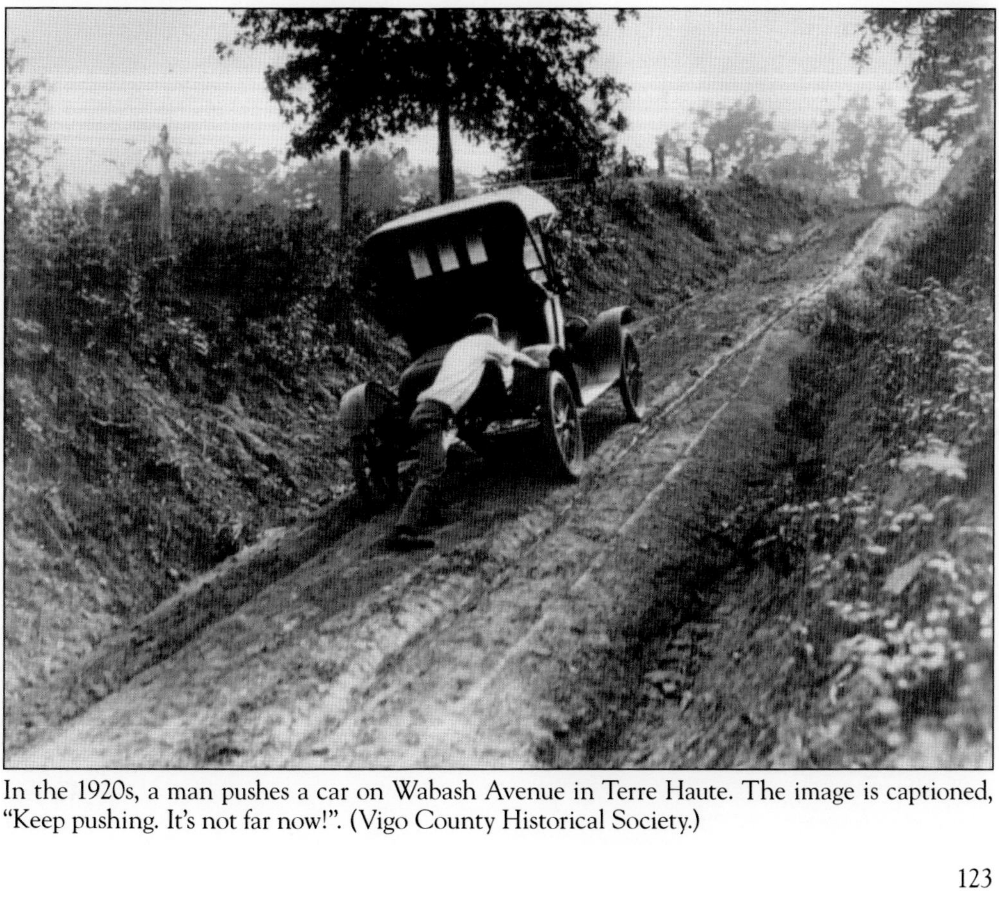

In the 1920s, a man pushes a car on Wabash Avenue in Terre Haute. The image is captioned, "Keep pushing. It's not far now!". (Vigo County Historical Society.)

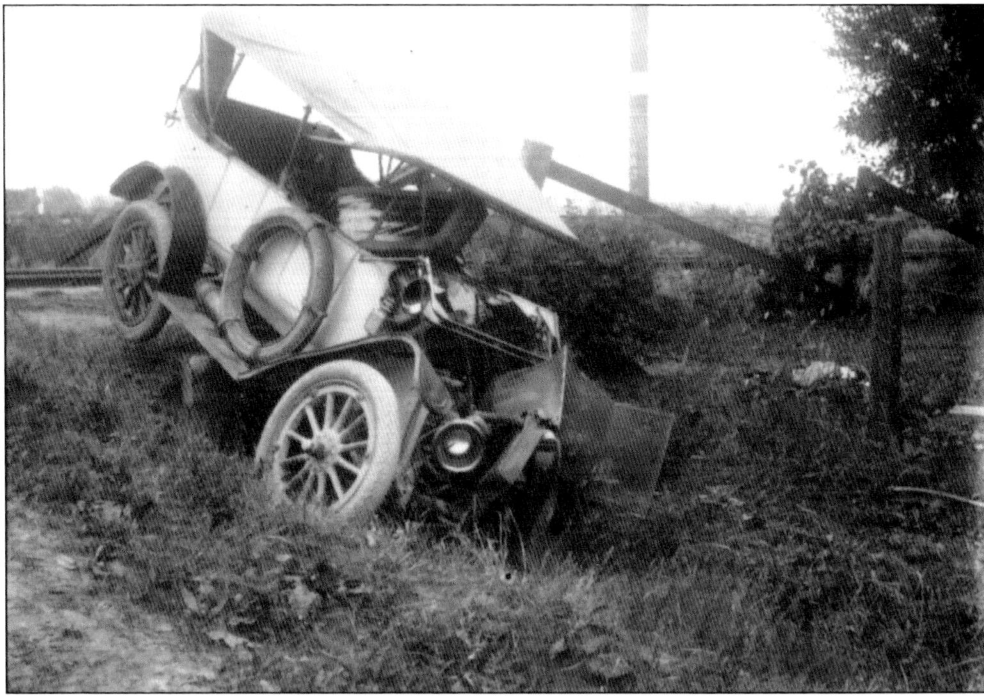

A photograph from about 1920 shows a wrecked car on Wabash Avenue just outside of Terre Haute. (Vigo County Historical Society.)

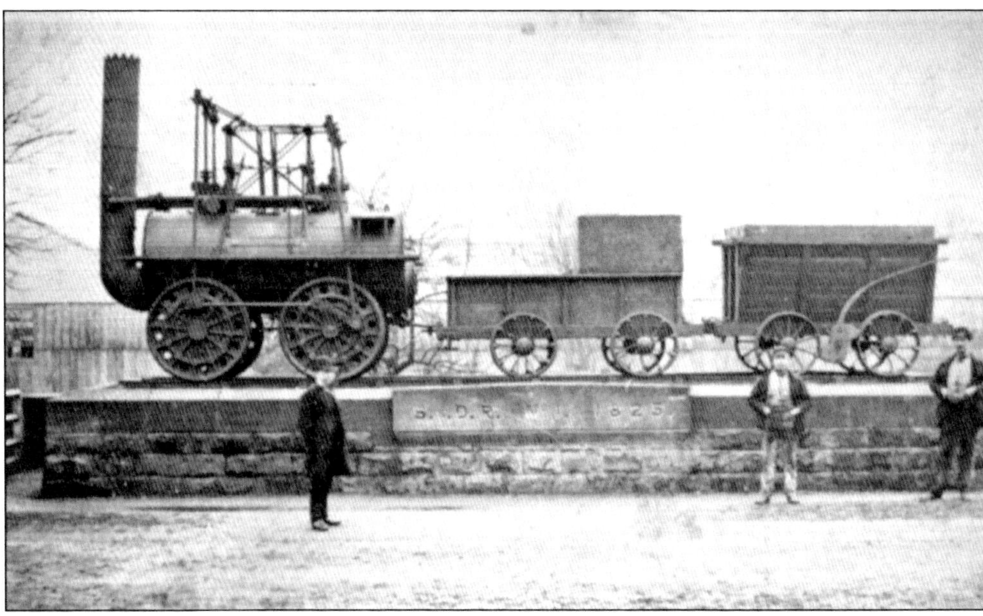

A cabinet photograph from around the 1880s is captioned, "Terre Haute—First train to cross bridge (No. 1 Engine S. and D.H. R. 1825) (Stockton and Darlington Railway-English) D.H. Wright Photographer 115 1/2 Main St. New No. 421 1/2 Terre Haute." (Vigo County Historical Society.)

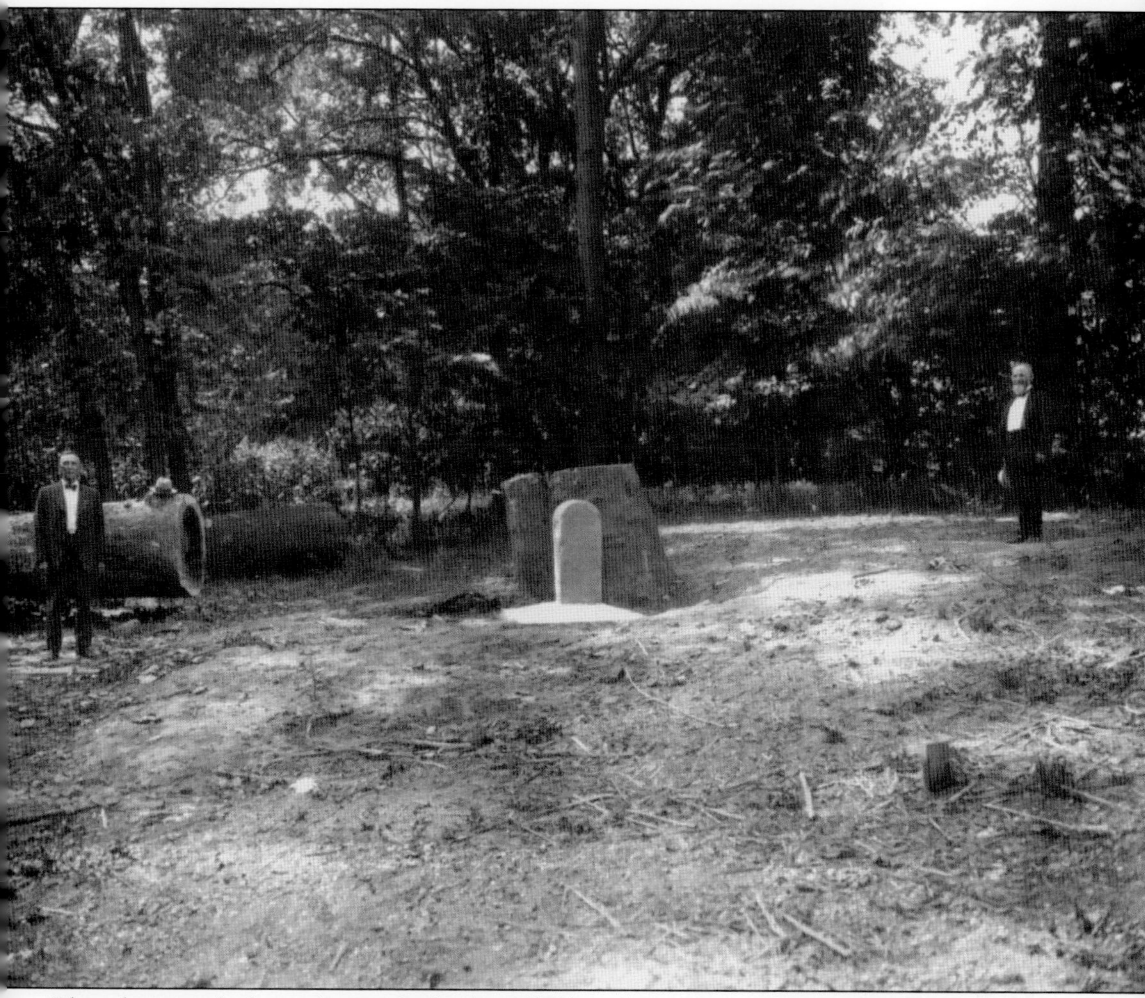

This photograph shows August Stukenberg (left) and George A. Scott at the boundary line between Indiana and Illinois. It is captioned, "Aug. Stukenberg East Side Monument Ind. And Ill. Statline at Wabash River Erected 1823." Looking west, the picture was taken by R.B. Hape of Terre Haute, Indiana, on September 13, 1928. Stukenberg is standing on the foundation prepared for a granite marker 15 feet south of the center of the old stone marker. George. A. Scott is standing on the same prepared foundation 15 feet north of the old stone marker. The original stone was set in 1823 by Guy W. Smith at the direction of the Illinois Legislature. This monument was reset September 4, 1928, by engineer C.H. Apple and C.S. Ward for Illinois and engineer C.C. Newsom and assistant engineer S.P. Stein for Indiana. This stone is located 150 feet north of the Wabash River's edge. (Vigo County Historical Society.)

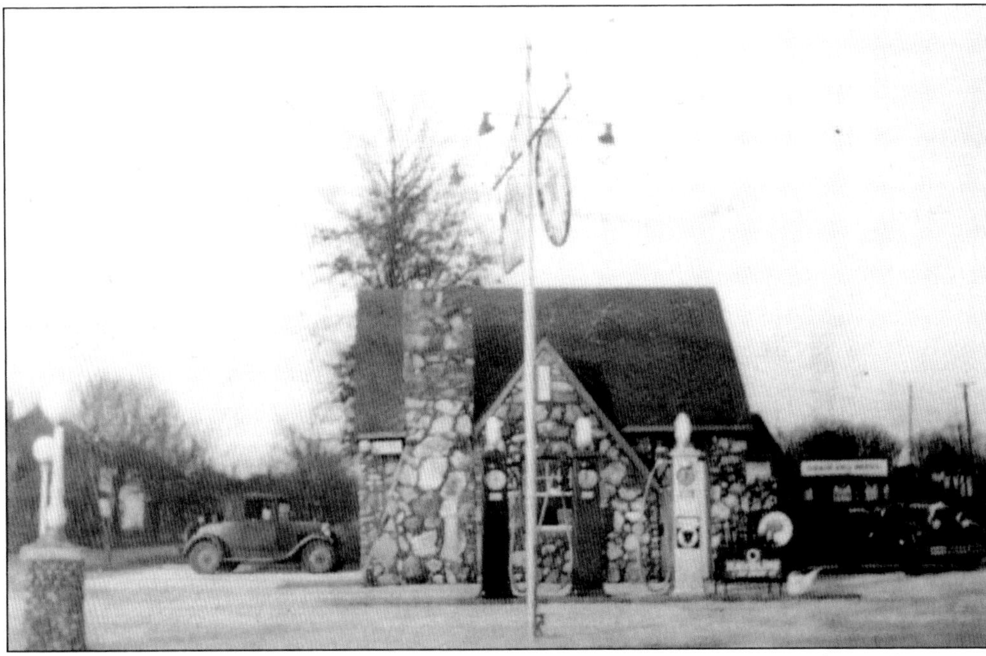

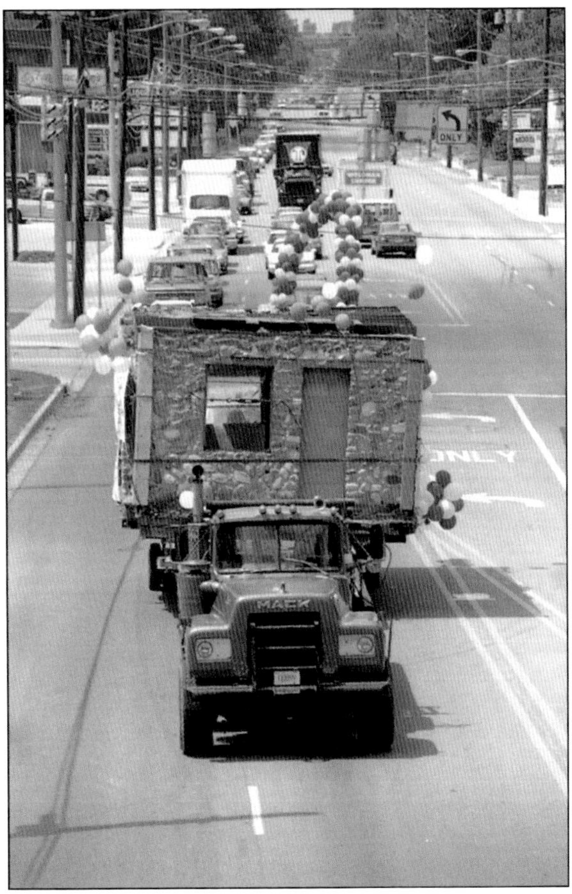

Another 1930s view shows the Texaco gas station on the National Road in Terre Haute. In the first decades of automobile travel, motorists often looked for a familiar place to stop—a place that reminded them of home. Consequently, many early gas stations were built to resemble small cottages and homes. (Indiana National Road Association.)

In 1999, the Indiana National Road Association and Rose-Hulman Institute of Technology saved the building from demolition by moving it from its original location to the Rose-Hulman campus. The move quickly took on a carnival atmosphere as the balloon-festooned building made its way slowly down the Historic National Road. (Trish Eccles.)

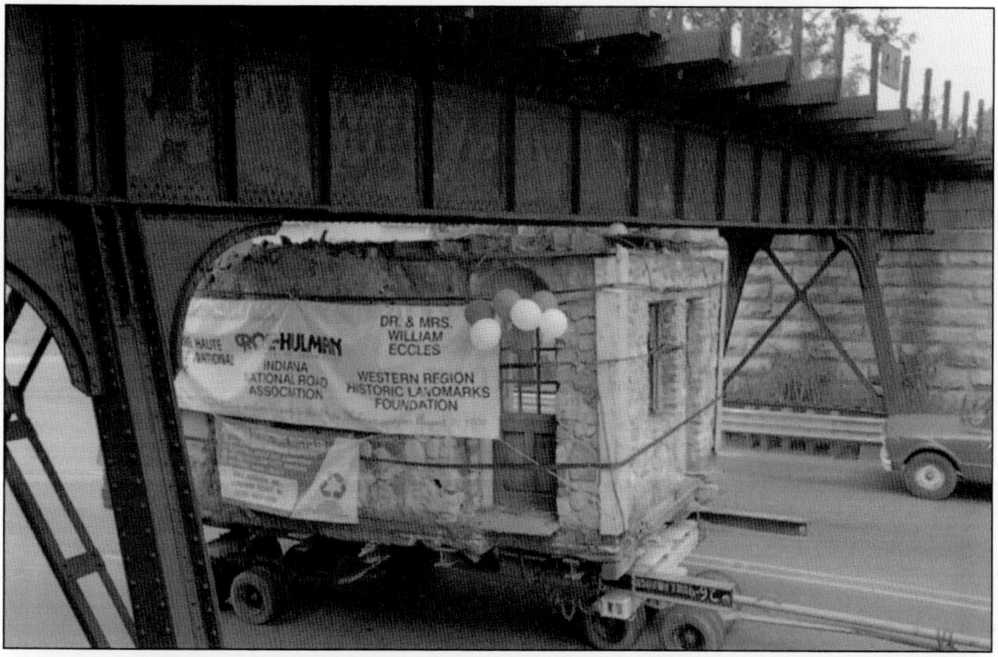

The move included many tight squeezes and close calls but ultimately resulted in a National Road preservation success story. This project would not have happened without the support of many partner organizations, such as Indiana Landmarks and Rose-Hulman, and local businesses, as well as the efforts of local advocates Joy Sacopulos and Trish Eccles. (Trish Eccles.)

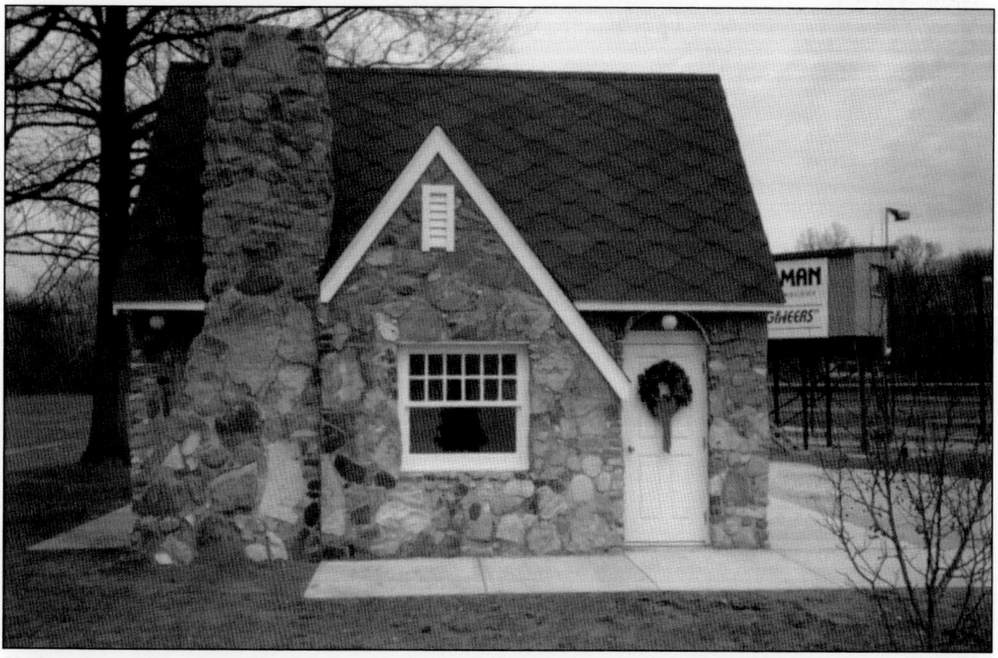

Today, the old gas station rests on the Rose-Hulman campus at 4480 Wabash Avenue in Terre Haute and is known as the Coffee Cottage. The building provides services for the school's baseball and soccer fields. It is also one site, among many across the state, that has interpretive signage to help tell the byway's story. (Trish Eccles.)

Discover Thousands of Local History Books Featuring Millions of Vintage Images

Arcadia Publishing, the leading local history publisher in the United States, is committed to making history accessible and meaningful through publishing books that celebrate and preserve the heritage of America's people and places.

Find more books like this at
www.arcadiapublishing.com

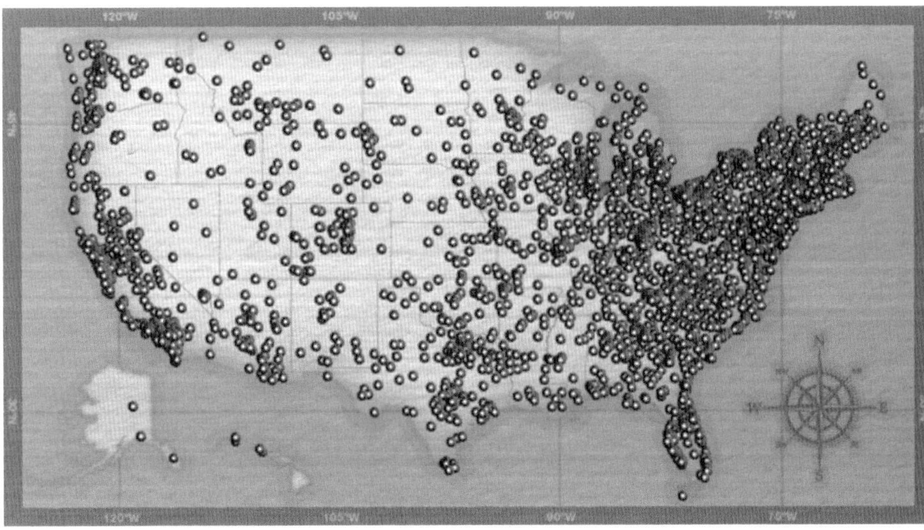

Search for your hometown history, your old stomping grounds, and even your favorite sports team.

Consistent with our mission to preserve history on a local level, this book was printed in South Carolina on American-made paper and manufactured entirely in the United States. Products carrying the accredited Forest Stewardship Council (FSC) label are printed on 100 percent FSC-certified paper.

MADE IN THE USA